BIBLE
PRESERVATION
AND THE
PROVIDENCE
OF GOD

492-TAGL

BIBLE PRESERVATION AND THE PROVIDENCE OF GOD

Sam Schnaiter
and
Ron Tagliapietra

492-TAGL

Library of Congress Number: 2002092564
ISBN :   Hardcover   1-4010-6248-2
                Softcover   1-4010-6247-4

Cover photo is used with the permission of Unusual Films. It shows a Hebrew scroll of the book of Esther from the Bowen Collection of Antiquities at the Bob Jones University Museum & Gallery.

This book was printed in the United States of America.

To order additional copies of this book, contact:
Xlibris Corporation
1-888-795-4274
www.Xlibris.com
Orders@Xlibris.com

CONTENTS

Introduction 7

UNIT I
Preservation of Scripture *13*

CHAPTER 1
DOCTRINE OF THE BIBLE 15
CHAPTER 2
PRESERVED SINCE ANTIQUITY 35
CHAPTER 3
PRESERVATION IN QUANTITY 45
CHAPTER 4
PRESERVATION THROUGH DISSEMINATION 55

UNIT II
Transmission of Scripture *71*

CHAPTER 5
HISTORY OF TRANSMISSION THEORIES 73
CHAPTER 6
GENERAL MODERN THEORIES 103
CHAPTER 7
REFINEMENTS 127
CHAPTER 8
EXTREME VIEWS 147
CHAPTER 9
COMPARING THEORIES 170

UNIT III

Translation of Scripture *185*

CHAPTER 10
    THE TRANSLATORS TO THE READER 187
CHAPTER 11
    TRANSLATION PRINCIPLES AND ISSUES 247
CHAPTER 12
    SELECTING VERSIONS 268
CONCLUSION 279
APPENDIX 1
    SCHNAITER'S REPLY TO ACCUSATIONS 283
APPENDIX 2
    QUOTATIONS 289
ANSWERS TO QUESTIONS 311
GLOSSARY 323
BIBLIOGRAPHY 333
INDEX 343

INTRODUCTION

A principle of physics states that every action has an equal and opposite reaction. It seems that this principle also applies to controversial theories, especially where it concerns Scripture. We seem to have reached a stage in Christian history where every possible viewpoint regarding the origin and transmission of Scripture is now being held by someone or some group, often in strong opposition to someone else or some other group. Accusations and counter-accusations sometimes of the most irreverent (and frequently irrelevant) sort have been hurled, by Bible believers against Bible believers, indiscriminately at times, all in supposed defense of God's Word.

For this reason not without misgivings we have undertaken to write a book on this subject. The misgivings arise, not out of uncertainty as to the need for it, nor even as to the direction which the book should take, but from the fact that an enormously important matter is at stake, which poses a sober responsibility toward its fair handling. We are well aware that by merely offering an opinion on this topic, we open ourselves to the possibility of an inordinate amount of criticism. Having read the vehement and often unwarranted remarks aimed at others who have written on this subject, we appreciate the laments of Miles Smith in his Translators' Preface to the Reader for the King James version produced in 1611:

> Whosoever attempteth any thing for the publick, (especially
> if it appertain to religion, and to the opening and clearing of

the Word of God) the same setteth himself upon a stage to be glouted upon by every evil eye; yea, he casteth himself headlong upon pikes, to be gored by every sharp tongue. For he that meddleth with men's religion in any part meddleth with their custom, nay, with their freehold; and though they find no content in that which they have, yet they cannot abide to hear of altering.

Nevertheless, encouraged by the kind words and prayers of friends and colleagues, we proceed. Critical ideas stand or fall, live or die on the sands of time. Throughout history, visionaries and conservatives have clashed, both making important contributions. Visionaries have made important discoveries and struggled for acceptance. Conservatives have been slow to change providing stability from the winds of doctrine of many self-proclaimed visionaries. Strong emotions on both sides have often clouded clear understanding. Usually, the calm reflection that accompanies the passing of time reveals the right or the wrong of something that emotional pressures prevent men from seeing immediately.

For examples, at one time godly men maintained that Mussolini must be the antichrist. They made quite a case for their belief, but now that Mussolini is long gone and antichrist is yet to come, no one makes that claim anymore. It was a viewpoint that simply did not stand scrutiny in the passing of time in spite of the strength of belief behind it. Likewise, in the early days of radio broadcasting, some of God's choice servants, preachers and evangelists, maintained for a time that radio was a satanic invention. Some supported their case with Bible verses like Ephesians 2:2 which refers to the Devil as "the prince of the power of the air." Today, Ephesians 2:2 is still in the Bible, but is not applied to radio even by the staunchest Bible believer that we are aware of. Most Christians recognize that radio can be easily misused to promote ungodly music. But it can also be used for God-honoring broadcasts. The invention of television, film, video, and the computer web has made the radio seem rather tame, and brought broader issues into focus. The passing of time has moderated intemperate allegations on this topic.

In the last five or six decades, we have seen among fundamental Bible believers a conflict in regard to the transmission of the text of the New Testament from its origins to our day. This conflict began from the first moment that the printed Greek New Testament edited by Erasmus hit the market. It has not let up. In 1881, when Westcott and Hort produced what they considered to be a carefully edited Greek text, the conflict revived in opposition to their text. As far as we know, no fundamentalist has written a book that articulates a good biblical balance in this complicated issue. Both authors of this text are fundamentalists who believe the cardinal or fundamental doctrines of the Bible to be true and who also believe the necessity of militant and obedient adherence to the clear-cut teachings of Scripture. We do not claim to keep God's commands perfectly. As sinners, saved by God's grace alone, we have often in our own strength failed the Lord. But we do not (nor does any true fundamentalist) dismiss or ignore God's commands even at those times where we might fail to measure up to them. The proper response for failure is always repentance.

The following, then, is intended to be something of a reference manual to clarify and evaluate the opposing arguments of this conflict from a fundamentalist perspective. We will examine the often puzzling and troublesome questions currently circulating about the transmission of the Bible from its autographic sources. We are not irretrievably committed to defending or advancing one position over another in this conflict. In fact, the co-authors do not favor the same theory. As far as we know, this is the first attempt at collaboration by people on opposite sides of the central textual issue. We hope that our attempt will shed light on the issue, provide balance, and prove that we prefer to sort out what is crucial to hold as part of the Bible believer's creed as distinguished from mere interpretative opinion.

At stake here, among other things, is the matter of our supreme authority. Authority is at the heart of one's religion and always poses a special sensitivity. Ultimately and inevitably a man takes direction from one of the following sources as his authority: (1) from other men perceived either rightly or wrongly as authorities (such as government officials, church officials, experts, or just tradition), (2) from himself (whether his reason, feelings, or other impulses), or (3) from God.

Unfortunately, it has often been difficult to avoid confusing God's authority from that of mere men at times. That which distinguishes Bible believing Christians from the world of men is their commitment to the written Word of God as their sole authority. Properly understood, the Bible is the final appeal in all matters on which it speaks to and commands men, and Bible believers have always understood this. Yet it has long been our impression that in the controversy concerning Greek texts and various translations of the Bible, much is passed off as God's authority which amounts to no more than men's impulses or opinions or interpretations of God's authority.

Men's opinions have their place. But they must not be allowed the same authority as God's Word. Scientific theories have a place, but they must be evaluated and tested first against the Word of God and then scientifically. Those who fail to make these tests with the help of the Holy Spirit will at best promote views that will die on the sands of time and at worst will cause God's children to stumble because of teaching "as doctrine the commandments of men."

Fifteen years ago, when we became independently interested in this subject, we were frankly quite appalled at the strength and rashness of many statements made largely by well-meaning crusaders. One benefit of the passing of time is that the brunt of those statements has for the most part been recognized as such. What remains are a few dozen troubling questions that come up in the minds of thoughtful, godly people when they are made aware of this subject and its controversies.

At one time such debate was considered appropriate only for seminary students. However, because the extreme positions have been advanced boldly and publicly, most Christians still struggle with textual issues at least occasionally. At present, every available book promotes the position of its author vigorously. This means that anyone wanting to hear all sides of the debate has to read at least a half dozen books. We hope (if only by putting the brakes on each other's interests) to provide a useful textbook in a calm encyclopedia style that will help people understand the issues and evaluate the positions.

What follows is an attempt to: (1) distinguish between the teachings of the Word of God on this subject and the opinions (however strongly held) of men, (2) build up believers as they see how God has providentially directed the discovery of manuscript evidence to vindicate his own promise of preservation, (3) present the major viewpoints, clarifying their strengths, weaknesses, and the issues involved, and (4) answer the troublesome questions about textual and translational matters of the New Testament.

UNIT I

Preservation of Scripture

Because the Scripture is a special writing with moral mandates and spiritual guidelines for the creature given by The Creator, any study which touches on it must have a special sensitivity to its nature and content. For the Christian, the authenticity and integrity of Scripture is necessarily bound up with the integrity of the God of Scripture. For this reason, careful Christians have been wary of anything "coming down the pipe" which would seem to attack the Word of God. Usually the most deceptive attacks have come from liberals, modernists, and cultists with some clever counterfeit to biblical faith. The battle-scarred warrior of the faith consequently anticipates attacks from these avenues and is on guard for some new anti-God idea masquerading as truth to deceive God's people who are not so on guard. History has often shown us that this is an unfortunate but necessary stance for a serious Christian. The Devil is cunningly deceitful in foisting his various ploys upon men.

It is no surprise then that so many of God's people have become alarmed by the translation and textual controversies revolving around the Bible especially in the past half century. We know dozens of pastors who are in a quandary about text types and translations. They have read disturbing articles by various other pastors on the subject. Most of them want to know what is going on and how to deal with the issues being raised over versions, the Greek manuscripts from which they were translated, and even the spirituality of the editors and translators involved.

Before one can research these questions and find satisfying answers, it is important to know the undisputable Bible facts upon which these questions stand or fall. In this unit, the first chapter covers the doctrinal basis of the issues, and the next three provide a survey of the ancient Greek manuscripts that have come down to the present. The chapters on the manuscripts are important because they provide background information necessary to the issues discussed in units 2 and 3 and also because they provide evidence that God has indeed preserved His Word as He promised.

CHAPTER 1

DOCTRINE OF THE BIBLE

The Bible is the only sure foundation for truth. Therefore it is important to begin any study with the biblical basis. This chapter presents the doctrines of inspiration and preservation from Scripture. Although a Christian should already be familiar with such basic truths, there is nothing like scrutinizing and applying them in detailed debate to engrave them in our minds. Controversy forces us to defend a position. If the specific meaning of the verses we depend on is muddled in our minds, it will become evident quickly. Since biblical doctrine is pre-requisite to discussion, a brief survey of inspiration and preservation follow with special emphasis on their relation to the controversial matters.

Inspiration

Scripture teaches inspiration in some detail. Key passages tell us that God inspired His Word and also inform us to a limited extent how He did it. The nature of inspiration, the process through which God inspired His Word, and the resulting product of inspiration.

The Nature of Inspiration

The Bible is unique among books because it is the Word of

God. No other book is divine, and no other shares with it its dynamic life and power. It is "quick (alive) and powerful and sharper than any two-edged sword" (Heb. 4:12). Peter says that the Word of God "liveth and abideth forever" (1 Pet. 1:23).

Jesus said "Thy Word is truth" (John 17:17), which makes it infallible. It is **inerrant**, or free from error, because God cannot lie (Numbers 23:19). There are those who deny these truths. Infidels deny the work of God at all in Scripture. Liberals deny all supernatural activity of God, affirming only that which can be buttressed by their own reasoning powers. Even some Evangelicals try to maintain an inspiration that applies to doctrine but is enslaved to the historical and scientific views of the apostolic age. They claim that the Bible is authoritative in spiritual matters, but not in historical or scientific details. But the illogical nature of such nonsense is demolished by the knowledge that the scientific and historical accuracy of Scripture is a doctrine of Scripture! Jesus said, "The Scripture cannot be broken" (John 10:35).

This declaration by Jesus was an incidental statement about the authority and inerrancy of the Old Testament based on Ps. 82:6. He said this in substantiating His claim to be the Son of God, and both claims are universal. In making such a statement, our Lord ratified the inerrancy of the Scripture. A document with errors can certainly be "broken" (the idea from the Greek word *luthenai* would indicate something like "dissolved," or "abolished," or "done away with"), but not the Scripture—according to Jesus.

The teaching of Scripture is inerrant and infallible, inspiration involves more than this. Jesus also verified that inspiration is both verbal and plenary. He claimed that the words and even the portions of words (jots and tittles) are reliable, not just the teachings.

For verily I say unto you, Till heaven and earth pass, one jot or one tittle shall in no wise pass from the law, till all be fulfilled. (Matt. 5:18)

Jesus practiced what he preached. In Matthew 22:31-32, He argued for the resurrection of the dead based on a present tense rather than a past tense. Similarly, Paul argued for the deity of Christ based on the fact that a word was singular rather than plural (Gal. 3:16). This dependence on the form of the words in Scripture illustrates that inspiration is **verbal** (applies to the words) and that it is **plenary** (complete or full). Inspiration refers to the words of Scripture and that means all of them.

On the basis of these and other statements in Scripture, we maintain that the Scripture is completely, infallibly, and verbally inspired. Though it does not exhaustively present all fields of knowledge (doctrine, history, science, etc.), it is nevertheless inerrant with regard to every point of doctrine, history, and science that it affirms.

The Process of Inspiration

> No prophecy of the scripture is of any private interpretation. For the prophecy came not in old time by the will of man: but holy men of God spake as they were moved by the Holy Ghost. (II Pet. 1:20-21)

This means simply that God's Word is not the invention ("interpretation") of any human philosopher. Nor did it arise as the product of any human will ("will of man"). Rather, it is the result of God's direct activity in the human authors as they "spake" God's Word at the prompting of the Holy Spirit. The Word of God was then written down (whether by the prophet or his scribe, called an amanuensis).

Peter here reveals certain aspects of the process of inspiration. That "holy men of God" were "moved by the Holy Spirit" (v. 21) means that God supernaturally intervened in the human process of writing. The verse first indicates that He chose as his agents particular members of this sin-cursed race ("holy men of God").

The word "holy" would indicate that these are men separated—to God and from the world, the flesh, and the devil. In popular usage, holy men include Tibetan lamas, Buddhist monks, Hindu fire-walkers, and Indian medicine men as well as Christians. Scripture uses a qualifier (Greek genitive) to eliminate any confusion, "holy men of God," thus affirming that they are in a unique way God's. They are "redeemed" men who belong to the true God. But not every redeemed man is in view here for these are God's holy men specially moved by the Holy Spirit for the explicit purpose of announcing the prophecies of Scripture.

The Lord Jesus indicated that the very process of divine inspiration mentioned in II Peter 1:21 would apply to His disciples (John 14:26). The Holy Spirit would teach them, remind them, and guide them into all the truth for them to record. Jesus reaffirmed this in John 16:31 of certain truths that up to that time He had not yet revealed to them. As a consequence of these promises, we have today the New Testament in addition to the Old.

The word, *moved* (pheromenoi) conveys the idea "being carried along." The same Greek word is used in Acts 27 (verses 17 and 27) of a ship "driven" by a cyclone. The human sailors are very active. They must lighten the ship, trim the sails, and bail water, or the ship will certainly be sunk. However, the feeble responses of the ship to the busy sailors affects the destination not one whit as the ship surges forward in the grip of the cyclone. The comparison makes the process vivid: the style of the human authors (human bailing and lightening) may be evident in their writings, but this in no way hindered God (the controlling cyclone) from bringing His Word into being exactly as he wanted it. The word contrasts the relative passiveness of the human authors with the activeness of the Holy Spirit. The implication is that the Bible is primarily a divine book, though it has a human element. A second conclusion to be drawn is that God did not dictate the New Testament word by word (as He spoke the ten commandments to Moses), but that he spoke through the human instruments he had chosen.

To summarize Peter's proclamation, then: God's Holy Spirit specially chose certain human instruments, and blocked any natural tendency they might have had to produce human errors. He very closely supervised His writers in such a way as to prevent any error from occurring in the words they spoke and ultimately penned. The result is that what they spoke (and later wrote) is the message of God to man.

The Product of Inspiration

As a consequence of the divine process we have the inspired product. The Bible tells us,

> *And that from a child thou hast known the holy scriptures, which are able to make thee wise unto salvation through faith which is in Christ Jesus. All scripture is given by inspiration of God, and is profitable for doctrine, for reproof, for correction, for instruction in righteousness: That the man of God may be perfect, throughly furnished unto all good works. (II Tim. 3:15-17)*

Whereas in Peter's discussion (already explained), the writers themselves were in focus, the subject of discussion in this passage is the written Word, (Greek: graphe). In all its more than fifty occurrences in the Bible, this word has reference to the inspired Word of God either in part or the whole. It is always the measure of truth and authority for the Christian as seen, for example, in I Corinthians 15:3 ("according to the Scripture"). The lesson here is that the inspired Scripture is **authoritative.**

In II Timothy 3:16, we are told of the origin of the graphe. It is the product of the divine breath of God, as evidenced by the word *theopneustos*, which translates "given by inspiration." As noted so often, theopneustos could be rendered "God-breathed" as a reflection of the sum of its compound parts (theos = God; pneustos = breathed). As the product of the very breath of God, it carries the supreme authority of God. It stands to reason therefore, that wherever it commands men, it is the manual for man's conduct. It is "profitable for doctrine, reproof, correction, and instruction." In all things it is our guide.

As with the phrase "holy men," we must not get the wrong idea of the term inspiration. Inspiration is not simply a great idea or a brainstorm written down. We sometimes say that some book inspired us, when all we mean is that it motivated us to begin an exercise program or simply made us feel good. The Word of God is inspired in a completely different sense. The biblical concept of **inspiration** refers to the theological fact discussed above—that the Bible is God-breathed. Only God's book is inspired in that sense; people never are.

The Bible, then, is authoritative as the inspired word of God. The Bible alone, not tradition or human leaders, is declared to be profitable and must be our guide. "Sola Scriptura," the cry of the Reformers, still rings today. The Bible is the sole authority for faith and practice.

Preservation

The doctrine of the preservation of the text of Scripture is something of a corollary to the doctrine of inspiration. With the completion of the revelation, God preserved his Word first by having his people recognize the inspired writings as divine, and then by protecting them from destruction and even from corruption. These aspects of preservation involve the canon of Scripture, the eternality of Scripture, and the integrity of Scripture.

Canon

The term canon refers to a standard or rule. The most important standard in the universe is the standard of the Word of God. It is essential for man that he recognize with God's guidance the books which God inspired. The list of sacred books is called the **canon** of Scripture.

By the time of Christ, the 22 books of the Hebrew Bible (Old Testament) had already been recognized as Scripture. Today we recognize the same 22 books, but have divided six of them into two parts each (besides the obvious splitting of Samuel, Kings, and Chronicles, Ruth has been divided from Judges, Lamentations from Jeremiah, and Nehemiah from Ezra). Finally, the twelve minor prophets are now counted as separate books instead of combined as one book (called the Twelve).[1] This means that our list of 39 books consists of exactly the same books recognized as Scripture in the days of Christ. Neither Jews nor Christians, Catholics nor Protestants have rejected any of these books since that time.

As with the Old Testament, the key characteristic of New Testament Scripture is divine inspiration. As soon as inspired books were written, believers recognized the voice of God with the help of the Spirit of God. Even the New Testament writers recognized their writings as divine. Peter classed Paul's writings as Scripture (II Peter 3:15-16), and both John (Revelation 1:1) and Paul (I Thess. 2:13) recognized their own teaching as divinely inspired.

Indeed, God promised to send the Holy Spirit for illumination—to provide understanding of the Scripture. He promised to guide his people into all truth (John 14:26, 16:13). The Holy Spirit helped believers recognize Scripture by giving illumination, by the mark of apostolic authority (authorship or approval), by the unique spiritual content of Scripture, and by its accurate fulfillments (Deut. 18:22). The universal reception by the churches of the inspired Scripture provided further evidence that aided the recognition of the New Testament canon. By the end of the second century, the universally received books numbered 27—the same 27 that we cherish today.[2]

God in his providence used the persecution of the early church to get His people to list the books of the canon. The partial list of the heretic Marcion (A.D. 140) showed the church the need for a complete list, while a few uninspired books that were accepted by some showed the churches the need for an accurate list. Further, the decree of Diocletian (A.D. 303) to burn the sacred books made it necessary for the church to know which books to protect.[3] It is important to recognize, however, that during these days of persecution, the church leaders could not hold councils to debate the issue.

During the third century, the East disputed the inspiration of Revelation, while the West disputed Hebrews. These disputes continued into the fourth century when councils were finally called. The Council of Hippo (A.D. 393), the Third Council of Carthage (A.D. 397), and the Second Council of Hippo (A.D. 419) all listed exactly the same 27 books of the New Testament that we have today. Such councils "did not confer upon them any authority which they did not already possess, but simply recorded their previously established canonicity."[4]

Since the fourth century, there has been no serious questioning of the 27 accepted books of the New Testament by either Roman Catholics or Protestants.[5] Together with the thirty-nine (as currently numbered) books of the Old Testament canon, we therefore have a collection of sixty-six inspired, infallible, inerrant, and authoritative books. The authority of the books is derived from the authority of God Himself. He has verified the unique errorlessness of those original writings.

Why, then, do Catholic and Protestant Bibles differ? The answer is not in the 66 canonical books. Bibles from both groups will contain all sixty-six. The difference is that the Catholic Bibles include some extra books. These books are called the **Apocrypha**.

Even the Catholics did not accept them during the Middle Ages. In fact, the first official recognition of these works by Catholics came at the Council of Trent (A.D. 1546). This was obviously a reaction against the Protestant Reformers. The books had been rejected for fifteen centuries since they had been written. Now, suddenly, they were dusted off to provide evidence for salvation by works and prayers for the dead.[6]

The Lord has clearly preserved his Word through the canon of Scripture. He did so through persecution and without the aid of councils, though the later councils recognized God's guidance and acknowledged the inspired books. For 1500 years after Christ, professed Christians of all types agreed on the 66 books of the canon as the complete revelation of God. What a testimony to the providence of God.

Eternal Preservation

The Scripture also has much to say concerning its own preservation. The Bible makes clear that God's Word will survive the most bitter and pointed opposition to it imaginable. Both Old and New Testaments affirm that Scripture shall stand forever (Psa. 119:89-90; Isa. 40:8; Matt. 5:18, 24:35) in contrast to the heaven and earth that will pass away (Luke 16:17; 21:33). Jesus Himself indicated that Scripture will always be available for man to live by (Matt. 4:4).

The doctrine that God's Word remains forever is the doctrine that it is **eternal**. However, the Word of God originated in heaven even before the world began. We know that, "In the beginning was the Word" (John 1:1) and in fact, "Thy Word is true from the beginning" (Ps. 119:160). This means that the Word has existed from eternity past in heaven.

How does this apply to the history of the world? These passages give us every right to believe that those who want God's Word are not now, nor ever will be, substantially without the Word of God. None of it is lost, if we are to believe Jesus' explicit teachings on the matter. For, if man is to live by every word that proceeds out of the mouth of God as Jesus told Satan (Matt. 4:4, citing Deut. 8:3), then that Word would have to be available for man in every age.

This means that God's Word was preserved for the Jews first in Hebrew and then in the Greek Old Testaments (after the dispersed Jews forgot their Hebrew). It would have to mean that God's Word was preserved for the Roman Empire in Latin, for the Coptic Christians in Egypt, and so on. Since it is God's promises that are at stake here, His promises must be applicable to the people who lived in Old Testament times, between the testaments, contemporary with the apostles, in the early church, in the middle ages, during the Reformation, in modern times—in every age. And indeed a sober reflection would conclude that God has indeed left His Word for all of these peoples in all of these places in all of these times. If we start scrutinizing and comparing versions from different ages one to another, we are bound to find some minor differences of translation as well as misprints, or "typos," as we would call them today. But we will also find that God has been true to His promises—to preserve His Word for His people—in spite of those minor differences.

Further, what is thus true for various peoples of differing languages, would certainly be no less true for people who speak the same language but reside in different parts of the world—as would be the case when Greek, followed by Latin, dominated the civilized world. Prior to the time of printed Bibles, we know that Greek speaking people in the Western part of the world had manuscripts of the New Testament which differed slightly from manuscripts used in the Eastern part of the world. Some 8,000 various manuscripts of the Bible testify to the same phenomenon in Latin. Strictly speaking, God's promises to preserve His Word are no less applicable to these situations then to that of people of varying languages.

We know God's Word is settled in heaven. Why study about the vagaries of history and translation? It would all be very easy if the original manuscripts of the books of the Bible could still be consulted. However, these original writings, called the **autographs**, have long since crumbled into dust. The loss of the autographs did not surprise God, and it is within God's providence that we do not have them. Though God may have had any number of reasons for letting them perish, even mere humans can see that if he had preserved them, men would tend to worship them (as ancient religious relics like the Shroud of Turin). God did not intend for men to worship the Bible, rather He wrote it so that man might read and obey it. By allowing the autographs to perish, God removed the possibility of their being worshiped and precluded idolatry toward His gift of Scripture. God's revelation is apparently not intended as an object of idolatry but to enable man to know God and to worship Him.

In spite of the loss of the autographs, there is plenty of evidence that God has preserved his Word through all generations. Copies were made of the autographs before they fell apart from use, and these copies continued to be copied until today. Copies made before the invention of the printing press are called **manuscripts**, meaning hand-copied. Manuscripts that have survived until the present are called **extant** manuscripts. Of course, many of the copies eventually wore out or were burned by pagan rulers, but the various extant copies provide ample evidence of preservation.

Besides the evidence from extant manuscripts, we also have evidence from our Lord's own example. The autographs of the Old Testament books were already lost when Jesus made His statements about the preservation of the Word of God. It is obvious that Jesus did not consider the lack of the autographs an important matter, and he called the extant copies inspired in spite of any "typos" in them. Since Christ never doubted the preservation of Scripture, we need not either.

Humanists and other enemies of Christianity love to point to the differences among versions and the lack of autographs to get people to doubt the authority of the Bible. It behooves the brethren to be aware of God's providence in preservation so as not to let the enemy get a foothold in shaking their faith.

Means of Preservation

If God has not preserved His Word by letting us check copies against the originals, how has he preserved it? More will be said in the next few chapters to strengthen your faith and display God's providence over the preservation of His Word on the earth. However, this chapter is concerned with preservation as doctrinal rather than providential. What can we know about how God has preserved his Word from Scripture?

In all the passages regarding the preservation of the New Testament there is no direct statement regarding the means of it. There is, for example, no indication that God supervised the copyists in a manner similar to His supervision of the inspired writers themselves (as in II Pet. 1:21). One does not read that "holy scribes of God were moved by the Holy Spirit" or anything equivalent to it.

As noted previously, the Lord was not disturbed by variations in copying. Christ quoted from several versions and different copies of different versions. He was aware of the "typos" and neither avoided nor condemned any. Such variations could not have even existed if the Lord had supernaturally intervened to make infallible copyists. In fact, any reader of any English translation can see that quotations of Old Testament passages were rarely word for word.

Quotations of the sense rather than the letter do not jeopardize what is written in any way.

Inspired copyists? In spite of this, some, such as Edward F. Hills, perceive differences of quotations as attacks on Scripture. In order to argue that there remain perfect copies without such differences, he builds a theoretical and speculative argument. Let's consider this doctrinal position. According to Hills, since God chose special believers to inspire His Word in the first place (II Pet. 1:20-21), He must have also chosen special copyists to preserve that same Word flawless. Who were these copyists?

Hills argues from Deuteronomy 31:12, 24-26 that God committed the copying of the Old Testament manuscripts to the Levitical priesthood. He says: But the duty of preserving this written revelation was assigned not to the prophets but to the priests [emphasis his]. The priests were the divinely appointed guardians and teachers of the law. Evidently the priests were also given the task of making correct copies of the law for the use of kings and rulers, or at least of supervising the scribes to whom the king would delegate this work.

However, careful reading discloses that these verses teach no more than the guardianship and responsibility to teach the law to the people. Though it is natural to suppose that some were also involved in the copying of it, it does not say that they were the only ones. He says the same of Deuteronomy 17:18, but again the work of copying is not delegated as a special work of priests. In fact, history shows that carefully trained Jewish scribes did the actual copying of the Old Testament. The Jewish groups that did the copying of Scripture are fairly well known: the Sopherim (scribes), the Zugoth (the "pairs" of textual scholars), the Tannaim (the "repeaters" or "teachers"), and finally the Masoretes (preservers of the masorah, or oral tradition). Of course, a priest could apply himself to careful training and become a scribe, but scribes were not all priests. Neither history nor the passages in Deuteronomy give indication that the priests were the designated copyists of Scripture. Furthermore, the priests eventually lost even their teaching ministry to the rabbis.

Assuming that God gave the scribal duties to the priests, Hills draws an analogy to the copying of the New Testament with the church as the counterpart of the Old Testament priesthood. In this way, the Holy Spirit preserved the New Testament text through the universal priesthood of believers. Those who reason this way do so to argue that the text of the New Testament, so providentially preserved in this fashion, is the Textus Receptus, as reflected in the majority of the manuscripts.

While it is certain that believers copied the New Testament, this view creates doctrine by overlooking or ignoring God's providence in history. There is no historical evidence to indicate that a true and flawless Bible was copied exclusively by members of the believer-priesthood and that its error-ridden rival was copied exclusively by unbelievers. Quite the contrary, during the same period of history, various sectors of the Church had Bibles with slightly different wordings from which to preach and all of the manuscripts were quoted by orthodox believers in their writings in spite of such variations in wording. The writings of even the earliest orthodox preachers quoted from various copies and versions without concern. Such variations did not shake the faith of these preachers in the inspiration of the originals, nor should it. They were but following the Lord's example, who had not been alarmed by variations in manuscripts during His earthly ministry.

Who had the "flawless" copy in the second century? Every copy had its "typos." The differences of wordings in a given passage resulting from these "typos" are called **variant readings** (or just **readings** or **variants**). When any two copies are compared, they will share at least one such "typo" that can be recognized by comparing both against other manuscripts.

The problem then is to achieve a proper perspective with regard to such variant readings—the textual problems of the New Testament. The correct view must not conflict with the promises of God concerning His preservation of Scripture, but neither may it reconstruct history to make its case. **Textual Criticism** is the comparison of manuscripts with the goal of eliminating "typos" and obtaining a copy of the autographs. Textual Criticism seeks to find the true history of God's providence over His Word. Every Christian is a textual critic, because we all must make judgments about translations and versions.

Textual Criticism is also called Lower Criticism to distinguish it from **Higher Criticism**. Higher Critics, in contrast, go beyond comparing manuscripts, and make judgments concerning the content of Scripture. Higher Critics contend that the words of the autographs (the true New Testament) are hopelessly lost amidst the readings of many error-ridden manuscripts. Textual Criticism helps to defend the Bible from this type of attack on the Word of God.

Wellhausen. **Julius Wellhausen** (1844-1918) is one of the most influential of the Higher Critics. One historian compares Wellhausen's theory of the Old Testament which prompted the modern revolution against Scripture to Darwin whose theory of evolution prompted the revolution against Creation.[7] Like other religious liberals, Wellhausen denies almost all the fundamental doctrines of the Christian faith.

Warfield. To this point in history, the landmark defense of the inspiration of the Bible was written by **Benjamin B. Warfield** (1851-1921). Warfield, after an education which included training at what later became Princeton University as well as at Edinburgh and Heidelberg, succeeded Dr. A. A. Hodge as professor of Systematic Theology at Princeton at a time when that school still maintained and taught the doctrines of God's Word. He brought to the study of the Bible a unique combination of immense scholarship, unexcelled knowledge of the attacks on the Bible from all positions, and unswerving commitment to the inspiration, inerrancy, and authority of the Scriptures. Warfield wrote several articles dealing with various aspects of the inspiration of the Bible. These articles were printed into a volume originally published by Oxford University Press under the title *Revelation and Inspiration*. Later the Presbyterian and Reformed Publishing Company reprinted the material under the title, *The Inspiration and Authority of the Bible*. It has long been recognized as a classic defense of Scripture from the attacks of Higher Critics.

Warfield also wrote *An Introduction to the Textual Criticism of the New Testament*. In this work, he distinguishes purity of doctrinal content (substantive purity) from purity of transmission (textual purity). It is important to realize that when textual researchers speak of corruptions in the text, they are not criticizing God's Word but are criticizing a phrase which they believe to be one of those "typos."

Though it may sound strange, it merely recognizes that a technical difference in sentence structure need not affect the message. Multilingual persons readily understand that one can say the same thing in several ways. For example, there is no substantial effect on the meaning of the statement "she denied her daughter permission to go," if the wording is altered to read "she refused to let her daughter go." But such a change in the text (more than a simple "typo") would consider the text with the error textually "corrupt" and the other "pure."

With this in mind, Warfield gauges the "purity" of the text of the New Testament by two measuring rods. First, he compares it to a modern book produced by modern proofreading methods, and with the original available for consultation. Compared to this the text of the New Testament is "sorely corrupt." The manuscript copyists had none of the valuable assistance of the modern printing press that virtually eliminates the introduction of new errors while old ones are being corrected. On the other hand, when he compares the New Testament to any other ancient writing, he finds it "marvelously correct."

Warfield goes on to point out that the text of Scripture is substantially unaffected by the variations. He observed,

> Such has been the care with which the New Testament
> has been copied,—a care which has doubtless grown
> out of true reverence of its holy words,—such has been
> the providence of God in preserving for His Church in
> each and every age a competently exact text of the
> Scriptures, that not only is the New Testament unrivalled
> among ancient writings in the purity of its text as actually
> transmitted and kept in use, but also in the abundance
> of testimony which has come down to us for castigating
> its comparatively infrequent blemishes. The divergence
> of its current text from the autograph may shock a modern
> printer of modern books; its wonderful approximation
> to its autograph is the undisguised envy of every modern
> reader of ancient books.[8]

Warfield has answered Wellhausen and shown that the true New Testament has existed in every age since the autographs and that the manuscript variations do not affect this fact. It is simply not true to say that the truth of Scripture is imperiled by the textual impurities of the sort found in the New Testament manuscripts.

In spite of such clearly defined battle lines between Christian and liberal theology, there are men who castigate both alike simply for discussing textual issues. David Otis Fuller denounces those who study the textual variations. He says, "THE BATTLE IS ON [emphasis his]!" "And Christian, the foundations of your faith and mine are now, this very moment, under bitter and vitriolic attack by the enemy of our souls. Other ages have witnessed vicious and malicious attacks upon the inspired Word of God, but never has any other age seen the attacks multiply with such rapidity."[9] By his exaggerated tone and language, he condemns Warfield and Wellhausen in the same breath. Such unwarranted rhetoric fails to distinguish liberal theology from thorny theoretical issues involving believers on both sides.

It was considered the greatest tragedy, during the two world wars in which our country was engaged, when occasionally out of confusion, our air force pilots mistakenly bombed or fired upon our own troops and killed many of them. Spiritually, men like Fuller, well-intentioned as they may be, have nonetheless caused division and brought about spiritual casualties among God's people through such indiscriminate and unsubstantiated attacks. Those who appear to love Christ and defend the truth in this way set a snare for believers on textual issues. This lure away from clear Bible teachings into controversy is second in seriousness only to doubts concerning inspiration caused by liberal critics such as Wellhausen.

In fact, we as authors do not hold the same view on the subject. But we invariably agree on the fundamental teachings of the Word of God, and we hope by collaborating in this effort to show Christians where the real targets are. By showing a willingness to understand views of other Christians, we hope that the artillery can be redirected against the true enemies: the army of liberal theologians who deny the word of God and the snipers among us, reactionaries that would divide the flock over these teachings of men. Rather than promoting our own positions, we wish to produce an informative book that acknowledges both the positive contributions of opposing views and the weaknesses of our own. In such a controversial field, this is no small endeavor. We ask only that our statements be taken in context and not prejudged. May the Lord be glorified for his providence over His Word.

Summary

The inspiration of Scripture is a clear doctrine of the Bible and includes the inerrancy of the infallible and authoritative Word of God. The verbal and plenary inspiration of the Bible is the foundation of our faith. This raises the question of its preservation. It is clear that God preserved His Word during its recognition and formation into the canon. It is also clear that God has promised to preserve His Word in heaven forever.

What is less clear is how God is preserving the Bible. Though the Bible describes a little of the process of inspiration, it does not describe in detail the process of preservation. Since God also chose in His providence not to preserve the autographs, it takes more effort to understand the process. The next several chapters will address important evidences of preservation.

Endnotes

1. Walter C. Kaiser, Jr., *Toward Rediscovering the Old Testament* (Grand Rapids: Zondervan, 1987), p. 37.

2. Henry Clarence Thiessen, *Introduction to the New Testament* (Grand Rapids: William B. Eerdmans, 1943, reprint 1987), pp. 8-9.

3. Thiessen, p. 9.

4. F. F. Bruce, *The Books and the Parchments* (Old Tappan, NJ: Fleming H. Revell, 1950, reprint 1984), pp. 103-4.

5. Josh McDowell, *Evidence that Demands a Verdict,* revised ed., (San Bernardino, Calif.: Campus Crusade for Christ, 1979), p. 38.

6. Norman Geisler and William E. Nix, *A General Introduction to the Bible* (Chicago: Moody Press, 1968), p. 172.

7. See Chapter 5 "Closing the Book: Julius Wellhausen," in Dave Breese, *Seven Men Who Rule the World from the Grave* (Chicago: Moody Press, 1990), pp. 89-104.

8. B. B. Warfield, *An Introduction to the Textual Criticism of the New Testament,* (London: Hodder and Stoughton, 1896), pp. 12-13.

9.   David Otis Fuller, *True or False?* (Grand Rapids: Grand Rapids International Publications, 1973, reprint 1978), p. 35.

Questions

1. Explain the doctrine of inspiration, especially the product, based on Bible verses.

2. Explain what each of the following terms tells us about the doctrine of inspiration: inerrant, infallible, authoritative.

3. Distinguish between the verbal and plenary inspiration of Scripture.

4. Explain which (if any) of the church councils decided on the canon of Scripture and justify your answer.

5. Identify some criteria that helped believers recognize the canon.

6. What does Scripture say about its preservation?

7. Evaluate the strengths and weaknesses of the theory of inspired copyists.

8. Distinguish Lower Criticism from Higher Criticism.

9. Who wrote the greatest defense of Scripture ever penned: *The Inspiration and Authority of the Bible?*

10. Describe the twin dangers for the students of the Bible regarding the preservation of the Bible.

CHAPTER 2

PRESERVED SINCE ANTIQUITY

Although God did not see fit to preserve the autographs themselves, God has providentially preserved some very ancient manuscripts of the Bible. This chapter will look at some of those manuscripts and see how their preservation glorifies Him.

Ancient Language

Most of the books of the Old Testament were written in **Hebrew**, the language of ancient Israel. Recall that the 39 books of our Old Testament correspond to the 22 books of the Hebrew Bible. Of these, 35 were written entirely in Hebrew. Two others were almost entirely in Hebrew since Jeremiah contains only one verse (10:11) and Genesis contains only two words (Jegar Sahadutha in Gen. 31:47) that are not Hebrew. Even the two remaining books, Daniel and Ezra, are largely in Hebrew but have longer foreign passages.

Although most of the Old Testament was first written in Hebrew, several portions were written in **Aramaic**. Aramaic is the language of the Aramaeans, the people from Aram. Because Aram is in western Syria, Aramaic is sometimes called Syrian or even Chaldee in English versions. The Aramaic portions include the two words in Genesis

31:47, the verse in Jeremiah 10 (v. 11), and several chapters of Ezra and Daniel. Thus, the main Aramaic portions of the Bible are Daniel 2:46-7:28 and Ezra 4:8-6:18 and 7:12-26.

Why are these passages in Aramaic? As the Babylonian kingdom grew, its Aramaic language became increasingly important for trade. Some men of Judah already knew it when the Babylonians invaded (2 Kings 18:26). Eventually, Aramaic became the international language, or *lingua franca,* and all the Israelites had to learn it when they came to Babylon as a captive people. When Ezra returned to Jerusalem, his letters to the king still had to be in Aramaic. Likewise, Daniel's prophecies against the nations had to be in Aramaic if other nations were intended to hear and understand.

By New Testament times, the Greeks and then the Romans had come to dominate the ancient world. Thus, the importance of Aramaic had diminished. However, Aramaic remained the common tongue in Israel. Some of the words Jesus spoke in Aramaic are preserved even in our English Bibles (Matt. 27:46, Mark 5:41, 7:34, 15:34). Most Christians also recognize the Aramaic words *Abba* (Father, Rom. 8:15, Gal. 4:6) and *Maranatha* (1 Cor. 16:22). Because Aramaic remained the common tongue in Israel, the word Hebrew refers to Aramaic in this period. Pilate's superscription on the cross of our Lord, then was in the dominant languages of the empire Greek and Latin, as well as the local tongue of the Hebrews, namely Aramaic (Luke 23:38).

All 27 books of the New Testament were originally written in **Greek,** the language of ancient Greece. Although, translations were soon made (see chapter 3), the most important manuscripts are still in Greek because details are always lost in translation. Any translation of Homer is adequate for those who want to read the story, but a person who wants to study Homeric themes or analyze his literary allusions will be greatly hampered without a knowledge of the original classical Greek.

In the same way, a good English translation is adequate for a Christian, but those who want to answer tough questions or prepare as a preacher need to learn Greek. This fact has been long known. When America was young, most schools required both Greek and Latin, because study of the Scripture was the main purpose for an education. Greek is still required for most seminary degrees.

Interestingly, though, until the late 1800s, it was thought that the New Testament was written in classical Greek just like Homer. Scholars then recognized that many sentences in the Bible broke the rules of classical Greek. Some concluded that the apostles spoke inferior Greek, while others assumed that it was a special language used by the Holy Ghost.

In the late nineteenth century, archaeologists began to discover many papyri with writing similar to the New Testament. They soon recognized that these papyri represented a form of Greek that displaced classical Greek, in some ways much as modern English replaced Old English. They immediately saw that this was the language of the common man during New Testament times, and they named this new stage of the Greek language **Koine,** which means common.[1] In His providential wisdom, God chose not the elitist, sophisticated, and difficult classical Greek, but the familiar language of the common man, Koine Greek, to reveal Himself and His Gospel to the Gentiles.

During both the Classical and Koine periods, two forms of written Greek were used. A cursive style was used for business transactions and letters. Literary works, however, were written in a formal style called **uncial.** This word derives from the Latin word meaning one-twelfth because an average line of text contained only twelve of these blocky capital Greek letters.[2] Scribes copied the New Testament using this formal literary style, and it should also be remembered that these copies had no spaces between words and no punctuation.

Ancient Books

Papyri

People of the ancient near east wrote on several substances. Notes could be written on bone, wood, or **ostraca** (shards of broken pottery), but such small surfaces were not appropriate for books. Clay **tablets** could also be used, especially for students in school, but more durable substances were desirable for important documents.

The most durable substances were stone or metal, but the effort required to write on these limited their use. Kings went to great expense and effort to etch their achievements in such monoliths, called **stele**. However, a book would be too lengthy for such treatment.

The most economical writing material was **papyrus**. Egyptians produced papyri economically because papyrus reeds up to fifteen feet high grew in profusion in the marshes of the Nile delta. Egyptians would cut the long reeds into foot-long sections, and then cut the pith into strips. By pressing two layers together with the top fibers at right angles to that below, they made a very strong fabric.[3]

Papyrus manuscripts could be written on more easily than on stone or metal, yet they were very durable compared to clay. Papyri could be linked end to end to form a **scroll** or collected in a book form called a **codex**. Either way, there was ample room for copying an entire book, unlike wood or ostraca. It is no wonder that Alexandria had the largest and most famous library in the ancient world.

Today, about 100 papyri containing portions of the New Testament are known. These have been numbered and are abbreviated by a "P" followed by the number as a supercript. Most papyri are fragmentary, but they are the oldest manuscripts of the New Testament that have come down to us. Only a handful of the papyri are remains of scrolls (such as P^{12}, P^{13}, P^{18}, and P^{22}). The rest were codices. Several of the oldest codices are of special interest.

The **Chester Beatty Papyri** date from the early third century and are now in the Beatty Museum near Dublin. In the 1930s some 30 papyri were known and a few were almost as old, but none contained more than a single leaf.[4] At the discovery of the Chester Beatty Papyri, for the first time a manuscript of most of the Bible became available that was older than the fourth century. They became the oldest relatively complete manuscripts of the New Testament. P^{45} contains 30 of the original 220 leaves of a codex of the gospels and Acts. P^{46} dating from the year 200 contains nine Pauline Epistles and Hebrews, while P^{47} contains ten leaves of Revelation 9:10-17:2.

The **Bodmer Papyri** include the oldest copies of several books. Published in the 1960s and now in the Library of World Literature near Geneva, these displaced the Chester Beatty Papyri in importance. The epistles of Peter and Jude (P^{72}) date from the third century, while P^{75} contains Luke and John and dates from 175-225. The portions of John 1-14 in P^{66} also date to about 200. P74 contains portions of Acts and the general epistles and dates to the seventh century. This is very recent for a papyrus, since only three more recent are known (all eighth century). The early Bodmer Papyri, in contrast, offer evidence of biblical antiquity, since the oldest known copies of Peter and Jude are in P^{72}, and the oldest copy of Luke is in P^{75}. P^{66} contains the oldest surviving extended portion of Scripture.

Another papyrus, P^{52}, the **Rylands Papyrus** is the oldest confirmed manuscript from the New Testament.[5] Dating to the first half of the second century, it currently resides at the John Rylands Library in Manchester, England. Although it contains portions of only five verses, John 18:31-33, 37-38, it offers important evidence of the antiquity of Scripture.

Liberals frequently attack the integrity of the Bible by trying to date the autographs to a time after the apostolic era. If the late date were correct, the New Testament books were not written by eye-witnesses during the apostolic age. This would mean that the orthodox should question the books as forgeries written after the apostolic era and foisted on the church. Late dates then undermine the integrity and canonicity of Scripture.

Ferdinand Christian Baur was one such infidel scholar who dated the Book of John at AD 160.[6] Unfortunately, the Rylands papyrus was not discovered during his lifetime, but it quickly silenced the liberal critics after him. This underscores the importance of the preservation of ancient manuscripts. The Lord clearly had a purpose for preserving this ancient papyrus.

Parchments

Pliny the Elder records that shortly after 200 B.C., King Eumenes of Pergamum desired to build a library to rival Alexandria. Ptolemy, placed an embargo on papyrus to nip the desire in the bud. Surely, without papyrus, Eumenes would not be able to have any books for his library. Instead, Eumenes popularized the use of parchments for writing.[7] Whether or not Pliny's history is accurate in every detail, parchment displaced papyrus completely by the eighth century.

Parchment is leather made of sheep, goat, cattle, or antelope skins, especially young ones. Preparation required scraping off the hair, washing the skins, smoothing them with pumice, and dressing with chalk.[8] The leaves or pages of a parchment codex alternated so that the darker hair sides always faced each other. Skins were available throughout the ancient world, unlike papyrus. This made parchment very practical, though still expensive. At least fifty sheep would be required to obtain enough parchment for a copy of the New Testament, and that does not count the labor in preparing the parchment and hand copying the text! Few could afford their own Bible at such a cost.

At least 274 uncial parchments are known. Distinctive styles in the ruled margins are among the factors that help scholars determine the date and sometimes source of the manuscript. These date from the second through tenth centuries (although one is known from the eleventh). Originally capital letters (English) were used to designate uncials (A, B, etc.), but after running out of both English and Greek capital letters, a new system was adopted. Caspar René Gregory (1846-1917, born in America) provided the current numbering system that designate uncials using an initial zero (to distinguish them from minuscules which you will learn about in chapter 3).[9]

The oldest uncials are 0189, 0171 (II or III centuries), 0212 (III century), and 0162 and 0220 (III-IV centuries). These are small fragments of books. For instance 0171 contains 23 verses from Luke 21-22, while 0220 consists of one leaf from Romans 4-5.

The most famous parchments are usually still referred to by their capital letter names. The two oldest almost-complete parchments of the New Testament date to the fourth century: codex **Vaticanus** (B) in the Vatican Library and codex **Sinaiticus** (ℵ) in the British Museum. More will be said about these in future chapters. The British Museum also contains a fifth century uncial, codex Alexandrinus (A), which is also almost complete. These held the place of oldest most-complete manuscripts of the New Testament until the discovery of the Chester Beatty Papyri.

Codex Ephraemi Rescriptus (C) is a fifth century parchment containing portions of every book except II John and II Thessalonians. The codex is an example of a **palimpsest**, a parchment that was "erased" and another book written on the same leaves. In this case, the New Testament was erased in the 12th century, and the sermons of St. Ephraem were then written. Eventually methods were found to read the erased text, and Tischendorf first read this particular manuscript. Another palimpsest is codex Nitirensis (R), a sixth century copy of Luke, that was overwritten in the eighth or ninth century with the treatise of Severus against Johannes Grammaticus.

Codex Bezae (D) is interesting for its many unique variants. It contains entire verses and even statements of the Lord not found in any other manuscript. Copied in the fifth or sixth century, Theodore Bezae presented this codex to Cambridge University in 1581.

The finest parchment is called **vellum**. These deluxe copies were dyed royal purple. Instead of simple ink, the reed pen would be dipped in silver or gold ink. Four important vellum manuscripts date to the sixth century. Codex Beratinus contains Matthew and Mark and uses silver ink. Codex Rossanensis has the same format but uses gold ink for the first three lines of each book. Codex Purpureus Petropolitanus (N) contains the gospels and uses silver ink, but the names of God and Jesus are in gold. Codex Sinopensis (O), its 43 leaves of Matthew at Paris, uses gold ink.

Although uncials originated in Bible lands, you have noticed that many currently reside in museums of Europe. In fact, the distribution is of some interest. The monastery at Mt. Athos, Greece, probably has the most (900), while Athens (national library) is a distant second (419). Mt. Sinai, another monastery, has a collection of over 200. Besides the museum at Athens, other large museum collections are to be found mostly among the colonial powers of Europe. Paris, London, Leningrad, and Oxford each have over 150 manuscripts. Rome also ranks high (fourth with 367), but that is because of the Vatican rather than colonial pursuits.[10]

Although almost 300 manuscripts reside in the USA, they are scattered among collections in many cities. The Smithsonian Institute at Washington, D.C., is the most notable, since it has the two most important manuscripts in the hemisphere. Codex W contains the gospels and dates to the fourth or fifth century. Codex I consists of 84 leaves of Hebrews and the Pauline epistles (except Romans) and dates to the fifth or sixth century.

Summary

This chapter has shown how God, in his providence, has preserved ancient texts for his glory. Man's study is but a feeble attempt to understand history, which is at once encompassed by God's omniscience. Scholars criticized the poor classical Greek of the apostles until they discovered that it was Koine Greek rather than classical. Liberal scholars tend to date New Testament books late as an attack on their authenticity, but God preserved ancient texts to silence them. He has also providentially preserved some manuscripts from every century, a clear indication of preservation throughout the ages since the autographs.

Endnotes

1. For a discussion of God's choice of Koine Greek, see Geisler and Nix, pp. 217-18, 220-21.

2. Bruce Manning Metzger, *The Text of the New Testament* (New York: Oxford, 1968), p. 9 including footnote 1.

3. Metzger, *Text*, pp. 3-4.

4. Kurt and Barbara Aland, *The Text of the New Testament* (Leiden: E. J. Brill, 1987), pp. 84, 87.

5. In 1972, Jose O'Callaghan identified eight scraps among the Dead Sea Scrolls found at Qumran as portions of the New Testament. Since very few letters remain, some scholars dispute his claim. If the fragments are from the New Testament, they are the oldest manuscripts since they definitely date from A.D. 50-80 (all the Dead Sea Scrolls are at least that old). The fragment *7Q5* probably contains Mark 6:52-53, and from that basis it is likely that *7Q4* and *7Q8* represent 1 Tim. 3:16, 4:1, 3 and James 1:23-24 respectively. Wilbur N. Pickering (pp. 155-158) defends these identifications but considers the other five identifications possible but strictly hypothetical. The five are Mark 6:48, 12:17, Acts 27:38, Rom. 5:11-12, and 2 Pet. 1:15 (see Cairns, p. 370).

6. Metzger, *Text*, p. 39.

7. Metzger, *Text*, p. 4.
8. Metzger, *Text*, p. 4.
9. Aland and Aland, *Text*, p. 73.
10. Aland and Aland, *Text*, p. 79.

Questions

1. Identify the three languages in which the autographs of the Bible were written.

2. Distinguish the languages of the New Testament and Homer.

3. Identify the oldest extant fragment of the New Testament and the two oldest nearly complete manuscripts of the New Testament. Explain the significance of each.

4. Define palimpsest and vellum.

5. Distinguish scroll and codex.

   Match the following base substances to the correct term.

   a. animal hides
   b. clay
   c. potsherds
   d. reed
   e. stone

6. Ostraca

7. Parchment

8. Papyrus

9. Stele

10. Tablet

CHAPTER 3

PRESERVATION IN QUANTITY

This chapter begins with a brief survey of Old Testament manuscripts for comparison. The focus of the chapter, however, is on the New Testament manuscripts. Topics include manuscript content, minuscules, and a comparison with ancient secular literature.

Old Testament Manuscripts

Just a century ago or so, men who denounced Scripture had little worry that their speculations and assertions could be proved wrong. **Archaeology** (study of ancient ruins and relics) and **paleography** (study of ancient writing) were relatively young sciences and had made more limited contributions. Such men as W. A. Irwin denied even the existence of the Babylonian exile and called it the fabrication of later writers. Since then, archaeologists have confirmed the details of the exile by excavating the cities conquered and paleographers have read Nebuchadnezzar's own inscriptions and royal archives.[1] Such speculations and groundless assertions against the historical record of Scripture often succumb to archaeological discoveries that confirm the biblical record.

Archaeological finds accumulated without locating more

ancient manuscripts of the Old Testament. The comparative rarity of Old Testament manuscripts suggests that Jewish scribes destroyed their older copy after making a new one. Even up until 1947, the Leningrad Codex, was the oldest known copy of the Old Testament, dating to A.D. 916[2] even though the last book of the Old Testament had been written about 400 B.C. This old codex and the fact that the scribes called Masoretes even counted letters to ensure accurate copying gave Christians a basis from which to argue preservation of this **Masoretic Text.** However, the Higher Critics simply scoffed.

The lack of more ancient evidence made it easy for the scoffers to speculate that the text had changed drastically over the ages. Such infidels condemned the stories of Adam, Noah, Abraham, and Moses as legendary traditions handed down and embellished for millennia. Wellhausen's theory is typical of such thinking. His *documentary hypothesis* affirmed that the Pentateuch actually consisted of four documents (*J, E, D, P*), two identified by which name the writer used for God (*J*ehovah or *E*lohim, as though no writer could use more than one!) and two identified by content (*D*euteronomical or *P*riestly-Levitical). He placed all four documents long after Moses and even after Solomon, dating them respectively 850, 750, 621, and post-exilic (after 500 B.C.).

The discovery of the **Dead Sea Scrolls** silenced much of this nonsense. The Dead Sea Scrolls consist of 400 scrolls discovered since 1947 in caves at Qumran by the Dead Sea. This community flourished from 100 B.C. to A.D. 70. Portions of every Old Testament book except Esther have been found along with many other ancient works. Thus, these manuscripts are about a millennium earlier than any previously known manuscripts. Since the scrolls agreed almost perfectly with the Masoretic Text, it became obvious that the careful scribal practices of the Jews enabled them to transmit exact wording over long periods of time. The transmission was not only free from embellishment, but virtually identical.

On the other hand, though the Dead Sea Scrolls became the oldest manuscripts and evidenced faithful copying, they did not undermine the late dates assigned to the biblical books by critics. The 1901 discovery of the Code of Hammurabi, which showed that the cultural traditions of patriarchal times were real and not later literary fabrications, made the Higher Critics revise their view. However, the critics still claimed the late dates for the four documents but admitted that they incorporated more ancient traditions.[3]

God made the critics backpedal more swiftly in the 1980s with the discovery of what remains the oldest portion of the Old Testament yet discovered. Archaeologist found two silver talismans etched with the blessing from Numbers 6:24-25. Found in a burial cave in Jerusalem, they date from before the destruction of the temple (586 B.C.). This flatly contradicts the post-exilic date which the critics had assigned to this blessing.[4]

New Testament Manuscripts

In contrast, the New Testament has not suffered from lack of manuscripts. Further, it is comparatively recent in date, so scoffers take a different tack. By focusing on variations between manuscripts they seek to undermine its authority. A careful examination exposes this ruse, but first it is necessary to obtain background information on this mass of manuscripts.

In fact, New Testament manuscripts are so numerous that they are divided by content into four parts. Textual scholars abbreviate the four parts with a lower case letter:

e the four gospels (or *euangellion*, Greek for gospel)
a Acts with the General Epistles
p the Pauline Epistles including Hebrews
r Revelation

Some two hundred manuscripts included the entire New Testament or lacked only Revelation. However, the order of the Acts, General, and Pauline Epistles occur in every possible permutation.[5]

Many manuscripts contain only one of the four portions of the New Testament. This should not surprise us since even today we can go to the store and buy a Gospel of John instead of an entire New Testament. In ancient times, before printing, obtaining major portions would have been even more important.

The most copied of the four portions were the Gospels. Manuscripts of the Gospels comprise about twice as many as all the other portions combined. However, even Revelation, the portion with the least manuscript support, can still be found in almost 300 copies, either alone or with the rest of the New Testament.

The reader will also recall that some manuscripts are simply fragments, such as the Rylands Papyrus. However, of 4000 manuscripts classified by Aland, only about 300 are considered fragments.[6] This is important because it documents the vast amount of textual evidence to God's preservation of the Bible.

Finally, it should be noted that some of the later manuscripts were written on paper rather than papyrus or parchment. Although the Chinese invented paper in the first century, it did not appear in the West until much later. The oldest New Testament manuscript on paper is dated in the twelfth century, and about a quarter of all the manuscripts are on paper (and a few others contain both parchment and paper leaves bound together).[7] By the late Middle Ages the use of paper had completely displaced parchment.

The Minuscules

About the ninth century, the cursive script developed into a very fluid and convenient writing system. The New Testament began to be copied in this script, and the resulting manuscripts are called **cursives** or **minuscules**. This script, in fact, became so popular that the uncial script died out completely after the eleventh century.

Most extant manuscripts are minuscules (whether written on parchment or paper). About 2800 of the 5300 manuscripts known by 1980 were minuscules.[8] Minuscules are designated by a number (like uncials but without the leading zero). Numbers ranged from 1 to 2795 in 1987, but more are continually discovered.

The vast quantity of textual evidence contained in 5300 manuscripts is beyond comprehension. It would take many lifetimes to read all of the manuscripts, much less painstakingly compare them all word for word. For this reason, many of them still have not been studied in detail. This is especially true of minuscules since there are so many of them, and since they are not quite so old. Still minuscules have important contributions to make, and more are being studied each year.

The oldest minuscule is manuscript 461, which dates from the year 835 A.D. and contains the gospels. Manuscript 33 is called the Queen of the Cursives because it was once thought to be the most valuable minuscule for scholarly study.

Codex 2 is one of the most influential manuscripts for the history of the English Bible. This minuscule dates to the twelfth century and is preserved in the library at Basle, Switzerland. Erasmus, who prepared the first Greek New Testament published on a printing press, depended upon this manuscript for the Gospels, only occasionally making changes based on another manuscript.[9] That printing eventually became the basis for our beloved King James Version.

There are also a few families of manuscripts among the minuscules. A **family** is named when some scholar groups together a number of manuscripts having distinctive similarities that he deems important. Family 1 (the Lake Group) consists of minuscules 1, 118, 131, 209, 1582, and others. Kirsopp Lake considered this group to represent manuscripts typical of a certain region (Caesarea).[10] Another group, Family M^a, is a large group of 74 manuscripts containing the book of Revelation. With similarities first recognized by Schmid, this group is still considered important by Zane Hodges.[11]

One interesting family is **Family 13** (the Ferrar Group), which includes manuscripts 13, 69, 124, 230, 346, 543, 788, 826, 828, 983, 1689, and 1709. The family is distinctive because the story of the adulterous woman, which our Bibles contain in John 7:53-8:11 appears in Luke (after 21:38)! William Hugh Ferrar first identified this family in 1868 based on four of the minuscules.[12]

Comparison to Other Books

In the last chapter, you learned that God providentially preserved some very old copies of the New Testament to silence the Higher Critics who tried to say that it was written much later. That this is a case of divine preservation is obvious when you compare this with other ancient books. However, the ancient manuscripts are not the only evidence of divine preservation. There are thousands of manuscripts of the New Testament compared to relatively few for other ancient works.

For instance, the Bible was completed when the apostle John finished writing Revelation about A.D. 95. About the same time **Tacitus** completed his *Annals*. Of the 16 volumes comprising the *Annals*, only ten survive and two others in part. The first six volumes of this work are preserved in only one manuscript dating from the ninth century, over seven centuries after it was written. The mass of manuscript evidence for the New Testament far surpasses any human book. God has intervened providentially.[13]

Similarly, the History of Herodotus was completed by 425

B.C., but the oldest remaining manuscript dates to 900 A.D., over 1300 years after being written. More surprising, its content depends on only eight known manuscripts. The same is true of the History of Thucydides (400 B.C.). F.F. Bruce comments that "No classical scholar would listen to an argument that the authenticity of Herodotus or Thucydides is in doubt."[14]

Bruce Metzger notes several stories of human preservation that survived by a thread. He notes that the "history of Rome by Velleius Paterculus survived to modern times in only one incomplete manuscript . . . and this lone manuscript was lost in the seventeenth century after being copied" and also that the only known copy of the early Christian *Epistle to Diognetus* perished in 1870 in a fire at the library in Strasbourg.[15]

Some will counter that lack of preservation of obscure works does not prove the preservation of the Bible. Consider then, the work with the most existing manuscripts of any ancient book other than the Bible. The *Iliad* by **Homer** boasts 643 manuscripts and is considered the most widely read book in antiquity. Homer, like the Bible, was quoted in religious debate, memorized, and used to teach reading. Some copies of both works were illustrated, others were supplemented with glossaries. Finally both inspired commentaries, allegories, imitations, and art (murals and frescoes).[16] Still it is obvious that the book most preserved by human means retained 643 copies compared to 5000 for the New Testament.

The reader should also consider the *Elements* (Stoicheia) by **Euclid**. Encyclopedia Britannica observes "It is sometimes said that next to the Bible, the *Elements,* may be the most translated, published, and studied of all the books produced in the Western world."[17] This textbook, written about 300 B.C., was used throughout ancient times, the Middle Ages, and into the twentieth century. This is no obscure treatise, as evidenced by the 1000 editions of it since the invention of printing. One historian says of it, "Perhaps no book other than the Bible can boast so many editions."[18] Although the most published human book in history, most existing copies are translations especially in Arabic and Latin (translated first in the eighth and eleventh centuries respectively). Of the Greek manuscripts, less than ten remain most of which date from the tenth to twelfth centuries and the oldest of which (at the Vatican) dates to A.D. 380. Three of Euclid's other works (*Surface Loci, Pseudaria,* and *Porisms*) have not survived at all. Euclid praised Aristaeus, a contemporary, for a great work on *Solid Loci,* which has not been preserved either.[19]

The following chart summarizes the comparison of the New Testament with other human works that have survived.[20]

Work	Date Completed	Oldest Copy	Time Gap (years)	Number of Manuscripts
New Testament	95 A.D.	125 A.D.	30	5300+
Euclid	300 B.C.	380 A.D.	680	10
Homer	900 B.C.	400 B.C.	500	643
Tacitus	100 A.D.	1100 A.D.	1000	20
Pliny the Younger	100 A.D.	850 A.D.	750	7
Herodotus	425 B.C.	900 A.D.	1300	8
Thucydides	400 B.C.	900 A.D.	1300	8
Aristotle	322 B.C.	1100 A.D.	1400	49
Plato	347 B.C.	900 A.D.	1200	7
Sophocles	406 B.C.	1000 A.D.	1400	193
Euripides	406 B.C.	1100 A.D.	1500	9
Aristophanes	385 B.C.	900 A.D.	1200	10

While a classical scholar is trying to conjecture what might have been written where there is a hole on his only manuscript, New Testament scholars have so much evidence for what was written that they have not sifted through all of it in four generations! In fact, the New Testament is more than eight to one than the next most frequent book. Such evidence proves that God has fulfilled his promise to preserve His Word.

Summary

The minuscules show God preserving His Word in great quantity. This is an important evidence of preservation that supplements the evidence from the oldest manuscripts presented in the last chapter. The amount of textual evidence for the New Testament far surpasses the quantity of evidence for any other book.

Endnotes

1. A. C. Schultz, "Exile" in *Zondervan Pictorial Bible Dictionary,* edited by Merrill Tenney, p. 427.

2. Alan Cairns, *Dictionary of Theological Terms,* (Belfast: Ambassador-Emerald International, 1998), p. 395.

3. Cairns, p. 199.

4. Amihai Mazar, *Archaeology of the Land of the Bible* (New York: Doubleday, 1992), pp. 517, 524.

5. Aland and Aland, p. 79.

6. Aland and Aland, p. 83.

7. Aland and Aland, p. 77.

8. Aland and Aland, p. 128.

9. Metzger, *Text,* p. 99.

10. Metzger, *Text,* p. 61.

11. Zane C. Hodges and Arthur L. Farstad, *The Greek New Testament According to the Majority Text* (Nashville: Thomas Nelson, 1982), pp. xxxiv, xlv.

12. Metzger, *Text,* p. 61.

13. F. F. Bruce, *The New Testament Documents: Are They Reliable?* (Downers Grove, IL: Inter Varsity Press, 1943, 1978), pp. 16-17.

14. Ibid.

15. Metzger, *Text,* p. 34.

16. Josh McDowell, *Evidence that Demands a Verdict* (San Bernadino, CA: Campus Crusade for Christ, 1979), p. 43 quotes both Metzger and Turner.

17. B. L. van der Waerden, "Euclid" in *Encyclopaedia Britannica* (Chicago: Helen Hemingway Benton, 1983), vol. 6., p. 1019.

18. Carl B. Boyer, *A History of Mathematics* (Princeton: Princeton University Press, 1985), pp. 111, 131.
19. Boyer, p. 112.
20. Table adapts (and adds Euclid to) McDowell, pp. 42-43.

Questions

1. Explain the importance of the Dead Sea Scrolls for a Christian.

2. Why are there so many New Testament manuscripts but so few of the Old Testament?

3. Into what four parts is the New Testament divided by ancient copyists and for purposes of textual study?

4. In what century were the first minuscules of the New Testament copied?

5. Contrast the terms *minuscule* and *parchment.*

6. Which manuscript of the Gospels had the greatest impact on the history of the English Bible?

7. What ancient book has the strongest comparisons with the New Testament including substantial amount of manuscript support?

8. What ancient book is called the most published and translated book in history after the New Testament?

9. Give the ratio of New Testament manuscripts to those of Euclid.

10. Revelation, being the last part of the Bible completed, is perhaps the part of the Bible most contemporary with Tacitus. Calculate the ration of extant manuscripts of Revelation to those of Tacitus.

CHAPTER 4

PRESERVATION THROUGH

DISSEMINATION

As is well known, the very oldest manuscripts of the New Testament tend to be found in Egypt because of its more accomodating climate. Yet God has preserved his word on a much grander scale. Ancient versions and quotations of early preachers also testify to the wide distribution of the Bible. Further, the Latin Vulgate of Jerome remains the translation of the New Testament with the longest continuous use in Western history.

Lesser Known Greek Sources

Besides manuscripts of the Greek New Testament, there are also quotations from the early church fathers as well as books of Scripture used for Scripture readings in churches.

Patristic Quotations

Of course, preachers and Bible scholars quote the Bible frequently and have always done so since the apostolic age. The writings of such preachers and scholars of the early church are called the Church Fathers, or **patristic** writings. Their writings from the centuries when Greek was the primary language are especially valuable because their Bible quotations can be checked against the Greek New Testament.

History records for us the lives of the great preachers and scholars of the early church. The century in which each lived, the place where they ministered, and their major travels are well known. When their Bible quotations are consistently in agreement with a given manuscript, it can provide evidence of the date and place of the manuscript.

Patristic evidence dates about as far back as the papyri do. The writings of Ignatius date back to about 110 A.D. He was the Bishop of Antioch and wrote seven letters (which quote Scripture) while being led to Rome for martyrdom. Justin, another Christian martyr at Rome, also left letters from the first half of the second century.

Heretics also quoted Scripture as did the **apologists** (defenders of the faith) who exposed their errors. Tatian and Marcion were early heretics (150 A.D.) who also left materials useful to Christians. Marcion left the earliest canonical list of books, and Tatian prepared the first harmony of the gospels, the *Diatessaron*, which is also useful in textual criticism. God raised up the apologists Polycarp and Irenaeus in defense of Scripture. Polycarp, Bishop of Smyrna, refuted Marcion but was burned at the stake as a martyr for his efforts. Irenaeus also defended the faith against the Gnostic heretics such as Marcion. He became the Bishop of Lyons and died about 200 A.D.

By the middle of the third century, five other important fathers had also died: Origen and Clement of Alexandria, Hippolytus of Rome, and Tertullian and Cyprian of Carthage. Of these, **Origen** is the most famous. His defense of Christianity from the first serious attacks of secular philosophy (Celsus) bring him credit. However, his sermons show a tendency to take Scripture symbolically and so he sets a wrong example for hermeneutics (interpretation).

Some of the better known fourth and fifth century fathers include Athanasius of Alexandria, Gregory of Nazianzus, Chrysostom of Constantinople, Theodore of Mopsuestia, Jerome, Augustine of Hippo, and the heretics Arius and Pelagius. In the region that is now Turkey, Chrysostom became known for his "golden-tongued" preaching, while Theodore gained a following for his theology and defense against the Monophysite heresy of Alexandria. Jerome is of special importance to textual criticism and will be discussed in detail later.

The two greatest of that period, however, were **Athanasius** and **Augustine,** both staunch defenders of the faith. Athanasius stood against Arius, the main rival of orthodox Christianity in his city (Alexandria). Athanasius's influence at the council of Nicaea against the Arians earned him the nickname "Father of Orthodoxy." Saint Augustine's *Confessions* relates his search for truth among the Manichaeans and his personal testimony of salvation by faith in Christ. This has made him the most famous of all the fathers, but his stand for truth against the Pelagians and Manichaeans is equally important. Thus, Athanasius and Augustine join Polycarp, Irenaeus, Origen, and Theodore of Mopsuestia as important apologists among the early church fathers.

Theologians continue to write to this day. However, church "father" should be restricted to the first millennium after Christ. In fact, patristic writings after Augustine are of relatively minor importance for textual criticism.

Lectionaries

A lectionary is not a normal New Testament in any language. Instead, a **lectionary** organizes passages to be read aloud in public services. The passages are selected topically, and there is no intent to read the entire Bible. Some portions were not read in the normal course of the year (such as Revelation), and even the included portions may be divided and read in different months and out of sequence. This should be no surprise, since your own pastor may interrupt his preaching from Romans for a special topic on Easter and another on Mother's Day.

Lectionaries are not useful for debates on the canon or on disputed passages, since some passages would not be there regardless. However, they are very useful in noting the wording of those passages that they contain. The Greek Orthodox Church still follows essentially the same pattern of reading found in the Greek lectionaries of the seventh and eighth centuries.

Lectionaries preserve an amazing amount of the New Testament and show that the New Testament was preached throughout all the centuries. The oldest lectionary dates to the fourth century, though only thirty-three are known from the eighth century or older (all of which use the uncial script). Over a hundred are known from each successive century until the sixteenth and the invention of printing. The total number of lectionaries known by 1987 was 2178.[1]

Ancient Versions

The Oldest Versions

A **version** is a translation of the New Testament from Greek into a language other than Greek. Since these languages change over time, many have had multiple translations much like English. This section will deal with the oldest extant version for each language.

For comparative purposes, here are a few comments on the oldest known English versions. The first portions of the Bible to be translated into English were the Psalms in the eighth century, while the Gospels did not appear until the tenth.[2] That such Old

English translations are no longer intelligible to us will be clear as you read Matthew 13:3b-4 translated in the tenth century.

> *Sothlice ut eode se sawere his saede to sawenne. And tha tha he seow, summu hie fellon with weg, and fuglas comon aeton tha.*[3]

However, the first complete translation of the Bible into English was made by Wycliffe by 1384. This version is more understandable to modern readers but still difficult as judged from Hebrews 1:3.

> *The which whanne he is the schynynge of glorie and figure of his substaunce, and berynge alle thingis bi word of his vertu, makyng purgacioun of synnes, sitteth on the righthalf of mageste in high thingis.*[4]

As you can see, English received the Bible rather late in history. The New Testament was first translated from Greek into the language of the Roman Empire, namely Latin. The fifty portions of the **Old Latin** version that remain date between the fourth and thirteenth century. However, patristic evidence (Jerome) proves that Old Latin versions proliferated in the third century, even though no manuscripts that old are *extant* (still remain). Since there were already many different Old Latin versions, it is likely that the first of these versions was substantially older. Most scholars date the first Old Latin translation to the second century, not too long after Paul wrote the epistle of the Romans to the church at Rome.

If the oldest translation was that of the dominant empire, it is not surprising that the next was done in a land adjacent to Israel. **Coptic** is the language of Egypt, which came to be written with the Greek alphabet in the first century. Coptic had two primary dialects. Sahidic, translated first, was used in Upper Egypt (south of Thebes), and those in Lower Egypt (around the Nile delta) spoke Bohairic. There is still a Coptic church in Egypt, though greatly persecuted. The Coptic translation is dated to the third century.

The Syrians, whose capital was Damascus, were also adjacent to Israel. The **Old Syriac** version survives in just a few fragmentary manuscripts. The **Syriac Peshitta,** or common Syriac version, followed, but its date is disputed. Several of the 350 extant copies of the Peshitta date to the fifth century (but some consider the Peshitta to date from the second century). During the fourth century, the Syriac language certainly had a New Testament, though the four shortest general epistles and the book of Revelation were never translated.

The Goths spoke a now dead East Germanic language. Ulfilas, the "Apostle to the Goths," translated the Bible into Gothic in the fourth century. The best copy of this version is at Uppsala, Sweden.

The gospel went into the Caucasus Mountains in the fourth century. The New Testament was translated into the two languages of the region in the following century: Georgian and Armenian. The oldest manuscript of the Georgian version is the Adysh copy of A.D. 897. The **Armenian** version is represented by over 1,200 manuscripts, which makes it the second best attested of any ancient version (after the Vulgate to be discussed shortly). Both Georgia and Armenia remain Christian nations to this day.

Ethiopian church history is as interesting as its eleven curious Lalibela churches hewn from rock outcroppings in the eleventh century. Ethiopian tradition claims that the royal line is descended from Solomon and the Queen of Sheba, whom tradition calls Queen Makeda. More intriguing, her son Menelik is said to have brought the ark of the covenant from Jerusalem, and that it now resides safely in St. Mary's Church at Axum.[5] It is at least clear that Ethiopia received the gospel early in church history, since the Bible records the salvation of the Ethiopian eunuch. In fact, Ethiopia was offended at the arrival of European Christians who wanted to convert them in the colonial era. In spite of this great heritage, the earliest known **Ethiopic** version dates to the sixth century.

In the ninth century, Cyril and Methodius left Greece and journeyed as missionaries to the Slavic lands north. These "Apostles to the Slavs" invented the Cyrillic alphabet and translated the gospels into **Old Slavonic** (Old Bulgarian). From here, the gospel eventually spread through Yugoslavia and Russia, all of which are still Christian (Eastern Orthodox).

About a half dozen other versions were translated in ancient times. The most important of these is Arabic. It receives little attention even though it dates to the ninth century and the translators definitiely used Greek sources. Ancient church historians spoke of an Old Persian version perhaps as old as the third century, but no ancient copies survive (though manuscripts in modern Persian exist). Unfortunately, only a few fragments remain of a sixth-century Nubian version (from Africa) and an undated Sogdian version (from central Asia). The versions in Old English, Old High German, and Provencal (Old French) are more complete but were probably translated from Latin rather than Greek.[6]

Jerome's Latin Vulgate

The great number of variations among the Old Latin manuscripts prompted Pope Damasus to commission an official revision of the Old Latin in A.D. 382. His goal was to have an official "ecclesiastical" text, and he delegated the work to a man named Jerome.

Jerome (ca. 347-420) was born near what is now Ljubljana in Slovenia, and his education was at home until the age of twelve. After about eighteen years of study in Rome and fifteen years of travel, he returned to Rome as secratary to Pope Damasus. He completed the official revision of the gospels about 383, the year after the pope's commission. His correction of the Old Latin gospels, his outspoken preaching, and his condemnation of the Roman clergy for selfishness and laziness provoked backlash of criticism. He moved to a monastery at Bethlehem in 386 and finished his translations there.

Jerome revised the Old Latin New Testament to reflect the common or vulgar speech of his day. His work therefore became known as the **Latin Vulgate.** He translated from the Greek as he revised the New Testament, and began to use the Greek Septuagint to revise the Old Testament but became dissatisfied with the result. He started over on the Old Testament from the Hebrew, and finally finished the entire Bible around 405.

Although his work had the official sanction of the pope, people were more familiar with the Old Latin and were reluctant to accept the new phrases of the Vulgate. During these early centuries it was not unusual for copies of the Vulgate to be altered to the characteristic phrasings of the older versions. These alterations might even vary from one geographic locale to another. This resulted in the cross contaminations and illustrates how strongly traditional wording patterns influence men.

Despite this fragile beginning, the Latin Vulgate eventually became as dearly beloved as the Old Latin version had once been. But about two hundred years passed before this officially sanctioned version became popularly accepted over the older Latin translations.[7] By the mid-sixth century, the entire Latin Vulgate Bible was commonly used bound in a single volume. For over a thousand years, it remained entrenched as the dominant text of Scripture for Christendom. In fact, in 1546, the Council of Trent decreed the Vulgate to be the exclusive Bible of the church.

Jerome's contributions include a high standard of translation based on the original languages and a love for the Scripture deep enough to challenge traditional interpretations (much as Jesus challenged the traditions of the Pharisees). The fruit of his careful research is still apparent. Some eight thousand manuscripts of the Vulgate remain for scholars to study.

Lessons from Scripture

Although the New Testament has no specific statements regarding New Testament versions, two key lessons can be drawn from the Bible regarding versions. Both the Old Testament and New Testament shed light on translations.

God's Principle of Communication

The Old Testament offers an important lesson on translation through the book of Nehemiah. The Jews had been taken captivity into Babylon, and many of them no longer spoke Hebrew. Instead, they spoke Aramaic, the language of the Babylonians who had taken them captive. Thus, when Nehemiah and Ezra led groups of Hebrews back from captivity into Israel, the people could not understand preaching or reading of Scripture in Hebrew. Translation had become necessary, even though all of the Jews knew that the divine words had been penned in Hebrew.

In Nehemiah 8:7, the Word of God says that the Levites "caused the people to understand the Law." And the next verse adds that "they read in the book in the law of God distinctly, and gave the sense, and caused them to understand the reading." It was not sufficient to simply read the inspired words in Hebrew if no one understood. God spoke in Hebrew for the purpose of communication, and when that no longer sufficed for communication, he provided for translation into Aramaic. In fact, the Levites developed an entire collection of text and commentary for the explanation of the Old Testament in Aramaic. These have come down to us as **targums** (Aramaic term for translations).

You have already learned that Koine Greek served as the language of the New Testament autographs. This is a second way that God shows His desire to communicate with man. By using the common language rather than the classical Greek of the scholars he showed that His Word was not just for the scholars and priests. Use of the trade language, much as His previous use of Aramaic, demonstrated God's desire to communicate with the man in the street and not just the priests.

A passage from the New Testament underscores this principle of communication in yet a third way. Paul wrote under inspiration: "Yet in the church, I had rather speak five words with my understanding, that by my voice I may teach others also, than ten thousand words in an unknown tongue." Without entering the controversy about the modern use of this passage in I Corinthians 14, it is clear that God intends to communicate.

God's Principles of Versions

Alexander the Great (356—323 B.C.), long after the Babylonian empire fell to the Medes and Persians, conquered the known world and made the Persian empire into the Greek empire. With the spread of Greek language, there came a need for a translation of the Old Testament that Greek-speaking Jews could understand just as there had been one for Aramaic-speaking Jews.

The first Greek translation of the Pentateuch (five books of Moses) was made by Jews at Alexandria during the reign of Ptolemy Philadelphus (285-246 B.C.). They continued to translate the rest of the books of the Old Testament until they had completed the whole sometime before 150 B.C.[8] This Greek version of the Old Testament is called the **Septuagint,** meaning seventy, because it is said that seventy (or perhaps seventy two) Jews participated in the translation work. It is usually abbreviated LXX, the Roman numeral for seventy. Before the time of Christ, the Hebrew and

Aramaic of the Old Testament was translated into Greek for the benefit of the Greek-speaking Jews.

The Septuagint, like any other version, is not a perfect translation of the Hebrew. The amazing thing is that both Jesus and Paul quoted it. Neither quoted it exclusively, though. When speaking to Hebrew speaking Jews they quoted the Hebrew, but when speaking to Greeks they quoted the Septuagint. The minor differences did not bother them—even when the wording was different.

For instance, in Romans 15:12, the phrase "Esaias saith" shows that Paul is quoting Scripture from Isaiah. Paul quotes, "There shall be a root of Jesse, and he that shall rise to reign over the Gentiles; in him shall the Gentiles trust." If you compare the words with Isaiah 11:10, from which Paul is quoting, most of the differences are a matter of translation into English ("which shall stand" in Isaiah translates the same wording as "he that shall rise" in Romans). However, two differences go beyond the English translation. Paul said one would "reign" where the Hebrew says that one would be "for an ensign," and Paul said in that one the Gentiles would "trust" where the Hebrew says that to that one the Gentiles would "seek." While the thoughts are related, they are not identical. Reigning interprets the type of sign or banner, while the word trust (translating hope) explains the result of the seeking (meaning inquiring). Paul chose to quote the Greek version perhaps because he thought the meaning would be clearer. Either way, his quotation under inspiration of the Holy Spirit, is certainly the correct interpretation.

The Lord Jesus himself also quoted the Septuagint even though it differed from the Hebrew. In Matthew 21:16, Jesus says, "Yea; have ye never read, Out of the mouth of babes and sucklings thou hast perfected praise." The phrase "have ye never read" shows that he is quoting Scripture, and indeed it is word for word the passage of Psalm 8:2 as it appears in the Greek translation. The Hebrew however, says "Out of the mouth of babes and sucklings hast thou ordained strength" just as it does in our English Bibles. Of course, Jesus made no mistake in his quotation, he simply saw no inconsistency between these translations. While "setting a foundation of strength" and "perfecting praise" are different words and thoughts, they are not contradictory. The perfect praise of infants is the strength that brings to nothing the might of this world. Both thoughts are inspired Scripture in our Bible. The Lord knew both the Hebrew and Greek wording and chose to quote the Greek here in spite of (or because of) its differences.

Lest you think that perhaps the Greek version is better than the Hebrew on this account, be assured that the Lord quoted the Hebrew more often than the Septuagint. There are over 300 quotations of Scripture in the New Testament, often introduced by such phrases as "it is written." Most such quotations follow the Hebrew, and less than one fourth of them follow the Greek of the Septuagint. As you can see from these examples, the differences do not cast doubt on whether God has preserved his word.

Even the most controversial quotation from the Septuagint will seem mild to most readers. Hebrews 11:21, says that Jacob (Israel) blessed the sons of Joseph, "and worshipped, leaning upon the top of his staff." This wording comes from the Septuagint. The Hebrew reads "and Israel bowed himself upon the bed's head," as you can see for yourself in Genesis 47:31. The aged Jacob bowed himself in worship, and probably he leaned both on the head of the bed and his staff. Either way, this quotation of the Greek is just as inspired as the Hebrew original, so neither should be accused of error.

The original Hebrew was inspired Scripture, yet Christians know that the New Testament is also inspired Scripture even when it quotes the Old Testament in a way seemingly at odds with the original. None of this requires that the Septuagint was inspired in the same way that the Hebrew was, but certainly where the New Testament quotes it, the quotations are inspired. Paul, a scholar himself, even went so far as to make his own translations on occasion when preaching instead of following either the Hebrew or the Septuagint. These translations and paraphrases of Paul are also inspired as part of the New Testament.

Neither Jesus nor the apostles worshiped a specific manuscript or translation of the Old Testament. The autographs were long gone, and they did not fret over it, nor doubt whether they had God's Word. They trusted God's Word in the languages of the day so fully, that "it is written" settled the issue. They used the Word of God in several languages in spite of minor wording problems. They did not tolerate deliberate tampering with Scripture either. Peter said that men did so "to their own destruction." Yet versions that honestly attempted to translate (rather than tamper) were accepted as the inspired Word of God.

Conclusion

With these facts in mind, we need never be ashamed to hold up an English Bible and declare "This is the inspired Word of God." God wants to communicate to all men his love and redemption. He has communicated these things and has preserved His Word for all. The patristic writings and lectionaries show us that the Bible was not just preserved on a shelf during the times of the church fathers but was in constant use for preaching and teaching. Even more importantly, the early versions show us the missionary interest of the early church and prove that the gospel had begun to spread. Christians should rejoice when the inspired Word of God is translated into each language. More will be said about versions in a later chapter. For now it is enough to note that God has preserved His Word in many versions for the purpose of spreading the gospel to "every people and nation and language and tongue."

Endnotes

1. Aland and Aland, p. 82.
2. F. F. Bruce, *History of the Bible in English* (New York, Oxford University Press, 1978), pp. 5, 7.
3. Bruce, *History of the Bible in English*, p. 8.
4. Bruce, *History of the Bible in English*, pp. 14-15.
5. John Baxter, Peter Clarkson, Elizabeth Cruwys, and Beau Riffenburg, *Wonders of the World* (Stamford, CT: Longmeadow Press, 1995), pp. 140-141.
6. Aland and Aland, p. 210.
7. Gordon D. Fee, "Textual Criticism," *Expositors Bible Commentary*, 10 vols., edited by Frank E. Gaebelein. (Grand Rapids: Zondervan, 1979), vol. 1, p. 426.
8. Ellis R. Brotzman, *Old Testament Textual Criticism* (Grand Rapids: Baker, 1994), p. 73.

Questions

1. What is a patristic quotation?

2. Name five early church fathers who were also apologists.

3. What is a lectionary?

4. Distinguish a version from a manuscript.

5. Name the three oldest versions of the New Testament.

6. What version has more copies than any other?

7. Who translated the common Latin version?

8. What were the translations with commentaries called that enabled Babylonian Jews to understand the Hebrew Old Testament?

9. What three lines of evidence show that God desires to communicate?

10. What do the New Testament quotations of the Old Testament teach us about Bible versions? Explain.

UNIT II

Transmission of Scripture

You have seen that God has preserved His Word. The issues among Christians involve the manner in which he did so. The first chapter in this unit presents historical background and views concerning how the transmission of Scripture was accomplished under God's providence. Chapters 6 through 8 present the seven modern theories usually promoted in the debate. In chapter 9, the seven views are summarized and briefly evaluated as theories.

CHAPTER 5

HISTORY OF TRANSMISSION THEORIES

Before considering modern theories of textual criticism, it will be helpful to be familiar with the history of the subject. To be sure, not all who have taken up textual research have done so out of concern for God and what He has to say to us as much perhaps for professional reputations or other selfish reasons. Still several notable scholars proceeded to invest their energies into research toward the goal of resolving from the variations amongst the many manuscripts the original text of the New Testament insofar as that is possible. These labors, hesitantly at first; more boldly as materials increasingly surfaced, spanned three centuries. This chapter presents this history in broad outline through the work of six key scholars.

Desiderius Erasmus
ca. 1466-1536

Desiderius Erasmus, was a Roman Catholic, a Humanist, and a Latin scholar from Rotterdam in the Netherlands. More importantly, however, he edited the first printed edition of the Greek New Testament ever published. Until 1516, whenever scholars consulted the New Testament in its original Greek, they had to study the handmade copies or manuscripts. Scribes and copyists had produced thousands of manuscripts over the centuries. Many of these manuscript copies were not complete, having been ravaged by the passing of time and by handling. By 1515, with the printing press nearly a century old and the Renaissance under a full head of steam, the world was more than ready for a printed Greek New Testament.

His Text

Erasmus was already involved in a project of his own to produce a fresh translation of the Bible into Latin as an alternative to the Latin Vulgate. He was incensed by the corrupt handling and traditional interpretations of the Vulgate by a corrupt clergy. It seemed to him that a fresh translation eliminating corruptions and traditions would help to reform some of the rottenness that had penetrated the Catholic Church. Already immersed in the research of manuscripts throughout Europe in pursuit of that goal, he did not find it an unreasonable request to consider editing from manuscripts the Greek New Testament into printable form.[1]

Johann Froben, a Dutch printer, was aware that the Roman Catholics in Spain were already preparing a printed Greek New Testament for publication as a part of their larger project to produce a complete Bible in a triglot (three language) edition. As a printer, Froben was interested in hitting the market with a Greek New Testament before the Spaniards' *Complutension Polyglot* came out. Froben knew of Erasmus: both his qualifications and his ambition to retranslate the Latin New Testament. He therefore offered to pay Erasmus a reasonable amount to undertake the editing of the Greek New Testament from manuscripts into a printed edition that all the (educated) world could read.

As a theologian and scholar upset by Catholic corruption already, Erasmus, no doubt had his own reasons for wanting to beat the Spanish Catholics to the market with a Greek New Testament. In any case, in the providence of God, Erasmus finished editing his New Testament in early March, 1516. As a matter of interest, the Spanish Catholics had completed the Complutension Polyglot New Testament in 1514, nearly two years before Erasmus even began his Greek New Testament, but it did not become available to the public until after Erasmus's third edition (1522) due to hierarchical "red tape."

In addition to being available to the public first, Erasmus's edition was also less expensive and less cumbersome (since it was not so huge and awkward to transport). For these reasons, it outdistanced its Spanish Catholic rival and soon took its place as the Greek New Testament all over Europe.

His Haste

To be sure, although Erasmus certainly had the credentials to perform the work he did, nevertheless, due to the urgency of his project (by his own admission) his New Testament was filled with numerous minor errors that required later editing to remove. For a manuscript of the Greek New Testament to work from, Erasmus had to make use of what he could get his hands on at the moment. He would have liked to have had one good manuscript at his disposal on which he could make all editorial (spelling, word omission, or duplication error) corrections as necessary. As it turned out, he had to use three twelfth century manuscripts—one of the Gospels, one of the Acts and Epistles, and one of Revelation— comparing them with a few others. His manuscript of the book of Revelation was missing the last leaf (page) containing the final six verses. Some other sections of the manuscript were faded or otherwise unreadable. At a loss for the Greek text of these passages, Erasmus had no time to locate other more complete manuscripts. Instead he simply used his Latin Vulgate version and translated these verses from Latin back into Greek!

As a result, the first printed Greek New Testament had some rather startling readings such as his invention of a Greek word (ἀκαθάρτητον) in Revelation 17:4.[2] The numerous errors grieved Erasmus, and he made the majority of the corrections himself. Most of these appeared in his fourth edition after he had opportunity to compare it with the less hastily prepared Complutension Polyglot. The Polyglot, in contrast to Erasmus's edition, from its planning stages to its actual public circulation occupied the greater part of two decades (1502-1520) under the preparation of not one, but several Scripture scholars.

In spite of the errors, the 1516 publication of Erasmus's Greek New Testament was so well received, especially on the continent of Europe, as to run through its first printing in a matter of months. Second and third editions were immediately forthcoming with as eager reception. However, opponents found his work easy to criticize. The clergy of the Roman Catholic Church, already outraged by his work on a new Latin translation, criticized the Greek New Testament for its numerous errors as well as its use of wording that would demand departure from traditional Latin translation.[3]

His Defense

The main controversy, however, involved a specific passage. Erasmus had not included a portion of I John 5:7-8, which was accepted as the traditional text by the Catholics using the Latin Vulgate. The traditions of men exert powerful influences, especially in religious disputes, and this became the most celebrated dispute of textual controversy. The portion in question (as translated into English) reads: "In Heaven, the Father, the Word, and the Holy Spirit and these three are in one. And there are three bearing witness on earth."

Erasmus had not included this verse in the first edition of his Greek New Testament on purpose. He knew that it was part of the traditional Latin Vulgate, but he felt that a Greek New Testament ought to follow the Greek manuscripts not the Latin. As far as he could tell it had never been part of the Greek. The few manuscripts at hand in Basel all lacked it. More importantly, though, during his years of inspecting manuscripts in libraries across Europe, he had never once found a Greek manuscript containing the phrase. In addition, Cyril of Alexandria had not known the passage,[4] and Erasmus had even found some Latin copies missing the words. Erasmus had therefore refrained from adding these words to the New Testament.

The key dispute, then, did not revolve around one of Erasmus's hasty errors nor a minor change in traditional wording. Rather it addressed the question of the genuineness of I John 5:7-8. Because of this controversy, the phrase in question has been named (in Latin) as the **Comma Johanneum.** Both sides accused the other of tampering with sacred Scripture. Catholics believed that Erasmus was removing words from Scripture based on the inspired Vulgate, while Erasmus argued from the Greek that the Catholics had already added a phrase to the Bible.

As debate raged, Erasmus sent to a friend in Rome to check for the suspect verse in codex Vaticanus kept in the library of the Vatican. Erasmus knew that Vaticanus was an uncial codex more ancient than any of the cursive manuscripts he had consulted. It is doubtful if Erasmus knew just how old Vaticanus was. Nevertheless the reply confirmed his suspicions. This ancient codex knew nothing of the Comma Johanneum.

His Detractors

As pressure to insert the verse mounted against him, attacks against Erasmus became vicious. Some of these attacks demonstrate the vehemence and stubbornness which may accompany a tradition. One of Erasmus's strongest opponents contended that "Erasmus's

New Testament foreshadowed the coming of Anti-Christ."[5] Another, Edward Lee, later to become Archbishop of York, complained that the omission of the verse would result in "heresy, schism, faction, tumults, brawls, and tempests."[6] In spite of the fact that Erasmus had not revised other relevant verses, Lee branded Erasmus with the heresy of Arianism (Arians deny that the Son is of equal substance with the Father). To this Erasmus astutely observed that the verse does not oppose Arianism anyway since the Comma Johanneum mentions nothing of the three heavenly witnesses's substance, only their testimony.

A professor named Dorpius opposed Erasmus's edition upon dogmatic grounds. He claimed that the church had used the Vulgate for all these years. Since the church is incapable of error, to change to anything else would be unthinkable. He wrote to Erasmus that, "it is unreasonable to suppose that the universal Church has been in error for so many generations in her use of this edition; nor is it probable that so many holy Fathers have been mistaken, who, in reliance upon it, have defined the most arduous questions in General Councils, which, it is admitted by most theologians as well as lawyers, are not subject to error in matters of faith."[7] He cautioned Erasmus not "to correct the Latin from the Greek," but said that the "Greek books were better emended from the Latin."[8]

Erasmus pointed out to Dorpius the problem of copyist errors that affect the text. Erasmus pleaded with him saying, "You must distinguish between Scripture, the translation of Scripture, and the transmission of both."[9] To his credit, Dorpius was finally convinced by Erasmus's clear thinking.

Another antagonist suggested, "If in one point the Vulgate were in error the entire authority of Holy Scripture would collapse, love and faith would be extinguished, heresies and schisms would abound, blasphemy would be committed against the Holy Spirit, the authority of theologians would be shaken, and indeed the

Catholic Church would collapse from the foundations."[10] Such thinking typified most of Erasmus's opponents. Unfortunately, such logic still circulates favoring use of a translation rather than the Greek New Testament.

Erasmus responded that prior to the Vulgate the church had survived without these dire consequences mentioned. He added, "You think it is all very well if a clumsy scribe makes a mistake in transcription and then you deem it a crime to put it right." He denounced such loyalty to a translation that would enshrine copyists' errors and said, "The only way to determine the true text is to examine the early codices."[11]

His Decision

After so much harassment, Erasmus wavered. He finally agreed to insert the controversial passage into the next edition if even one Greek manuscript could be found supporting it. In a short time, such a manuscript was brought to his attention, a codex (Greg. 61) which now resides at Trinity College in Dublin, Ireland. Erasmus, true to his word, inserted the verse into his third edition (1522). However, Erasmus regretted his promise and along with the passage, he included an extended marginal note conveying his suspicions that the manuscript had been specially prepared for the occasion.

There can be no doubt that the pressures of tradition working in the minds of men were chiefly responsible for the inclusion of what is now admitted on all sides as the most textually indefensible passage in the entire Bible. Even so traditionally minded a man as John W. Burgon (who argued forcefully for the Textus Receptus and against the Westcott-Hort text for most of his life) did not defend this passage. However, due to ecclesiastical pressure exerted upon Erasmus to include it, the passage remains with us today. The Comma Johanneum is certainly the most famous passage to come into Erasmus's text via the tradition of the Vulgate.

His Contribution

Erasmus, though more a humanist than a Christian, made several key contributions to the study of manuscripts. First, like Jerome, he stressed the importance of the original languages. Second, though his hasty production resulted in numerous errors, he showed his higher standard by spending many years and editions in correcting it. Third, though he included the Comma Johanneum against his will, his marginal note documented for readers its unlikely authenticity.

The most important result, however, came more from the invention of printing than from Erasmus's own scholarship. Since his printed Greek New Testament was both the first and the most popular, it became the standard against which later editions could be measured. It is always very difficult to keep track of differences in readings in a lengthy work. However, with the vast number of manuscripts of the New Testament and with no accepted standard, any systematic study of the differences was well-nigh impossible. Erasmus's text provided a standard for comparison of variant readings. The systematic comparison of manuscripts and organizing the variants is called **collation**. Erasmus's text provided textual researchers the tool they needed to collate manuscripts. Many more would soon be discovered and stimulate rapid growth of textual research. Yet only since Erasmus gave us a printed Greek New Testament has textual research become a viable science.

In 1633, long after Erasmus's death, the Elzevir Brothers of Holland printed a Greek New Testament which was essentially a reprint of the work of Erasmus. Though otherwise unimportant, the preface of this edition contained a Latin phrase which can be translated "You have therefore the text now received by all." The phrase **Received Text** or **Textus Receptus** (in Latin) traces to this preface. It has come to refer to the Greek text of Erasmus.

J. A. Bengel
1687-1752

Johann Albrecht Bengel, a director of an orphanage, was a German theologian who founded Swabian pietism. When he saw thirty thousand variants in the Greek New Testament of John Mills (1707), he became alarmed about the preservation and plenary inspiration of the Bible and began to study. As he studied Mills's collations and did more of his own, he became aware that the more recently discovered manuscripts found in Egypt differed in certain phrases or verses from the familiar manuscripts used by Erasmus. He then naturally asked (1) how the differences of text arose and (2) which variants more likely reflected the original.

His Theory of Text Types

Bengel first theorized that manuscripts like evidence in a courtroom must be "weighed." If one witness tells another witness what to say, their combined witness is not stronger than one alone. Likewise, he argued, extant manuscripts cannot be presumed independent witnesses to the text because some were merely copies of others. "Weighing" means simply recognizing that each manuscript must be evaluated in terms of its relationships to every other.

Manuscript Genealogical Chart

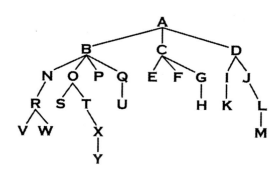

For example, from the chart above, suppose A represents the autograph and every other alphabetical letter a copy or a copy of a copy. Then B, C, and D would be copies directly from the autograph; E F G H would all be copies of C; I J K L M would all be copies of D; N O P Q R S T U V W X Y would all be copies of B.

Now suppose a reading in manuscript E is slightly different from that of N. A textual researcher checks that the E manuscript agrees with F G H as well as with I J K L M and the N reading agrees with O P Q R S T U V W X Y. By merely counting manuscripts without weighing them, the majority of manuscripts would favor the N reading by a 12 to 9 ratio. By checking manuscripts B, C, and D for their testimony, the majority is still in favor of the N reading by a 13 to 11 ratio. By knowing the genealogical relationships: that manuscripts N through Y are simply copies of B; E through H are copies of C; I through M are copies of D, Bengel considered the original reading to favor the E reading by a 2 to 1 ratio.

Bengel grouped manuscripts together in families to evaluate their evidence. He thought that by comparing the variants he could identify different parts of this ancestral family tree of New Testament manuscripts. He divided them into two classes or families, called **text types**. A text type is a group of manuscripts with shared readings that differ from other group[s] at those particular shared readings.

Bengel named the text type of the Egyptian manuscripts *African*. He noted that the Greek text used by Erasmus drew on a few manuscripts from the *Asiatic* family. The Asiatic type includes the overwhelming majority of manuscripts. Bengel weighed them as providing little if any evidence because they were not as old. Thus dismissing in a moment great masses of manuscript evidence.

Bengel also formulated a **canon** of textual research still considered primary to critical thinking today. Canon means standard or rule, and his standard is very basic: to prefer as more likely original the harder reading to the easier one. Bengel recognized a simple truism of scribal habit: a scribe, aside from accidental error, will invariably make a reading easier rather than harder. Or to phrase it the other way around, there is scarcely any reason, aside from a simple blunder, why a scribe would take an easily readable text and convert it to a text that is more difficult to read.

Bengel produced in 1734 a Greek New Testament that weighed the variants according to his principle of scribal habits and his principle of text type. He placed much evidence on codex Alexandrinus (A), which was the oldest then known. Since modern textual criticism stresses scribal habits, genealogy, text types, and the oldest manuscripts, Bengel is rightly considered "the father of modern New Testament textual criticism."[12]

His Defense of Preservation

Bengel, as many other scholars since, found after much collation, that the thousands of manuscripts with all their differences did not undermine preservation.

While Mills reported 30,000 variants, the number has risen. However, only ten thousand places are affected each with several alternative variants. Scholars of every conceivable position acknowledge that seven out of every eight verses in the New Testamanent have no textual problems.[13] In other words, over 87% of the words of Scripture are not in doubt no matter what manuscripts or groups of manuscripts you think are the best.

Of the remaining 12.5% where some variants exist, about 7.5% are insignificant. Most of these involve variant spellings of proper names, spelling variants in other words (such differences were not deemed "errors" until modern dictionaries), and certain changes in word order, which was more flexible in Greek. None of these variants affect meaning much less doctrine. This means that only one verse in twenty contains a variant that may affect meaning.[14] Thus 95% of the Greek New Testament is free from variants that affect meaning.

Even the remaining five percent that may affect meaning rarely result in an alternate meaning of importance. For instance, it is possible to paraphrase with different literal meaning without affecting the sense of the passage. Robertson estimated that only one line per thousand contains a variant where meaning would be significantly affected (or about 20 lines in the entire New Testament).[15] This means that 99.9% of the Greek New Testament is free from variants that significantly affect meaning.

The most important conclusion is that even those few variants that affect meaning do not affect doctrine. Rarely is the main point of the passage affected. Even the exclusion of the Comma Johanneum would not change the message of 1 John 5, much less change a doctrine of Scripture. Many other verses teach the doctrine of the Trinity whether or not one accepts the Comma. The only two lengthy passages in dispute involve Mark 16:9-20 and John 7:53-8:11. These are the only passages in which the main point of the passage would be affected, but again, the doctrines taught in these passages can easily be found in other passages. It cannot be stressed too heavily that not one textual variant affects even one single teaching of Scripture. Fully 100% of the Greek New Testament is free from variants that alter doctrine.

After years of intensive textual study, Bengel also concluded that no doctrinal change resulted from the variations. Though fewer variants were known in Bengel's day, he was perhaps the first to address this reasonable concern. He reached the same conclusions as others since and for the same reason. God has preserved the integrity of His Word, and everyone who studies the issue recognizes this fact. Thus, Bengel found the answer to his concern over the many variants and made a lasting contribution. Ironically, though defending the Scripture, many viewed his theories of text types as an attack on the Holy Scripture.[16]

Constantin von Tischendorf
1815-1874

Perhaps the most illustrious name in textual research is that of **Lobegott Friedrich Constantin von Tischendorf**. Tischendorf, a German, pursued the discovery of new manuscripts relentlessly through the libraries of Europe and the Near East. He then collated them and published his findings in no less than eight editions of the Greek New Testament.

Between his seventh and eighth editions, Tischendorf hit upon his most famous discovery. While visiting the monastery of St. Catherine on Mt. Sinai in 1846, he noticed some old parchment leaves in a wastebasket, thrown there by monks who had no ability to read the ancient Greek it contained. A careful look revealed parts of the Septuagint in old uncial script. Some leaves had already been used for kindling, but he recovered 43 leaves and returned to Leipzig. Seven years later he returned, but found no trace of the manuscripts.

With financial backing from Russia, he returned one last time in 1859. This time, the steward of the monastery fourth century showed him numerous Greek uncial manuscripts. He immediately recognized Bible passages and negotiated a purchase of the manuscript for about $7000. He returned to tsar Alexander II with his prize and soon identified complete Old and New Testaments together with some apocryphal books and two early Christian works (the Epistle of Barnabas and the Shepherd of Hermas). This manuscript is known today as **Codex Sinaiticus** (and abbreviated by ℵ). In 1933, during the Soviet era, the British Museum purchased this codex for $100,000.[17]

Tischendorf then published his eighth and final edition (1869-1872). This edition was marked by two striking features. First, its comprehensive critical apparatus remains unmatched today for its citation of Greek manuscript evidence, patristic evidence, and evidence from the versions (different early translations of the New Testament like Syriac, Egyptian Coptic, and Latin Vulgate).[18] Second, it relied so heavily upon the manuscript Sinaiticus that it differed in over 3,500 places from his seventh edition. This serves as a lesson on the temptation to over-value one's own discoveries.

Tischendorf's contributions, however, included the discovery of many Greek manuscripts including Sinaiticus, the oldest most complete manuscript yet known. He published his findings including twenty-one uncial manuscripts. He also collated or copied at least twenty others and made the most complete collation of manuscripts ever assembled.[19]

B. F. Westcott and F. J. A. Hort
1825-1901 and 1828-1892

In 1881, two Cambridge scholars published a two-volume work entitled *Introduction to the New Testament in the Original Greek*. The book would soon become the standard in the field of textual criticism. The two Englishmen, **Brooke Foss Westcott** and **Fenton John Anthony Hort**, were both Anglicans as were many Christians of their day. Westcott, in fact, served as a preacher (bishop of Durham) and wrote commentaries on Ephesians, John, and Hebrews. Using his thorough knowledge of Greek, Westcott wrote in depth studies of those Bible books with such depth that they are still being used. Most surprisingly, however, neither of the two men ever collated a single Greek manuscript.

Their Theory

Westcott and Hort brought together the results of a number of previous scholars and textual traditions. By their time, much collation had already been done by men like Bengel and Tischendorf. Others, such as Johann Jakob Griesbach (1745-1812), had formulated some fifteen more "canons" of textual research beyond Bengel's first canon.

Griesbach had also identified a third text type, which he called **Western**. The Western type is frequently identified with Greek manuscripts found in Italy and the Old Latin version translated from them. Griesbach was only one of a steady stream of scholars whose textual views influenced Westcott and Hort.

Westcott and Hort used Bengel's genealogical method to group the manuscripts. They found four text types, three of which had been previously identified by Bengel and Griesbach. Besides the Western type identified by Griesbach, they identified both a *Syrian* and an *Alexandrian* text type corresponding to Bengel's Asiatic and African types.

The fourth type they called **Neutral**, because they believed it to be unprejudiced by the variants in the other regional streams. This neutral text type consisted primarily of two codices: Sinaiticus (א) and Vaticanus (B). They explained that:

> "(1) the readings of א B should be accepted as the true readings until strong internal evidence can be found to the contrary, and (2) that no readings of א B can safely be rejected absolutely."[20] In fact, where these two manuscripts disagreed, they tended toward the reading of Vaticanus alone.[21]

To justify their Neutral text type as best reflecting the original autographs, they would need to show its priority over the other three. However, they knew that the main issue would be its priority over the Syrian text, from which the Textus Receptus derives. To address the Syrian text type, they noted that only the Syrian text type lacks manuscripts older than fifth century.[22] Of course, this does not preclude the finding of older manuscripts, so they went on to construct three arguments for the lateness of the Syrian text type.

First, they displayed eight variants of the Syrian type that combined phrases from the Western and Alexandrian text types.[23]

They termed this **conflation,** and claimed that this meant that the conflate reading must be more recent than the two which had been combined. Second, they pointed out that Syrian readings are never found quoted by the church fathers before A.D. 350, a clear evidence of late text.[24] Third, they characterized the Syrian text as "full" and "smooth,"[25] and concluded that the harder readings of the Neutral type should be preferred according to Bengel's canon. Similarly conflations and other longer fuller readings would be deemed late according to another canon of scribal tendency ("shorter reading preferred"). Scribes would tend to retain both variants rather than risk losing some words of Scripture.

Finally, since they believed they had proved the lateness of the Syrian text, they sought to explain how it came to be. They postulated that the vast number of manuscripts exhibiting such obviously late readings must be due to a **recension,** that is an official edition of the Bible such as that made by Jerome. A recension could well explain why a given reading would proliferate. They did not identify the leader who commanded the recension to be made, but suggested that perhaps it was Lucian, who died in 311.[26]

Westcott and Hort did not produce a critical apparatus for their text, but rather used Tischendorf's collations to a large extent.[27] They obviously depended upon the work of Bengel and Griesbach for the concept of genealogy, text type and canons of scribal tendency.[28] However, though they did not devise a new text entirely their own, their theory was the first to unify the strands into a cohesive convincing position.

Their Influence

In their second volume Westcott and Hort set forth in detail the factors by which they determined their text. Although much of what they used was dependent upon the work of earlier scholars, the insight and judgment that they applied to textual research has ruled the field of textual thinking from their day to the present. Their influence has been so great, in fact, that modern scholars recognize that even the most recent modern editions of the Greek New Testament are substantially based on Westcott and Hort's Greek text.[29]

Westcott and Hort are to be congratulated not for their particular edition of the Greek New Testament but for promoting use of a critical text to work backwards through the scribal errors and alterations to approach the original autographs. In fact, Westcott and Hort were the first textual scholars to attempt to identify the wording of the autographs. Before them scholars hoped only to obtain the wording of the Bible as it was known in the fourth century or in the oldest available texts.[30] All Christians should agree that this is a proper goal, whether or not they agree with the methods and results obtained by these men.

Indeed, as Erasmus himself had understood, unless God chooses to give us some special revelation on the subject, the only objective way to determine whether the Textus Receptus or the Westcott-Hort text is closest to the originals is through the application of sound critical research principles.

Along with the arrival of the Westcott-Hort Greek text came the first major revision of the Bible in English since 1611. The English Revised Version (ERV) editors had before them pre-publication copies of the Westcott-Hort text and made major revisions on the basis of it. In fact, almost without exception, modern translations produced since the 1881 Greek text of Westcott and Hort reflect it.[31] The Westcott-Hort text has thus effectively replaced the one Desiderius Erasmus edited in 1516-22.

John W. Burgon
1813-1888

The Dean of Chichester, **John William Burgon,** immediately challenged the Westcott and Hort theory and text. He along with Edward Miller (his student) sought to disprove Westcott and Hort's theories at the outset. Burgon and his students were not the only opponents of Westcott and Hort, but they were certainly the most outspoken and most formidable. He was in England "the leading religious teacher of his time."[32] Burgon was no ignorant rabble-rouser. He collated the famous manuscript D himself and his index of quotations of the church fathers is still the most exhaustive ever compiled—with a total of 86,489 quotations.[33]

His Critiques

Burgon attacked the genealogical foundation of the theory of Westcott and Hort and exposed some unproven assumptions. While the principle of genealogy cannot be disputed (since manuscripts were certainly copied from earlier manuscripts), no existing manuscript has been shown to be a direct copy of another existing manuscript. Burgon pointed out that the principle of genealogy does not determine its application to existing manuscripts nor does it prove which witnesses are independent.[34]

Further, Burgon criticized the principle of genealogy from which text types derive. Westcott and Hort applied the dictum "identity of reading implies identity of origin."[35] However, recalling the small number of variants, the primary conclusion of this dictum is that all manuscripts point back to the autographs from which they have variously descended. He pointed out the inconsistency of classifying several hundred Syrian manuscripts as a single voice because of similar readings while counting Vaticanus and Sinaiticus as independent witnesses in spite of their similar readings.[36]

Burgon and followers such as Edward Miller also pointed to the Syriac Peshitta as evidence that the Syrian text type is not as late as Westcott and Hort claim. Since the Peshitta is grouped with the Syrian type, Burgon mentioned its second century date with relish.[37] This point defused some of Burgon's critics at the time. However, by 1901 Syriac scholars had concluded that the Peshitta dates to the fourth century. This is still disputed by a few, but most concede that Burgon was wrong in this.

Burgon also rejected all three arguments against the Syrian text. He maintained that conflation is not the only explanation for Syrian variants which combine Western and Alexandrian types. Accidental omission of different phrases by Western and Alexandrian scribes is a far simpler explanation (whether adequate or inadequate). He even claimed that three of Westcott and Hort's eight sample conflations were not conflations at all and two others were doubtful.[38] Next, he drew on his vast compendium of quotations from the church fathers to supply early Syrian quotations. He even produced many from Origen, whom Westcort and Hort had claimed never used Syrian readings.[39] Third, he rejected the application of Bengel's canon. The canon says that the harder reading is preferred *if* it is an intentional change rather than a simple copying error. For Westcott and Hort to apply the canon to the entire Syrian text, they must first know that the changes were primarily intentional rather than unintentional, which they cannot know.[40]

Burgon identified the recension idea of Westcott and Hort as completely speculative. There is no historical evidence of any authoritative revision during that time period. The historic decree of the pope for the making of Jerome's Vulgate can be read to this day, and Burgon demanded similar historic evidence from Westcott and Hort if they wished to claim a similar recension by the fourth century.[41] Burgon first quoted Hort's own words that "it was probably initiated . . ." and that it "may perhaps have found a Patron . . ." He then exposed such expressions as speculation.[42]

Burgon's impassioned rebuttals could not contrast more sharply with Hort's calm and scholarly-sounding speculations. Burgon claimed that the Textus Receptus represented God's preservation of Scripture.[43] This put scholars on the defensive and many failed to consider his important and detailed critiques.

His View of Preservation

Burgon's reference to the Greek text underlying the KJV as the "Traditional Text" is a clue to his view of its preservation. He conceived of the text as handed down from God to the Church and by the Church handed down through the ages by tradition. He further conceived of the Word of God as early on the object of severe attack and corruption. He wrote,

> Calumny and misrepresentation, persecution and murderous hate, assailed Him [Jesus] continually. And the Written Word in like manner, in the earliest age of all, was shamefully handled by mankind. Not only was it confused through human infirmity and misapprehension, but it became also the object of restless malice and unsparing assaults.[44]

Now, one might think, in reflecting on the history of the Christian Church, that by "restless malice and unsparing assaults," he meant the official persecutions wrought by ungodly Roman emperors and their efforts to destroy Christianity and the Word of God along with it, or that perhaps he meant the scoffing sneers of pagan philosophers, or the intense hostility of the Jews towards Christians and their New Testament. On the contrary, by this strongly worded description Burgon refers instead to readings here and there which differ in wording among the manuscripts from what he considers the true text of the New Testament. He reckons these as so mutilated by heretics that no conscientious Christian could conceivably have anything to do with them. His reference is to the early uncial manuscripts, notably Vaticanus and Sinaiticus, as deliberate falsifications of the New Testament during the second and third centuries.[45] Of these textual variants he continues, the Church under Him has watched over them with intelligence and skill; has recognized which copies exhibit a fabricated, which an honestly transcribed text; has generally sanctioned the one, and generally disallowed the other.

Burgon, then, viewed God as committing to the Church the task of superintending the transmission of the New Testament text just as He entrusted to the Jews the Old Testament text. The Jews rejected all spurious works from the Old Testament (including the Apocrypha) and transmitted the text through meticulous care in the copying process. The Church has indeed watched over the text of the New Testament and rejected all attempts to change its message as for example in the case of such a man as Marcion. It has carefully delineated the canon of twenty-seven books just as the Jews did.

But we have not just two or three conflicting texts to choose between, but somewhere in excess of five thousand manuscripts of varying length and description. Each of these manuscripts varies from every other in certain minute textual details; there are no two of them that agree in every particular. One estimate is that even the nearest two manuscripts (members of the Majority text) vary from each other as many as six to ten times per chapter. Further, none of the autographs exist (a point which no one disputes) and, as far as is known, no single, absolutely flawless copy of the autographs exists either. Since God has not seen fit to indicate to us in any objectively verifiable manner which of the various manuscripts exhibits "the one true text" as regards these wording differences, the Church down through the ages has reasonably concluded that God's Word remains undisturbed in spite of those minor wording variants. That is to say, as far as satisfying the promises and integrity of God, and the authority and inerrancy of His Word is concerned, the variants leave these matters largely undisturbed.

Burgon also proposed seven "Tests of Truth" for identifying the original text of Scripture. Notice that both antiquity (age of manuscripts) and internal evidence are recognized but are not the sole arbitrators. The seven tests follow.[46]

1. Antiquity, or Age of Witnesses
2. Number, or Consent of Witnesses
3. Variety, or Catholicity (from all countries and ages)
4. Weight, or Respectability of Witnesses
5. Continuity, or Unbroken Tradition
6. Context
7. Internal Evidence, or Reasonableness

These seven points evaluate each reading by asking respectively, How ancient is the reading? How many manuscripts support the reading? How widespread is the support? Are the manuscripts independent witnesses showing evidence of faithful copying? Is the reading supported throughout church history? How sensible is the reading in the context? How reasonable is the reading in the light of logic and grammar.

Scholars disagree on the application and order of importance of these principles. However, even those who disagree with Burgon recognize that these criteria are valuable in the defending the preservation of Scripture based on the extant manuscripts.

His Influence

Although Burgon exercised admirable thoroughness in examining textual evidence, his refutation of Hort's procedures and conclusions convinced few textual researchers. Gradually the furor over the new text subsided. In spite of Burgon's efforts, Westcott and Hort's Greek text dominates scholarly circles and has become a tradition among scholars to which they now hold as strongly as they once held the Textus Receptus and the Vulgate.

Later scholars recognized the need to address Burgon's detailed and knowledgeable criticisms. Those who agree in general with Westcott and Hort began to refine the theory at its weakest points. Those who agree in general with Burgon also refine their positions in response to the heirs of Westcott and Hort. Thus, Burgon's influence continues, and his books remain in print through the efforts of some of his own modern heirs.[47]

Burgon marked the polarization of textual scholars into two camps. The wide range of modern textual theories presented in the next chapters developed from this parting of the ways. Unfortunately respectful and constructive communication between the camps (which often helps both grow) has decreased. When there is communication at all (rather than cynical or supercilious silence), it is rarely reasoned debate but more often vitriolic propoganda and bitter retorts. It is our hope that the discussion of the various views in the next chapters will encourage reasoned debate once more.

Burgon's lasting contributions include his extensive study of patristic evidence and his seven tests of truth. However, his most important contribution was simply to critique Westcott and Hort. He focused attention on their underlying (and often unacknowledged) assumptions in both methods and conclusions. No matter which side one takes, such questioning and evaluation is worthwhile and necessary for the growth of a science.

Conclusion

The goal of this chapter has been to present the historical background for modern theories of textual criticism. Six men decisively influenced this history. Erasmus prepared the first printed Greek New Testament to be published, which became the successful industry standard. Bengel proved that manuscript variation does not affect doctrine, and his theories earned him the title Father of Textual Criticism. Tischendorf discovered many ancient manuscripts of the New Testament. Westcott and Hort contributed the first comprehensive theory of text transmission. Burgon raised the first scholarly voice of caution against the speculations of his predecessors.

We have not argued which of their theories is correct, because it should be clear that all of them had weaknesses. However, each of these six men made important contributions both to textual research and to the defense of the Scripture whether or not their theories are correct. Two extremes should be clear.

First, one may exaggerate the importance of his own speculation or theory. Tischendorf speculated on the value of Sinaiticus rather beyond its due respect, and Bengel also treated his theories so seriously as to dismiss in effect most textual evidence. Westcott and Hort hypothesized a Syrian Recension trying to bolster their larger theory. None of these theories contradict Scripture, and such blind spots toward one's own work can be difficult to detect. Present scholarship has abandoned these weak points of the theories. Nevertheless, these men made valuable contributions, which remain with us as will be apparent in the next chapter.

Second, it is easy for men dealing with the Word of God to be dominated by tradition and thereby to resist changes. It is tempting to cling to an accepted standard even though evidence indicates that the standard does not reflect the original wording as well as it could. Erasmus buckled under the pressure of tradition regarding the Comma Johanneum. Burgon also erred in adopting tradition as evidence of preservation. By Burgon's time, the text of Erasmus (like that of Jerome before him) had also became traditional in contrast to the attitude of Erasmus himself. These men also made outstanding contributions to textual scholarship, and more recent scholars have also improved upon their work.

Perhaps the most important conclusion drawn by all of these men is that the Word of God has been preserved. Though they disagree on the manner and details. All of them agree that not a single doctrine of Scripture is in question.

Erasmus: "Does it not happen frequently that from several faulty manuscripts—though not faulty in the same way—the true and genuine reading is found?"[48]

Bengel: "1) By far the most numerous portions of the sacred text (thanks be to God) labour under no variety of reading deserving notice. 2) These portions contain the whole scheme of salvation, and establish every particular of it by every test of truth."[49]

Tischendorf: "The chief end of such inquiries, however, lies in its enabling us to find out the very words and expressions which the holy apostles either wrote or dictated to their amanuenses. If the New Testament is the most sacred and precious book in the world, we should surely desire to possess the original text of each of its books, in the state in which it left its author's hands, without either addition or blank, or change of any kind . . . If you ask me then, whether any popular version, such as Luther's, does or does not contain the original text, my answer is, Yes and No. I say Yes, as far as concerns your soul's salvation; all that is needful for that, you have in Luther's version. But I also say No, for this reason, that Luther made his translation from a text which needed correction in many places."[50]

Westcott and Hort: "With regard to the great bulk of the words of the New Testament, as of most other ancient writings, there is no variation or other ground of doubt, and therefore no room for textual criticism."[51]

Burgon: The provision, then, which the Divine Author of Scripture is found to have made for the preservation in its integrity of His written Word, is of a peculiarly varied and highly complex description. First,—By causing that a vast multiplication of copies should be required all down the ages,- . . . He provided the most effectual security imaginable against fraud. . . . Next, Versions . . . Lastly, . . . Patristic Citations accordingly are a third mighty safeguard of the integrity of the deposit.[52]

Endnotes

1. Metzger, *Text*, pp. 95ff. for a detailed disucssion.
2. Ibid, p. 100. Also see Tregelles, p. 21.
3. Interesting and amusing examples of this can be found in biographies of Erasmus by Froude, Bainton, and Seebohm.
4. Tregelles, p. 22.
5. Hall, p. 105. In *Erasmus* by T. A. Dorey.
6. Bainton, pp. 136-37.
7. Faulkner, p. 127.
8. Faulkner, pp. 127-28.
9. Bainton, p. 135.
10. Ibid.
11. Ibid.
12. J. Harold Greenlee, *Introduction to New Testament Textual Criticism* (Grand Rapids: William B. Eerdmans, 1964), p. 73.
13. Brooke Foss Westcott and Fenton John Anthony Hort, *Introduction to the New Testament in the Original Greek* (Peabody, MA: Hendrickson, 1882, 1988 reprint), p. 2.
14. Ezra Abbot quoted in Geisler and Nix, *General Introduction*, p. 365.
15. A. T. Robertson, *Introduction to the Textual Criticism of the New Testament* (Nashville: Boardman, 1925), pp. 21-22.
16. Ibid., cf. Metzger, *Text*, p. 113.

f g

17. Metzger tells the story of its discovery in some detail, *Text,* pp. 42-46.
18. Fee, "Textual Criticism," *Expositors Bible Commentary,* vol. 1, p. 427.
19. Greenlee, p. 76.
20. Westcott and Hort, *Introduction,* p. 225.
21. Westcott and Hort, *Introduction,* pp. 230-50 discuss the singular readings of Vaticanus and Sinaiticus, but three-fourths of the space is devoted to Vaticanus. On this basis, Sturz describes Vaticanus as the "leading" manuscript of Westcott and Hort's Neutral texttype. See Sturz, *The Byzantine Text-Type* (Nashville: Thomas Nelson, 1984), p. 20. 22. Westcott and Hort, *Introduction,* pp. 92-93.
23. Ibid., pp. 104.
24. Ibid., pp. 114-15.
25. Ibid., p. 135.
26. Ibid., p. 137.
27. Jack Finegan, *Encountering New Testament Manuscripts: A Working Introduction to Textual Criticism* (Grand Rapids: Eerdmans, 1974), p. 64.
28. Hort described his method as follows: "The proper method of Genealogy consists, . . . in the more or less complete recovery of the texts of successive ancestors by analysis and comparison of the varying texts of their respective descendents, each ancestral text so recovered being in its turn used in conjunction with other similar texts, for the recovery of the text of a yet earlier common ancestor . . . Genealogical method . . . reduces within narrow limits the amount of variation which need occupy an editor when he comes to the construction of his text: but it leaves him in the dark, as all criticism dealing only with transmitted variations must do, as to the amount of correspondence between the best transmitted text and the text of his author." Westcott and Hort, *The New Testament in the Original Greek,* 2 vols. (New York: Harper, 1882), vol. 2, pp. 51-58.
29. See, for example, articles by Eldon J. Epp, "The Twentieth Century Interlude in New Testament Textual Criticism," *Journal of Biblical Literature,* XCIII (1974), p. 389 f. and Zane C. Hodges, "Rationalism and Contemporary New Testament Textual Criticism," *Bibliotheca Sacra* CXXVIII (January-March, 1 71), p. 27.
30. Thiessen, p. 32.
31. Most modern translations use the United Bible Societies Greek New

Testament or the Nestle-Aland New Testament, both of which are the Westcott-Hort text with modifications. See Unit 3.

32. E. M. Goulburn, *Life of Dean Burgon*, 2 Vols. (London: John Murray, 1892), vol. 1, p. vii.

33. Pickering, *Identity*, p. 66.

34. John William Burgon, *The Revision Revised* (Paradise, PA: Conservative Classics, 1883, 1977 reprint), p. 358.

35. Westcott and Hort, *Introduction*, p. 46.

36. Burgon, *Revision Revised*, p. 255.

37. Burgon, *Revision Revised*, p. 9.

38. Ibid., pp. 257-65.

39. Burgon, *The Traditional Text of the Holy Gospels Vindicated and Established* (London: George Bell & Son, 1896), pp. 99-101, 118-121. Cf. Frederick Kenyon, *Handbook to the Textual Criticism of the New Testament* (Oxford: Clarendon Press, 1977), pp. 321-22 for a summary of Miller's study of Burgon's compilation of patristic quotations. He notes that 4383 quotations of passages with variants distinguish between texts, and 2653 favor the TR. Among the oldest fathers, 151 of 235 variants favor the TR.

40. Burgon, *Traditional Text*, p. 67.

41. Burgon, *Revision Revised*, p. 293-94.

42. Burgon, *Traditional Text*, quotes from pp. 133-34. Subsequent exposé follows "But then, since not a shadow of proof is forthcoming that *any such Recension as Dr. Hort imagines ever took place at all,*—what else but a purely gratuitous exercise of the imaginative faculty is it, that Dr. Hort should proceed further to invent the method which might, or could, or would, or should have been pursued, if it *had* taken place. Having, however, in this way (1) Assumed a `Syrian Recension,—(2) Invented the cause of it,—and (3) Dreamed the process by which it was carried into execution,— the Critic hastens, *more suo*, to characterize *the historical result* in the following terms:—`The qualities which the Authors of the Syrian Text seem to have most desired to impress on it are lucidity and completeness.'"

43. Metzger, *Text*, p. 135.

44. Burgon, *Traditional Text*, p. 10.

45. Burgon (*Revision Revised*, p. 319) explains that if Vaticanus and Sinaiticus had been highly prized, they would have worn out from use. Mauro later

added that the Sinaiticus has been corrected some ten times, and handwriting analysis suggests that some of these correctors were contemporaneous with the main text while others date from the sixth century or later. For a vellum manuscript to be subjected to repeated alteration suggests that the owner found sufficient errors to necessitate marking it up and depreciating its monetary value. Mauro concludes that its owners "from the very first, and for some hundreds of years thereafter, esteemed it to be so impure as to require correction in every part" (in Fuller, *True or False*, p. 75).

46. Burgon, *Traditional Text*, pp. 28-29 for the list; pp. 40-67 for extended discussion of the seven tests.

47. Burgon, *The Revision Revised*, collects three articles: (1) "The New Greek Text," (2) "The New English Version" (meaning the Revised Version), and (3) "Westcott and Hort's New Textual Theory." David Otis Fuller reprinted parts of these articles in his book *True or False?* Besides his book on *The Traditional Text*, two other books by Burgon were published posthumously, *The Causes of the Corruption of the Traditional Text of the Holy Gospels*, and *The Last Twelve Verses of the Gospel According to St. Mark*. Fuller condensed the latter along with "Pericope de Adultera" from the former in his book *Counterfeit or Genuine? Mark 16? John 8?*

48. Erasmus quoted in James R. White, *The King James Only Controversy*, p. 57.

49. John Albert Bengel, *Gnomon of the New Testament* (Edinburgh: T. and T. Clark, 1877), vol. 1, p. 18.

50. Constantin von Tischendorf, *Codex Sinaiticus* (London: Lutterworth Press, 1934 reprint), pp. 84-85.

51. Westcott and Hort, *Introduction*, p. 2.

52. Burgon, *Revision Revised*, p. 8-9.

Questions

1. Which textual scholar first theorized text types and a canon of scribal tendencies?

2. To which text did Tischendorf cling most closely? Westcott and Hort? Burgon?

3. List Westcott and Hort's three key arguments against the Syrian text type.

4. Which textual scholar seems most bound by tradition?

5. Which textual scholar seems most speculative?

   Match the scholars to their major contribution.

   A. Bengel
   B. Burgon
   C. Erasmus
   D. Tischendorf
   E. Westcott and Hort

6. attacked speculation among other scholars

7. greatly added to manuscript discovery and collation

8. Father of New Testament Textual Criticism

9. unified and popularized a theory of textual transmission

10. produced a text basic for comparative research on the Greek

CHAPTER 6

GENERAL MODERN THEORIES

Two competing textual views arose early as heirs to Burgon's debate with Westcott and Hort. Critical Eclecticism developed as a result of Burgon's addressing some of the weaknesses of Westcott and Hort. Similarly, the Textus Receptus view developed from the views of Burgon. Several points will provide background needed for the consideration of these two views.

First, in addition to the Alexandrian, Syrian, Western, and Neutral text types of Westcott and Hort, B.H. Streeter defined a **Caesarean** text type as the text familiar to Origen. It is the most controversial and least verified type. It has been identified primarily in the synoptic gospels, and many scholars do not acknowledge it as a separate text type at all.

Second, there are a limited number of possible theories explaining textual variants. One view promotes a single manuscript or version as the best, one adheres to a single text type as the best, and one selects readings from different manuscripts or text types on the basis of various theoretical criteria.

Third, and most important, none of these views necessarily disturbs the orthodoxy of the Christian faith as plainly taught in the Scriptures. Good Christians can hold to any of these views without compromising one's faith. Those who hold to other views do so based on theory rather than theology. These two viable positions, like all other positions, have both strengths and weaknesses. Any weaknesses described are offered in the spirit of finding and evaluating the strongest position. Good causes are never served by weak arguments. Even the most ardent supporter of a position must recognize that some facts are more difficult to explain than others and so should be willing to seek the best explanation possible. Chapter 9 will explain how to compare some theories, but for now we want to consider the strong and weak points.

Critical Eclecticism

Eclectic means selecting items from varied sources. For example, Americans like to be eclectic both in their shopping and frequently in their philosophy. In a competitive market, eclectic or comparison shopping is good since in this way one is more likely to find the best buys from different stores. Eclectic philosophy however fails to recognize that the Bible is the only source of Truth; those who select from various religions and books end up adrift on the winds of doctrine. In textual criticism, the term eclectic simply describes the process of selecting readings from various manuscripts and text types.

Bruce M. Metzger and **Kurt Aland** were among the editors of the Greek New Testament produced by the United Bible Societies. This edition of the Greek has become the standard used worldwide—much like the edition of Erasmus was used in times past. Both men have also written textbooks on textual criticism (Aland with his wife Barbara). Though sympathetic with Westcott and Hort, these men acknowledged some valid points raised by Burgon and sought to improve the theoretical basis of Westcott and Hort.

Position

Recall that there is only a small proportion of passages where manuscripts substantially disagree. However, it is important to Christians to know which reading is correct in these passages. It is especially important to preachers who preach phrase by phrase through a passage. Metzger and Aland believe that such problems are best resolved by evaluating all available evidence, which includes date and place of manuscripts as well as author's style and scribal habits.

Such evidence is handled much as in a court of law. Legal matters in the Bible required multiple independent witnesses. The greater the number of witnesses, the less likelihood of a wrong judgment. In a courtroom, the jury listens to each witness as the witness gives his personal (or internal) testimony. The jury also knows external things about the witness apart from the testimony. They know how old the witness is, where he lives, and where he works. They know if he has a criminal record or bad credit. They also notice mannerisms, attitudes toward the defendant and the judge, and a shifty or honest demeanor. These signals provide clues concerning the reliability of the witness.

In textual criticism, the manuscripts are the witnesses, and the evidence is divided into external and internal evidence. The words written in the manuscripts compare to the personal testimony. This is **internal evidence,** which shall be discussed shortly. The **external evidence** involves things we can know about the manuscripts such as its age and the place it was found. The textual critic desires to determine the number of independent witnesses, the age of the witnesses, the places where the witnesses came from. The basic idea is that the reading with the most independent witnesses from the most time periods (including the oldest) and geographical regions is most likely authentic.

The internal evidence deals with evidence from the text of the document itself. This evidence is also subdivided into two categories. **Intrinsic probability** refers to the style of the author. The goal is to identify how the human author would probably have worded the autograph based on his known tendencies. For example, Luke has a very classical and scholarly style with long sentences and complicated grammatical constructions. John has the simple style of a fisherman. Each of the gospels is known for a different theological emphasis, while other authors such as Paul are known for characteristic phrases (grace and peace be unto you). Identifying an original reading based on consistency with the theological emphasis, style, grammar, and word choice of the author's other writings is the goal of this type of internal evidence. The textual critic prefers the reading that best fits the context and is most consistent with the author's style, vocabulary, grammar, and theology.

By contrast, **transcriptional probability** refers to the typical habits of copyists. Since no two manuscripts agree perfectly, and since the autographs were perfect, there have obviously been scribal errors. Many of these are accidental. If copying by hand, the scribe may have mistaken the letters of one word for another (error of the eye). Sometimes a room full of scribes took dictation (the ancient version of mass production). In this case, a scribe may have mistaken the sound of one word for another (error of the ear). Or he may forget part of what he intended to copy (error of memory causing omissions).

In Eclecticism, intentional errors receive more attention than the unintentional errors above. This does not mean that the scribe was intentionally trying to add or subtract from Scripture, but that he made a well-meaning choice that resulted in an error. For instance, he may have misunderstood a marginal note and caused an error thinking he was correcting an error. Three of these types of errors are famous, and are used as rules of thumb.

Prefer the shorter reading. This rule is the most famous and was mentioned in the discussion of Westcott and Hort (chapter 5) as a central part of their conflation theories. Researchers use this canon extensively. They claim that a reverent scribe, impressed with the authority of God's Word and faced with readings which differ, one longer than the other, would naturally prefer to include the longer reading rather than risk the possibility of leaving out what very well might be a portion of God's Word. The textual researcher reasons that the shorter reading would more likely be the original one. In other words, the overall tendency for scribes was to lengthen rather than shorten the text out of their very reverence for it. That being the case, the longer text tends to reflect added material, rather than the shorter text reflecting omitted material. But the demonstrable tendencies of the scribes to add to rather than to (deliberately at least) omit material from the copies they produced seemed reasonable to textual researchers as a basis for use of the canon, "prefer the shorter reading."

As an example, consider how people refer to the Son of God. His given name is Jesus (Matt. 1:21, 25; Luke 2:21). Jesus is the Greek equivalent of the Old Testament name, Joshua, which means literally something like "Jehovah is salvation" or more simply, "God saves." He is distinguished from other people with the name Jesus by his [supposed] town of origin, "Jesus of Nazareth" (Mark 16:6). He is the Messiah, a title taken from the Hebrew word for "anointed one," as God's special anointed person to both redeem and inherit the world. The Greek equivalent of Messiah is Christos which comes into English as Christ. So Jesus the Messiah eventually simplified to Jesus the Christ or Jesus Christ. In addition, spiritual men who worship the one true God recognize him as Lord (John 20:28, And Thomas answered and said unto him, My Lord and my God.). So that when Peter preached his sermon at Pentecost, he informed his listeners that they—and all men—must deal with Jesus of Nazareth (Acts 2:22) whom God has established as the anointed one and the Lord of all (Acts 2:36). Many of the reverent Christians, who copied the New Testament manuscripts, became conditioned by their religious training to refer to Him as the Lord Jesus Christ. It is therefore quite natural that such scribes, upon seeing "Christ" or "Jesus" or "Christ Jesus" or "Jesus Christ" in a manuscript might inadvertently write down instead their own familiar phrasing of his name and/or titles. On this basis, in passages where manuscripts differ concerning the Lord's name or title, textual researchers of the Eclectic school often consider that the shorter name or title more likely reflects the autographic text than the longer title. One of the authors teaches Greek and has often observed this phenomenon. Students may translate the name of Christ with a phrase set in their minds by long use instead of the wording of the passage.

Prefer the harder reading. Scholars developed this rule from the idea that scribes tend to smooth out difficulties. Spelling or grammar that does not make sense would be viewed as a previous scribal error and corrected. Today, we too would have difficulty copying a sentence with poor grammar. We may do so unintentionally (reading what we expect and not even noticing a "typo" in our source) or intentionally (either by making a change or by using our modern marginal "sic"). This extends beyond "typos" to passages made difficult by seeming discrepancies of parallel or quoted passages, or that appear to conflict with clear doctrines. (For instance, how many sermons have you heard from the theologically difficult verse "be not righteous over much" in Eccles. 7:16?)

Prefer the less harmonious reading. This rule of thumb derives from the tendency to write the familiar. Having memorized a passage from Matthew, a scribe may write from memory when he gets to that part of Luke. This changes the original wording to harmonize the passage with Matthew's account. Some scribes may do so deliberately to remove what seemed to them inconsistencies in quotations.

Another example involves harmonizing to familiar names. The partaking together of the bread and the cup has several names. The early church called this the "Eucharist." It came to be called "Communion" among some groups, and the "Lords Table" or the "Lord's Supper" among others. Roman Catholics call this service the "Mass." These differing terms reflect some different emphases, but the heart of the matter is that you will tend to call it what you are used to hearing. When copying material down from another source, it is not easy for one accustomed to one term to avoid writing that term even though he saw another term for the same thing.

Summary. As in the courtroom, some evidence is subjective. Different jurors evaluate the attitudes of each witness differently. However some subjective evaluations (such as rebellion toward authority) may not only be true but essential to recognize. Likewise each type of textual evidence can be very important. Internal evidence is more subjective than external evidence, which is why both types of internal evidence are called probabilities. Yet within internal evidence, transcriptional probability is less subjective than intrinsic probability, since typical scribal copying errors are better known than the styles of the human authors themselves.

Hence the phrases say "prefer, as more likely original," which is not an absolute dictum. Like most rules, they have exceptions and modifications as all textual critics have acknowledged from Griesbach to the present. The rules do not necessarily explain or even apply to every variant reading. At times, the rules must even be reversed, but each arises often enough and consistently enough to be regarded as useful in evaluating certain kinds of variants. Based on the historic evidence of this kind of thing, it will not do simply to dismiss with a wave of the hand the likelihood, that in a sufficient number of these cases, the longer reading reflects an addition to the autographic text. Neither therefore is it fair to charge Westcott and Hort (or Griesbach or Tregelles or Bengel) with demeaning the Lord by shortening his title. Whatever theological emphases existed among these men, denying the Lord Jesus Christ was not one of them. They simply sought the original text from these variants, and believed that they had evidence for the shorter text. The rules must be applied judiciously, but cannot be dismissed summarily.

Since the Eclectic Text became popular, many variations have developed. Some are more conservative views (see the next chapter), while others are more liberal views (see Chapter 8). The term **Critical Eclecticism** distinguishes the position of Metzger and Aland from other Eclectic theories. Some prefer the term Reasoned Eclecticism[1], but the term *critical* is more appropriate. While the terms reasoning and critical thinking are synonymous, the term critical is tied to the theory in three important ways. Metzger and Aland are probably the best known modern textual critics, their resulting Greek text is always called the *critical text*, and their practices developed from the *critical method* of Westcott and Hort. Keep in mind that a "critic" in this discipline is attempting to determine the original readings as objectively as possible.

Objections

Metzger acknowledged Burgon's thorough patristic studies as evidence that Westcott and Hort had overstated their case. He even acknowledged Westcott and Hort's error, especially regarding Origen, but would not drop the patristic argument against the Syrian text type.[2] In fact, both Metzger and Aland ignored Burgon's warnings about speculating on a recension, and both men specifically identified Lucian as its agent.[3]

Of course, Metzger and Aland also disagreed with Burgon concerning the use of internal evidence. While Burgon condemned it as subjective, these scholars relied heavily on the canons of scribal tendency (transcriptional probability) and the considerations of the human author's style.[4] They consider applications of these principles to prove that the Syrian text is late and secondary (as did Westcott and Hort).

The emphasis on intrinsic probability shows up clearly in their treatment of Acts 16:12. In this verse, based on their view of Luke's style, they adopted a reading not found in any manuscript. This practice is termed **conjectural emendation**. Admittedly their use of this practice on one word in one verse in the entire New Testament does not typify their regard for the mass of manuscript evidence. Nevertheless taking this liberty even once suggests a weaker view of preservation than fundamentalists take. It shows that they do not consider the mass of manuscript evidence to have definitely preserved the Word of God to the present.[5]

The points above are symptoms of the primary failure in the writings of these men. Like Westcott and Hort, they never say even a word about either inspiration or preservation. Without attacking the spiritual condition of these men, we must question the wisdom of such a presentation. They have left themselves open to criticism from Bible believers for undermining the authority of Scripture without ever once claiming otherwise. They spend an entire book discussing the variants from a human perspective without ever attempting to reconcile their findings with Scripture or to show their readers how their findings fit in the larger scheme so that God is glorified. Unless the limited scope of the variant readings is repeatedly stressed and put in its proper context, such an approach is bound to put doubts in the minds of Bible believers. Perhaps this tactic was employed for marketing as a text at secular universities, but for whatever reason it has done a disservice to the cause of Christ.

Aland in particular displays a liberal view regarding Scripture. He refers to the second century, "when the New Testament text was not yet regarded as 'canonical,' much less as sacred . . ."[6] Of course, the New Testament books were regarded as sacred Scripture as Peter testifies to this fact in his quotations regarding inspiration and the epistles of Paul.[7] Aland also says, "1 Peter and 2 Peter, for instance, were clearly written by two different authors."[8] This denies the inspiration of the opening verse of at least one of the two books.

Contributions

Metzger and Aland have contributed to the field through their Greek text and textbooks which have summarized modern research and have disseminated knowledge of extant manuscripts across the world. Their widely used texts have helped scholars shift away from Westcott and Hort on at least five points.

First, Metzger and Aland noted the obvious bias in the choice of the name "Neutral" text type by Westcott and Hort. The Neutral text was not neutral and could not even be proved to be a separate type from the Alexandrian type. Westcott and Hort were so blinded in their defense of this type's neutrality, that in the nine instances where they followed a Western reading[9] rather than a Neutral text reading, they "could not bring themselves to refer directly to 'Neutral interpolation,'" and instead called them Western non-interpolations.[10] Metzger and Aland recognized this bias and abandoned the Neutral text type. They refer to an **Alexandrian** text type that encompasses both the Neutral and Alexandrian types defined by Westcott and Hort (or Bengel's African type). This broader Alexandrian family explains some variant readings identified but not explained by Westcott and Hort.[11]

Second, their popular books have served to stabilize terminology in the field. The bewildering maze of names for the text types has now settled at four: the *Alexandrian* type (in the modern sense of Metzger and Aland), the *Western* type (of Westcott and Hort), the *Caesarean* type (of Streeter), and the *Byzantine* type. The **Byzantine** type is the type called Syrian by Hort and Asian by Bengel. Griesbach called it Constantinopolitan, but the name Byzantine derives from the older name of Constantinople (Constantine renamed Byzantium after himself, but the Muslims have changed the name of this city in Turkey to Istanbul). Burgon referred to these manuscripts as representatives of the Traditional Text, but the term Byzantine has become standard for this type.

We have previously pointed out that these types are named for regions, and that a manuscript need not come from that region to be classified in the type. Nevertheless, some manuscripts within each type do come from the region in question. Whether or not one agrees with the theory of text types, these regional categories stress yet another aspect of God's providence: the fact that all manuscripts have a close agreement in spite of coming from various parts of the ancient world.

Third, Metzger and Aland emphasized that any existing manuscript is bound to have some copying errors. They argued the weakness of tying a text type to a single manuscript so well, that no one has practiced a single manuscript approach to textual criticism since—not even during the rage of new papyri discoveries. Hort's preference for Vaticanus and Tischendorf's for Sinaiticus is no longer acceptable among scholars.

Fourth, the same applies to text types. Metzger recognized that at least occasionally the Western type may preserve the original wording more accurately than the Alexandrian. In fact, every text type has some characteristic readings that are probably scribal errors. This major concession together with the rejection of the Neutral type has made it unpopular if not impossible to promote a single text type approach to textual criticism. Of the four modern text types, none are promoted as always closest to the autographs. While Burgon and Hort debated the Alexandrian versus Byzantine types, the basis for such arguments today has shifted. These terms occur only in the context of broader discussions. It is not an Alexandrian position that is argued, but an Eclectic position that frequently adopts Alexandrian readings. Again, it is not a Byzantine position, but a Textus Receptus position that frequently adopts Byzantine readings. Few scholars have promoted the Western text type,[12] and no scholar has promoted the precedence of the Caesarean text type. Apparently, the days when Westcott and Hort could promote the priority of a single text type have ended.

Fifth, in keeping with their view of the limitations of any single manuscript or type, Metzger and Aland moved to an eclectic text. While Westcott and Hort had stated essentially the same criteria, they had applied their criteria to text types as a whole. Having arrived at what they considered the most reliable type ("Neutral"), they had followed the then oldest known representative of that type Vaticanus. In effect, then, Westcott and Hort had evaluated types rather than manuscripts, and the net result was a single-type theory.

In contrast, Metzger and Aland advanced the position that the textual scholar should "choose the reading which best explains the origin of the others."[13] This provides a theoretical basis less tied to a single type. It permitted them to select readings from any text type. Although they typically preferred Alexandrian readings, they did herald a major shift at least in attitude. Readings from all text types were evaluated and sometimes non-Alexandrian readings were adopted.

Their text included more readings from Alexandrian manuscripts other than Vaticanus or even Hort's Neutral type. They included the eight Western readings without apology (or recourse to Western non-interpolations) and added a ninth from Mark 14:25. They even adopted a reading with only Caesarean text type support in Matt 22:34-35. Most surprisingly they sided with the "suspect" Byzantine type in three passages (Matt. 12:47, Luke 20:1, and Heb. 7:1) against the Alexandrian.[14] This move toward an eclectic text is probably the most important influence on textual criticism in this century.

Textus Receptus

Burgon had referred to the Traditional Text. By using this term, he meant to trace the Greek text as it was popularly accepted since the apostles. This included the Byzantine manuscripts, the Textus Receptus of Erasmus. In English, the KJV is the traditional text, which is based on Erasmus. The Byzantine manuscripts form the vast majority of all Greek manuscripts.

However, the terms are not the same. The KJV is an English version, the Textus Receptus is the Greek text which Erasmus edited from manuscripts, the Byzantine Text is a text type which has similar readings at key points of variation in the New Testament, and the Majority Text reflects a selection criterion for comparing variants. While these are related in various ways, arguments for or against one may not apply to another.

The Textus Receptus (TR), which came from a handful of manuscripts of the Byzantine type, includes a peculiarity here and there not typical of the entire Byzantine family or text type. We have already seen examples of this in the Comma Johanneum and the translation from Latin of the six verses at the end of Revelation. Similarly, the KJV is a translation of the TR and occasionally does not reflect the Greek of the TR as well as it might. Likewise the Byzantine text type occasionally includes several large groups of manuscripts that differ in a given passage. In such places, it is possible for the reading of the Byzantine type to disagree with the majority of manuscripts. This is rare in general, but does occur especially in the book of Revelation, where there are fewer known manuscripts.

Position

In 1956 **Edward F. Hills** published a paperback defending the King James Version of the Bible. Hills modified Burgon's tactics and focused solely on the Textus Receptus. By claiming the TR to be closest to the autographs, he defended the KJV from the original Greek and still addressed preservation by pointing to the vast number of Byzantine manuscripts.

Recall, however, that the Textus Receptus includes the Comma Johanneum, which is absent from most manuscripts, and also includes Erasmus's own Greek translation of the Latin at the end of Revelation. For many of the words in Revelation 22:16-21, the TR matches other manuscripts, in other spots the word used is a minor variation of the word in the manuscripts, however in verse 19 Erasmus uses the word "book of life" rather than "tree of life." These variations are not a reading of the Byzantine text type nor of the majority of manuscripts. Thus, Hills could not address the preservation of these unique readings in the Textus Receptus by pointing to the many Byzantine manuscripts. To defend every reading of the Traditional Text required that he go beyond an argument from the majority of manuscripts and Byzantine text type.

Hills observed that in nine passages (including the "book of life" in Rev. 22:19)[15] Erasmus had followed the Latin Vulgate rather than the majority of manuscripts. Since the Latin Vulgate was the traditional text used by the Holy Spirit for centuries, Hills suggests that the Holy Spirit guided Erasmus in retaining these readings.

Likewise, Hills justifies the inclusion of the Comma Johanneum. He points out that the Comma does have early support in the patristic writings. Besides a disputed reference from Cyprian (about 250), it is cited by two Spanish bishops of the fourth century and several fifth century writers including Cassiodorus. It is also in some Old Latin versions of the fifth and sixth century. On the basis of the Old Latin, it was incorporated it into a later edition of the Vulgate (about 800). Hills suggests that this was the work of the Spirit, correcting the human error and a correction he would later guide Erasmus to as well.[16]

In the final analysis, Hills argued that God preserved His Word miraculously and providentially through the Textus Receptus as it came down through church history from the autographs through the Latin Vulgate and Erasmus and culminated in the King James Version. He observed that a Bible-believing Christian has an altogether different line of thinking about the Bible from an infidel. He pointed out that we cannot view the Scriptures as strictly human compositions. We reason things out from biblical presuppositions, which gives us a **logic of faith**. This view was later aptly expressed by another:

> The New Testament is not like any other ancient text. The New Testament is unique! It is breathed out by a living God. It is inerrant as it came from the pen of its inspired authors. Moreover, the logic of faith demands that documents so unique cannot have had a history wholly like that of secular writings. As they cannot have avoided the attack of supernatural principalities and powers of evil, so they cannot have lacked the superintending providence of the God who authored them. It [Hort's reasoning] is also an expression of unbelief in the kind of overruling divine providence which is inescapably implied in the very nature of the Word itself.[17]

Objections

Although the main point of Hills' is sound, the concept of the logic of faith has been misapplied to draw several unnecessary conclusions. First, since the Bible is God's revelation of Himself to man, it must be that God has always preserved it by multiplying it into the most dominant text in every age. Hills has equated the true autographic original text with the Traditional Text used by God's people.[18]

It is essential that a theory not contradict Scripture, and in that sense the view of Hills is biblical. However, to claim that only one view is biblical, it is necessary to show that no other view is compatible with Scripture. Has Hills proved this? Certainly not. The Scriptures he cited prove only that God has kept His message pure to the present and do not say anything about how God preserved it. Nothing in the verses cited requires the text to be without any variation in wording. As we discussed in Chapter 1, Matthew 24:25, "Heaven and earth shall pass away, but my words shall not pass away" does not identify any manuscript or text type, or whether the preservation will be achieved through popular texts, traditional texts, old texts, or simply some text somewhere on earth or in heaven. These authoritative words of Jesus guarantee only that His Word shall be preserved and that none of His words shall be lost. In absence of Scripture, then, whether the method involved the Textus Receptus, the Alexandrian text, or the mass of manuscripts is not a matter for dogmatism but for diligent prayer and careful study.

Hills also applied his concept of the logic of faith to polarize textual theories as competing philosophies. He claimed that spiritual men recognize the true reading by the logic of faith, and any other readings are naturalistic and by implication ungodly. By "naturalistic" he means the textual researchers' process of comparison of manuscripts to determine which reading is more likely to reflect the autographic text. The idea is that such a study is appropriate for other human writings such as ancient classical works but not for the Scriptures which were superintended by God Himself. In summary, "naturalistic" New Testament textual criticism is incompatible with the providential preservation of the New Testament text.[19] However, Hills quotes no textual scholar who denies the preservation of Scripture because none deny it. Instead he is accusing some scholars of denying preservation simply because they view the manner of preservation differently than he does. He begs the question. What is at issue is not whether God preserved His Word but how God superintended the preservation of His Word.

Hills applied the logic of faith a third time to try to show that the Traditional Text is correct, and that competing text types are tools of Satan. This point is fallacious on three grounds (besides the fact that the argument depends on the previous weak argument concerning the method of preservation). First, the fact that the early church used all the variant readings of competing text types is evidence that they do not constitute a satanic attack. Second, satanic attacks against the Greek text have been ineffective because the distortions are either blatant and easily spotted by Christians (Marcion's tampering with the text got him branded as a heretic very early and quite vocally) or too little to affect doctrine. As has been noted no text type variants affect doctrine. Third, the real satanic attacks on the Word of God during the manuscript period took the same form that they take today: denying, misinterpreting, mistranslating, and misapplying the Word. These points will be discussed more in a later chapter, but the manuscript variants are simply not in the same category.

Finally, the logic of faith claims that the pure text must be the one that God has blessed. This equates preservation with use. Though having some appeal, this argument is quite subjective. For what determines that God has blessed a certain version of His Word beyond the fact that He has simply blessed His Word? Hills concluded, "Hence the text current among believers must be the true text."[20] If this were true, then the Hebrew Masoretic text was the true text for Israel, the Septuagint and the Alexandrian text was the true text in the fourth century in Egypt. The Vulgate was the true text for over a thousand years for virtually all of Western Christendom (not just for the Catholics; for men like Wycliffe as well). The Byzantine text was the true text in Constantinople for over eight hundred years and so on. In other words, this argument ignores the differences among these texts, and yet all were at one time or place the "current text" of believers. To be sure, God blessed each of these texts, if usage of them is a criterion for blessing. If it is a question of how much usage, then perhaps the truest text would be the Latin Vulgate (from which Wycliffe's version was translated).

Whatever one's criteria for God's blessing on texts, the fact is that God has historically blessed more than one type of text, even where there has been some disagreement between texts. The Greek text of the Old Testament varies from the Hebrew text. Was the Hebrew text used by David replaced by the Septuagint used by the apostles? In fact, the apostles used both the Hebrew and the Greek in spite of their differences. Furthermore, at times the King James Version follows the Hebrew text in the Old Testament but the Septuagint in New Testament quotations. The apostles knew that these variations in the Old Testament did not affect the message, and the same is true of the differences among New Testament text types. Remember, as we have shown, that the variants by no means diminish the power and authority of the Word of God. The variants have minimal importance to preservation because they are comparatively few and because no Christian doctrine is affected by them. Recognizing this ought to return our focus to more important matters, such as obeying the clear commands of the Word of God and sharing the gospel with a lost world.

The most serious problem with Hills' position is his lack of charity toward his brethren. He is certainly entitled to advocating his position on the Greek text and to advocate it strongly. It is, however, unfair for him to condemn another believer's faithfulness to Christ simply because that believer may not agree with Hills' opinion. In order to denounce another professing Christian, he should be able to demonstrate from Scripture that his view about the preservation of the text is exclusively God's view on the matter, something he has not accomplished. He has attempted to make a spiritual battle out of a theoretical debate. Like many crusaders for causes—real or imaginary—Hills has simply argued beyond the basis of clear, undeniable scriptural evidence. By so overstating his case, Hills has done great disservice to believers who happen to differ from him regarding the nature of preservation and accused them of lacking spirituality. Such slurs against other believers give an otherwise viable position a bad reputation.

The reader should recognize that the primary objections to the Textus Receptus view involve applying the logic of faith to make absolute statements concerning preservation and in denouncing other views as satanic. It is quite possible to hold the Textus Receptus view without appealing to the logic of faith and without condemning other positions. Such a position is a viable theoretical alternative.

Contributions

The Textus Receptus view retains some popularity with such men as Hills and Alfred Martin. Hills has contributed the most thorough defense of the position, but others such as Alfred Martin have also published a defense of certain points.[21] The view has made at least four lasting contributions.

First, by advancing a well-thought out position, these scholars clarified some confusion between the Byzantine, Majority, Textus Receptus, and KJV positions. He made clear that his position focused on the TR as the primary text that God preserved.

Second, Hills paid attention to the dispute concerning the date of the Syriac Peshitta. Research had cast doubt on its second century age, and it became no longer tenable as evidence of the

Byzantine text type in the second century. He recognized the force of scholarship and ceased to cite the Peshitta as evidence. He considered its evidence unnecessary because the rest of Burgon's arguments still stood against the key points of Westcott and Hort.

Third, the Textus Receptus position identifies several of the weaknesses of Critical Eclecticism. For instance, Martin flatly denounces all use of conjectural emendation and condemns the oft-heard speculation on Byzantine recension.[22]

Fourth, addressing the issue of preservation is probably the greatest contribution of the view. These scholars properly stress the importance of preservation and divine providence, points too often ignored or de-emphasized by scholars holding the critical eclectic view.

The major points are sound. God has certainly superintended His New Testament in a unique way. No Christian familiar with the power and spirit of the Scriptures would question this point. The New Testament (along with the Old Testament) is a unique book. As God's Word, it is subject to supernatural attacks of Satan, and we have already seen how God has providentially preserved it from those attacks. No doctrine is lost, all of the words are preserved in the mass of manuscript evidence, and it has been preserved across the known world and in each time period. This stress filled an important void left by eclectic scholars.

Endnotes

1. David Alan Black, *New Testament Textual Criticism: A Concise Guide* (Grand Rapids: Baker Book House, 1994), pp. 37-40.

2. Metzger, "Explicit References in the Works of Origen to Variant Readings in N.T. MSS."

3. Metzger, *Text*, p. 141; Aland and Aland, *The Text of the New Testament* (Leiden: E. J. Brill, 1987), p. 65.

4. Metzger, *Text*, p. 210; Aland and Aland, pp. 275-76.

5. Although conjectural emendation is never justified in New Testament passages, the rejection of the practice deserves a minor qualification for Old Testament studies. Most extant Old Testament manuscripts represent the Masoretic Text, and only limited corroborating evidence is available from other sources (Samaritan Pentateuch, Dead Sea Scrolls, ancient rabbinic commentaries, Septuagint versions, etc.). Thus, in the very few instances where the Masoretic Text appears to have suffered in transmission, the plethora of manuscript evidence for New Testament variants is not always available. The most difficult such instance occurs in 1 Samuel 13:1. The Hebrew says that "Saul was one year old when he began to reign." Textual scholars must either make an interpretation here (which is not supported by other uses of the word in Hebrew but is the explanation given by Jewish tradition) or explain the problem as a copyist error. Those who suspect a copyist error may leave an blank for Saul's age (acknowledging that they do not what it should say) or they may employ conjectural emendation based on knowledge of Saul's life from other passages (for fuller discussion, see *Biblical Numerology* by John J. Davis, pp. 86-87). Since none of the three options is fully satisfactory, Christians should be charitable toward all conservative scholars regarding their handling of this most difficult of preservation problems.

 While few conservatives would recommend conjectural emendation even in this extreme instance, they should be slow to condemn those who employ it if this is the only passage in which they do so.

6. Aland and Aland, p. 51.

7. The Scripture was recognized as canonical by the original recipients as soon as they were written. Though a few books (antilegomena) were disputed for some time, none were ever rejected by all Christians. Most remained recognized by all Christians, and a few were for awhile recognized by only some Christians. Even so, it is too strong to say that the text was *not* regarded as canonical (by anyone?) during the post-apostolic age. While there is a kernel of truth in the claim that the canon remained in dispute, the further claim that the books were not even considered sacred

does not accord with the fact that it was the authority in all of the disputes of the early church councils.

8. Aland and Aland, p. 49.

9. Westcott and Hort, *Introduction*, p. 295.

10. Metzger, *Text*, p. 134.

11. Namely, the "Western non-interpolations." See Metzger, *Text*, p. 134.

12. Metzger (*Text*, p. 211) cites a 1902 work in German by Adalbert Merx that does so. In contrast, Aland rejects even the existance of the Western type (pp. 68-69).

13. Metzger, *Text*, p. 207.

14. Metzger, *Text*, p. 238-40. The first passage also has Western support, but the other two are accepted as preserved by the Byzantine type alone.

15. Edward F. Hills, *The King James Version Defended* (Des Moines: IA: Christian Research Press, 1956, 1973), pp. 197-99. The other eight passages are: Matt. 10:8*, 27:35, John 3:25*, Acts 8:37, 9:5, 9:6, 20:28*, Rom. 16:25-27*. In some of these passages (marked *), the TR departs from the Majority of manuscripts but does agree with the oldest manuscripts. Also, in Matt. 27:35, the TR agrees with Caesarean manuscripts against both the majority of manuscripts and the oldest manuscripts.

16. Hills, *King James Version Defended*, pp. 204-08 explains how the Comma Johanneum entered the TR, documenting its early support and also speculating on its possible authenticity and why it might have been dropped out of the traditional Greek text.

17. Hodges, Zane C. "Rationalism and Contemporary New Testament Textual Criticism." *Bibliotheca Sacra*, 118 (1971), pp. 29-30.

18. Edward F. Hills, *Believing Bible Study* (Des Moines, Iowa: Christian Research Press, 1967, 1977), p. 61. "Because the Scriptures are God's revelation of Himself, eternal, forever relevant, and infallibly inspired, they have been guarded down through the ages by God's special providence, preserved not secretly but in a public way. The logic of faith leads us to this conclusion, and this logic is confirmed by the promises of our Lord and Saviour. Till heaven and earth pass, one jot or one tittle shall in no wise pass from the law, till all be fulfilled (Matt. 5:18). And it is easier for heaven and earth to pass, than one tittle of the law to fail (Luke 16:17). Heaven and earth shall pass away, but my words shall not pass away

(Matt. 24:35; Mark 13:31; Luke 21: 33). The true Bible text, therefore, has been preserved in the majority of the Hebrew and Greek manuscripts, and in the King James Version and other faithful translations. When we read this text believingly, then the Holy Spirit assures us by His testimony that we hold in our hands the true Word of God."

19. Hills, *Believing Bible Study,* p. 55. He says, "For if we ignore the providential preservation of Scripture, then we can be no more sure of the text of the New Testament than of the text of any other book. And this skepticism will grow and eat away like a cancer until our whole Christian faith is well nigh gone. For if we no longer believe in the providential preservation of the New Testament, how can we believe in the infallible inspiration of the original New Testament manuscripts? For why would God infallibly inspire these original manuscripts if He did not intend to preserve their texts by His special providence down through the ages?"

20. Hills, *Believing Bible Study,* p. 187.

21. Alfred Martin, "A Critical Examination of the Westcott-Hort Textual Theory" in *Which Bible?* (pp. 253-82), edited by David Otis Fuller.

22. Martin, in *Which Bible?* edited by David Otis Fuller, p. 269-71, 280. See also Edward Miller, *A Guide to the Textual Criticism of the New Testament* (Collingswood, NJ: Dean Burgon Society, 1886, reprinted 1986), p. 65.

Questions

1. What data made the Westcott and Hort theory inadequate and in need of refinement?

2. What is the major difference between the four text types used by Westcott and Hort and the four types used today? What scholars can be considered responsible for this change?

3. Name two well-known textual scholars of the twentieth century who have written major books on textual criticism.

4. What is the most serious weakness in the writings of these two men.

5. What was the most influential contribution of the century to textual criticism.

6. Distinguish internal from external evidence, and explain the subdivisions of internal evidence. Give an example of each. Rank them all from most to least subjective.

7. Why do no modern writers hold to a strict oldest manuscript theory?

8. What are Edward F. Hills' main contributions to the textual debate?

9. What is the major weakness of Hills' view?

10. Have five people copy by hand the book of Colossians (or II Peter, Titus, or II Thessalonians). Read their work; how many errors do you find? Are they accidental omissions and spelling errors or are there some wording and grammatical errors caused by memory? Compare the five manuscripts. Do you find patterns of errors among the scribes? Did any scribe produce a perfect copy even in punctuation (which would compare to marginal notes in ancient manuscripts)?

CHAPTER 7

REFINEMENTS

This chapter will consider three views which have refined the views of the previous chapter. All three are held by Christian scholars who are not afraid to defend the fundamentals of the faith including the inspiration and preservation of Scripture. All three are vast improvements over previous views, and all have made major contributions to the field.

Majority Text

In 1977 **Wilbur N. Pickering** published *The Identity of the New Testament Text*. Pickering's view is called the **Majority Text** position because rather than promoting a text type, he believes that the correct reading is most likely preserved in the majority of Greek manuscripts. Thus, he reconstructs the autographs by comparing all the manuscripts and selecting at each variant the most frequent reading.

The Majority Text view opposes the Eclectic position on numerous points. For instance, Pickering questioned evidence for the existence of text types. He rejected the idea that the genealogy of existing manuscripts can be traced usefully. He argued, as did Burgon before him, that none of the text types are meaningful, and text types should not serve as the basis of a theory. He opposed the Lucianic Recension theory because it lacks any historical verification. He also contended that the agreement of the mass of so-called Byzantine texts is inexplicable unless it reflects the autographs.[1]

Pickering also rejected the canons of scribal tendency. For instance, he believes that the longer reading is to be preferred. He reasoned that careful scribes would not tamper with the words intentionally, but like anyone may have accidentally left words out. Considering accidental omissions to be the most common scribal error, he viewed the longer readings as most likely original. Similarly, he considered the so-called conflations to be genuine and explained the shorter readings as accidental omissions of different parts of the combined original. He also rejected the other canons (harder reading preferred and the less harmonious reading preferred).

The most visible obstacle to the theory involves the fact that the oldest manuscripts contain variations from the Majority, and that no equally early manuscripts contain the reading of the majority. Pickering rightly reasons that the agreement of a mass of manuscripts points to a copy from which they came earlier than any one of them. He also argued based on mathematical probabilities that the majority reading was most probably the oldest. This argument is often misquoted. He did not argue that the majority reading is always the oldest. Rather he argued that rejecting the majority repeatedly and consistently (as Westcott and Hort did) requires an explanation so complex as to be improbable. He also noted that such old manuscripts are found only in Egypt because only such dry climates are conducive to preserving papyrus. In light of this, the lack of equally old manuscripts from other regions is no surprise.

Concerning scribal tendency, Pickering emphasized that careful copyists carried out the task of copying Scripture reverently. He theorized that in general, at any reading, hundreds of manuscripts should agree and a few dozen manuscripts would display divergent readings often resulting from accidental omissions. He rejected the eclectic canons of scribal tendencies in favor of the view that the most frequent scribal error was omission. He claimed that the agreement of ninety percent of the manuscripts evidenced this and cited the variants at 1 Timothy 3:16, emphasizing that 300 manuscripts read "God" while the other eleven are divided among themselves (seven read "who" and the other four offer three other readings).[2]

Since manuscripts agree in about 90% of the text, Pickering deemed any similarities among the small numbers of randomly distributed errors insignificant. He therefore opposed the grouping of such haphazard errors as text types. His rejection of text types then removed the need for explaining criteria for identifying the types (even eclectic scholars do not all agree on the existance of the Caesarean or even the Western types). By focusing on the primary stream of transmission (90%), he also avoided the need for explanations for why a few dozen manuscripts should be correct as opposed to the many (whether by recension or process). Thus, Pickering sought economy of theory by replacing all these constructs with a single construct explaining why the oldest manuscripts are among the divergent few.

Pickering studied at Dallas Seminary under **Zane Hodges**. Hodges can be credited as the first textual scholar to expound the Majority Text theory. Hodges published a Greek New Testament as an alternative to the much used UBS text of Metzger and Aland. *The Greek New Testament according to the Majority Text*, edited by Zane C. Hodges and Arthur L. Farstad, is a major contribution and should be welcomed by all scholars. Even those who disagree with their conclusions may be interested in the footnoted readings, many of which are not noted in the UBS[3] . The views of Hodges are laid out in the introduction and a few other articles, but because he wrote relatively little concerning his theory, Pickering's book has become the standard defense of this position.

A more recent contributor, **Alan Cairns**, also aptly expounds the Majority Text position. He goes a step further than Pickering in attempting to present a theory that applies equally to both testaments. Since there are far fewer copies of the Old Testament surviving than the new, and since the scribes in Israel (such as the Masoretes) had a far more detailed system of transmission than the scribes in the church, the transmission for the two testaments have typically been considered separate issues with few points in common. Cairns is perhaps the first to move toward the synthesis of Old and New Testament textual theories. Such innovative steps claim to combine the simplicity of Pickering's theory with the power of broad application. Regardless of one's conclusions on this matter, the attempt to unify the subject is a noble effort worthy of consideration and response.[4]

Contributions

The Majority Text advocates improved on the positions of Burgon and Hills in several ways. First, it focused on the Greek Text rather than what is simply traditional. This is important. The Comma Johanneum has become traditional but has little support from any Greek texts. Erasmus had very few Greek manuscripts available, and many passages depended on a single manuscript. The Textus Receptus, therefore, depended on some readings which may have been easily improved if more manuscripts had been collected. Such criticisms of the Textus Receptus do not apply to the Majority Text, because the reading must appear in the majority of manuscripts in order to be adopted as authentic. In fact, Cairns claims that the TR and KJV contain only three verses that are not supported by the Majority Text.[5]

Second, Pickering did not rely on the logic of faith argument promoted by Burgon and Hills (see Chapter 6). This is especially important since some proponents of the Majority Text appeal to the logic of faith for additional support.[6] Pickering's defense of the Majority Text shows that the position stands on its own without this weak support. Pickering specifically states that he believes the Scriptures concerning inspiration and preservation, but he acknowledges that in the Bible "no intimation is given as to just how God proposes to do it."[7]

In fact, Cairns goes another step and argues that it is inconsistent of those who promote the Textus Receptus to criticize eclectic texts for adopting readings with limited manuscript evidence and to justify those traditional verses with equally limited manuscript support. Cairns demands objective manuscript evidence and is willing to let the evidence speak for itself, even though it may cut both ways (against both modern scholarly opinion or against familiar traditional readings).[8]

Third, Pickering's summary of the remaining difficulties of the Westcott and Hort position consists of showing that the main points upon which Westcott and Hort rested their case are controversial even among Eclectic scholars. He viewed such controversial foundations as suggesting a need for overhaul involving alternative assumptions and theories.

For example, Pickering strongly objected to Hort's use of conflation to discard the Byzantine text. He called conflation a "pseudo-issue"[9] because, as he claimed, (1) there are not enough examples to support it, and (2) there is too much intermingling of text types in the manuscripts. He complained that Hort tried to build a generalization on only eight examples. Hort also neglected the factor of mixture, which occurred when a scribe copied from more than one manuscript (of different text types). Pickering cited Colwell to show that such mixture known to occur among the manuscripts would tend to nullify the generalization by which

Hort dismissed the Byzantine text as secondary. Pickering and Colwell argued that to claim a generalization, dozens of examples should be demonstrable, yet the list has not grown in the century since Westcott and Hort. Majority text scholars point to the weakness of the evidence from conflation and therefore think its use against the Byzantine text type should be abandoned.

Further, Pickering did not simply try to refute other theories as Burgon and Hills had done but set forth an alternative theory in detail. He pointed out weak points in opposing theories and exposed weakly supported assumptions. He cited studies in support of his own points, and also cited opponents who commented on key points. He foresaw objections and addressed them head on. He even included an appendix[10] with a mathematical argument using probabilities to support his view that under normal circumstances the original wording finds its way into more copies than a copyist error.

Pickering cited several studies to support his claim that scribes tended toward omissions rather than interpolations. E. C. Colwell had made intensive investigations into scribal habits in early papyri and published an article in which he demonstrated rather decisively that P45, P66, and P75 give evidence of editorial omission or in the case of P66, just plain old sloppy copying.[11] Pickering viewed this study of editorial omission as support for his position.

Whether or not scholars agreed with Pickering, they took notice that his theory and critiques demanded response. Other things being equal, a simpler explanation always puts a burden of proof on a more complex one. Rejection of prevailing notions often forces a healthy reevaluation. As Westcott and Hort pulled together prior research into a cohesive theory, so Pickering pulled together the work of Colwell, Scrivener, Burgon, Hodges, and others, into an equally cohesive opposing theory. His critiques of eclecticism encouraged greater caution in statements and practices of textual scholars. Perhaps Pickering's greatest contribution was to marshall the evidence against the dogmas that had developed among eclectic scholars, thereby prompting a reevaluation and a fresh look at the Majority position.

Objections

Perhaps the most important weakness in Pickering's presentation is his treatment of inversion. **Inversion** occurs when either the Western text conflates readings from the Alexandrian (Hort's Neutral) text and the Byzantine text, or where the Alexandrian text conflates readings from the Western and Byzantine texts. Hort had said that no instances of text type inversions existed. Pickering cites Hort's own reference to the conflation of D (a Western manuscript) in John 5:37 and B (an Alexandrian manuscript) in Col. 1:12 and II Thess. 3:4. Thus, Hort seems blithely unaware that he contradicted himself. What Pickering failed to discern here is that these examples he found in Hort are places where the manuscripts do not reflect the text type. They represent valid conflations in the manuscript but not valid inversions of the text types.

Knowing that all manuscripts contain scribal errors, Hort never claimed that all Alexandrian manuscripts were free of conflation, but only that text type conflation (when it occurred) always went against the Byzantine. This is why Hort could on the one hand claim that no inversions exist and still acknowledge conflations in the verses that Pickering cited against him. This particular argument then is not as Pickering claims, "fatal to Hort's purpose." While Pickering denies the existence of types, he cannot show inconsistency in Hort unless it can be demonstrated that the Western and Alexandrian text type readings show conflation as Hort claimed the Byzantine did. This Pickering has not shown.

Pickering's error is frequent among those who do not hold to

Eclectic views, so it bears emphasis. Every manuscript varies from every other manuscript in various ways. Some differences reflect the group from which the original was copied and are text-typical variants. Others, however, reflect only mistakes of the copyist of that particular manuscript and are not representative of the text type. The manuscript B (Alexandrian type), for instance, has variants that reflect the text-type and distinguish it from other types. However, even when compared with another manuscript of its own type (such as A), they can disagree at a given place in three ways: A can reflect the type, but not B, or vice versa, or neither may reflect the type. Examples of inversions put forth by opponents are often irrelevant because they illustrate disagreements between manuscripts within types rather than between types.

Another weakness in Pickering's presentation involves quotations. The most serious of these involved a quotation of Hort. Pickering asserts that Hort, who did the lion's share of the work, was prejudiced against the Textus Receptus from the beginning. As evidence, he cites some intemperate statements of Hort who referred to the Textus Receptus as "vile" and "corrupt" and the like.[12] He thus portrays Hort's theory as unobjective, biased, and therefore untrustworthy. While Hort was unwise to express himself this way, he was speaking in private correspondence as one textual scholar to another and did not mean what he appears to mean. The term **corrupt** when used of textual issues need refer to no more than scribal errors. Excited about manuscripts (such as Vaticanus) which he believed to have fewer scribal errors, he simply described Erasmus' text as having many more.

Another example of quotation without the full context involved the early findings of A. C. Clark. Clark, like Hort, treated biblical writings like classical writings in terms of textual principles. Pickering criticized Hort for this, but did not acknowledge that Clark approached his studies with the same presuppositions. More to the point, not only were Clark's conclusions refuted by Frederic

G. Kenyon at the time, but Clark himself abandoned his own conclusion about the text of Acts being longer in its original form! Pickering refers in a footnote to the critiques of Clark's work by Kenyon, but he omits the significant reversal of Clark's work by his own subsequent labors in the same field. Pickering should have acknowledged the final conclusion of Clark as well as the one that he originally held, but abandoned. His failure to do this, makes it appear to be more a matter of propaganda than of judicious weighing of evidence.

Again, Pickering quoted Vaganay to support his rejection of the canon that prefers the shorter reading. Vaganay, however, merely provided exceptions to the general rule as cautions. Pickering focused on these exceptions without acknowledging that Vaganay affirmed that scribes tended to extend the text rather than shorten it. Similarly, Pickering countered each of the Westcott-Hort appraisals of the text with quotations from various textual scholars who express some dissatisfaction with their theory. However, any honest scholar will express areas where he feels improvements can be made or where more research is warranted, and such declarations do not constitute admission that one's theory has failed.

Finally, Pickering tends to lump the various eclectic views together, failing to distinguish them from one another and from Westcott and Hort's. He correctly traces Eclecticism to Westcott and Hort,[13] and aptly summarizes the Westcott and Hort theory.[14] However, the discussion of eclecticism revolves around the practices of radical eclectics (to be discussed in the next chapter), which are not representative of any of either critical or conservative eclectic scholars. Such lumping is another common pitfall of those who do not hold eclectic views, but it is quite unfair to the various Eclectic scholars.

However, the key weakness of the Majority Text position is not any weak arguments against eclecticism but rather the lack of ancient manuscripts supporting it. If its proponents could hold up an ancient manuscript as a proof of its antiquity, its detractors would be silenced. Instead, its claim of antiquity depends on the agreement of numerous later manuscripts, an argument which eclectic scholars consider weak. The lack, then, of a "Byzantine" manuscript dating before the eighth century is the primary problem with which the theory must wrestle.

Conservative Eclecticism

Some who hold the Eclectic view are far quicker to publicly defend the inspiration, inerrancy, and preservation of the Bible than were Metzger and Aland. For instance, **Stewart Custer** is a long time faculty member of Bob Jones University and his defense of inspiration and preservation is well known. Custer teaches an eclectic position but remains conservative in doctrine and decries the silence of the critical Eclectic scholars on such essential doctrines as inspiration and preservation.

Contributions

Scholars who apply **conservative Eclecticism** agree with the Critical Eclectics on most points. Both distinctives relate to inspiration and preservation.

First, conservative Eclecticism takes a clear stand for divine inspiration and preservation of the Scripture. Custer states "God's Word is preserved in the sum-total of all the manuscripts (over 5000) which have been so far discovered."[15] Similarly, **D. A. Carson** defends both inspiration and inerrancy[16] and acknowledges its authority, bowing "in reverent submission to the Scriptures".[17] He calls himself, "a confessional evangelical with a high view of Holy Scripture."[18]

Second, conservative eclecticism adopts no conjectural

emendations in the New Testament. Custer opposes conjectural emendation altogether on theoretical grounds believing that the Scripture is preserved in the mass of manuscript evidence. Carson, while not rejecting the possibility of an emendation, accepts none in the New Testament, thereby agreeing in practice that the Scripture has been preserved in this mass of evidence.[19] Since manuscript evidence is abundant especially for the New Testament, one's policy toward emendations of it reveals one's stance toward preservation.

The conservative scholars, then, differ with Metzger and Aland and do not share their liberal tendencies. Their repudiation of every New Testament use of conjectural emendation (whether on theoretical or practical grounds) and their public defense of inspiration and preservation stand as refinements of critical Eclecticism. These key contributions address major weaknesses of Eclecticism. In fact, criticisms of Eclecticism for being weak on inspiration or preservation or for employing conjectural emendation simply do not apply to these scholars.

Objections

Conservative Eclectic scholars share the major weakness of previously discussed Eclectic positions—the difficulty of explaining the agreement of the many later manuscripts. While they do not resort to recensions used by earlier eclectic scholars, the explanations offered by eclectic scholars remain unconvincing to scholars holding non-eclectic views. The agreement of the mass of manuscripts is the key problem confronting eclectic scholars.

Also like other Eclectic scholars, conservative scholars tend to use the terms Majority Text, Byzantine, and Textus Receptus interchangeably. This is as inaccurate as Pickering's failure to maintain distinctions between the Alexandrian Text and the various positions within Eclecticism (radical, critical, and conservative).

Conservative eclectic scholars readily acknowledge that accidental scribal errors occur and that several canons of scribal tendency apply only to intentional errors. However, by excluding the (accidental) errors of omission from the canons, they imply by their terminology that scribes tend toward intentional rather than accidental errors. They certainly view more variants as due to interpolation (adding to the text) than would a non-eclectic scholar. Non-eclectic scholars regularly object to this persistence in referring to these intentional errors as "canons of scribal tendency" rather than "canons of intentional scribal errors."

The function of canons in any field is to describe and summarize typical (rather than exceptional) patterns. We could easily state an *e* before *i* rule for English spelling with numerous examples of words which it correctly describes, but the canon *i* before *e* is taught to students because it is more typical, applying to far more words. Pickering objected to Westcott and Hort's claim that interpolations are much more numerous than omissions.[20] Pickering considered their claim to give undue emphasis to what Westcott and Hort called "canons of textual criticism." However, if most errors were accidental, then the first "canon" should be to prefer the longer rather than the shorter reading. Eclectic scholars now treat the canons as standards of intentional errors. It would be fairer, then, either to rename the set of canons as "canons of intentional scribal errors" or to offer evidence that such intentional errors are indeed more common than accidental omissions.

Remember that every textual position is a theory and that every theory involves assumptions. If conclusions could be proved absolutely, they would be facts rather than theories and would involve no assumptions. To their credit, when asked directly, conservative eclectic scholars usually acknowledge that their views are theories, but unfortunately, it is rarely obvious from their writings. The impression often remains that they consider their theory to be fact.

The theoretical assumptions related to scribal tendency were mentioned above. Other examples include the derivative nature of distinctively Byzantine readings and the explanation of the agreement of the mass of manuscripts. The most basic theoretical construct, however, is the very existence of text types. Pickering observed that text type classifications are artificial and arbitrary, and even quotes Aland's admission of this.[21] Pickering's point is that a differing view of the criterion passages can alter a manuscript's text-type classification. In fact, he argues that the few shared peculiarities used for classifying often mask substantial disagreements, and that the "extent of disagreement is equally germane to any effort at classification."[22] He thus considers the evidence for text types insufficient to bear the weight of a theory. In discussing the conflation aspects of text types Pickering should have avoided examples of inversion that were not text typical, yet it is unfortunate that his real criticisms were ignored on the basis of what were deemed poorly chosen examples.

However, the key weakness of conservative eclecticism is a weakness shared with other forms of eclecticism, namely the dearth of Alexandrian manuscripts, upon which some selected readings are based. If its proponents could hold up numerous manuscripts as a proof of its wide distribution and acceptance across the ancient world, its detractors would be silenced. Instead, its claim for authenticity depends on a handful of manuscripts, though very ancient ones. The lack, then, of a large quantity of manuscripts with these disputed readings is the primary problem with which the theory must wrestle.

Independent Text Types

In 1984, **Harry A. Sturz** published *The Byzantine Text-Type and New Testament Textual Criticism*. In this book, he attempted to combine elements of both the Eclectic and Majority positions.

Sturz believed the Byzantine text to be very ancient in spite of the lack of individual ancient manuscripts. He argued that even Kilpatrick (see next chapter) recognized that most variants of interest existed by the second century. He pointed out that text-typical Byzantine readings have been found in Western manuscripts and even in Vaticanus. Most importantly, some of these Byzantine readings have been found in the oldest papyri. Evidence from papyri was unavailable to Westcott and Hort, but must be considered by present scholars.[23]

In addition, Sturz claimed that early conflate readings have also been found in the Alexandrian text type. This together with the lack of evidence for recension convinced him that the Byzantine type "did not originate through the mixture of Alexandrian and Western texts as conjectured by WH [Westcott-Hort], but that it is an independent witness to the second century tradition of its locale."[24]

Thus, Sturz, like Metzger and Aland recognized the weaknesses of the Westcott and Hort Theory for dismissing Byzantine readings. While Metzger and Aland accepted a few Byzantine readings, they continued to agree with Westcott and Hort that most Byzantine readings are secondary. Like Burgon and Hills, Sturz rejected this approach. On the other hand, Burgon and Hills argued that the Byzantine text is primary on the basis of God's providence. Sturz saw the weakness of this argument and did not consider the Byzantine text to be primary. Instead of following contemporaries in evaluating the Byzantine text type as greater or lesser in value as compared with the Alexandrian and Western types, he ranked it as having equal value.[25]

Sturz, then, treats the Alexandrian, Western, and Byzantine types as three independent testimonies from across the ancient world. He treats each text type witness as casting one vote and selects the reading with the most votes as most probably that of the autographs. By always using readings typical of a type, he never indulges in conjectural emendation; and by polling the types he only rejects the Byzantine tradition in the face of a substantial amount of evidence (the Western and Alexandrian types agreeing against it). This method of counting text-typical readings is often called the **Independent Text Type Theory.**

This view provides an interesting variation between the Majority and Eclectic positions. Like the Eclectic view, it recognizes text types and selects readings from different manuscripts. Unlike the Eclectic view, however, the Byzantine text has equal weight with the other types. Like the Majority Text view, the selection of the correct reading is based on quantity. However, unlike the Majority view, text types rather than manuscripts are counted in support of a given reading.

Contributions

Because manuscript collation (compiling the variants in a manuscript) can occupy years, scholars hoped to identify the best manuscripts and study those first. Nevertheless, every manuscript deserves detailed study. God's providence over existing manuscripts suggests that each offers evidence worthy of attention. Indeed, even poor witnesses are given a hearing before their testimony is evaluated. Sturz has provided additional motivation toward the collation of all manuscripts including the much neglected Byzantine manuscripts.

Perhaps the main contribution of this position is that by combining arguments from two opposing views, it has opened a channel for discussion. His method provides conclusions acceptable to a wide variety of scholars when the Byzantine and Alexandrian types agree (with or without support from the Western type).[26]

Objections

In Sturz's view, only five cases are possible (see chart). All three types may agree, any one of the three types may be overruled when the other two agree, or no two types may agree.

Of course, no objections arise when all the types agree. Further, since the Western type is not the basis of any theory, no objections arise when the other two agree against it. However, when the Byzantine type is rejected, non-eclectic scholars object using the same arguments that they raise against eclectic views. Similarly, when the Alexandrian type is rejected, eclectic scholars object with the arguments against non-eclectic views.

Text Type Agreement Cases in Sturz's View		
Alex = Alexandrian, Byz = Byzantine		
case	description	objections
1	All 3 agree (Alex + Byz + Western)	none
2	Alex & Byz agree v. Western	none
3	Alex & Western agree v. Byzantine	by non-eclectics[1]
4	Byz & Western agree v. Alexandrian	by eclectics[2]
5	No 2 agree (Alex v. Byz v. Western)	by all

[1] If the total number of these is few, Majority scholars may not object since no repeated and continual statistical overturning of the Majority would be apparent.

[2] Since Eclectic scholars evaluate evidence on a case by case basis, they would not immediately reject all such conclusions. However, they would not adopt them solely on this basis so objections remain. See the reply to Sturz by Gordon Fee, *Journal of the Evangelical Theological Society,* June 1985, pp. 239-242.

The most serious objection to the theory, however, involves the case when no two types agree. The basic principle offers no guidelines for resolving a three-way split among text types and other principles must be invoked. Of course, whatever principles are invoked provoke further objections. It is this point that undermines its attempt at retaining a neutral ground between the eclectic and non-eclectic views. Whether for this reason or others, the position has not been widely accepted.

Conclusion

The three positions presented in this chapter build on the positions previously presented. The Majority Text view of Pickering and Hodges build a stronger case even than the Textus Receptus view of Burgon and Hills while still retaining its strengths. Likewise, the Conservative Eclecticism of Custer and Carson avoid the most serious criticism of the Critical Eclectic views of Metzger and Aland while retaining its strengths. Finally, the Independent Text Type theory of Harry A. Sturz attempts to combine the strengths of the Majority and Eclectic positions. It is hoped that criticisms leveled at each theory have helped the reader see that each is still a working and developing theory but also that criticisms of these theories are less pivotal to the theories than criticisms of previous theories. A more thorough comparison of the seven modern theories is postponed to Chapter 9.

Endnotes

1. Wilbur N. Pickering, *The Identity of the New Testament Text* (Nashville: Thomas Nelson, 1980), pp. 44-48. See also Alan Cairns, p. 380.

2. Pickering, p. 118. See pp. 116-19 for overview of topic.

3. Hodges and Farstad (p. xv) explain that the footnotes preserve some of the analyses of von Soden as a provisional arrangement until more detailed studies can be made.

4. Alan Cairns, "Textual Criticism," *Dictionary of Theological Terms* (Belfast: Ambassador-Emerald, International, 1998), pp. 371-402.

5. Luke 17:36, Acts 8:37, and I John 5:7 (though the verse in Luke is

parallel to Matt. 24:40). Beyond these complete verses, substantial phrases from about two dozen other verses are also unsupported. Though the Majority Text lacks key phrases in Acts 9:5-6, those phrases do appear in the text of Acts 26:14 and 22:10 (see Cairns, pp. 393-94).

6. Hodges, "Rationalism and Contemporary New Testament Textual Criticism," *Bibliotheca Sacra*, 188 (1971), pp. 29-30.
7. Pickering, p. 153.
8. Cairns, p. 394.
9. Pickering, p. 62.
10. Appendix C "The Implications of Statistical Probability for the History of the Text" by Hodges and Hodges is printed in Pickering, pp. 159-69.
11. Pickering, pp. 82-83.
12. F. J. A. Hort, comment to a friend in a letter, "Think of that vile Receptus leaning entirely on late manuscripts; it is a blessing there are such early ones." See Arthur F. Hort, *Life and Letters of Fenton John Anthony Hort*, vol. 1, p. 211. This must be taken in context with his other statements, such as "An exaggerated impression prevails as to the extent of possible textual corruption . . . which might seem to be confirmed by language used here and there in the following pages, . . . much of the New Testament stands in no need of a textual critic's labours." See Westcott and Hort, eds., *The New Testament*.
13. Pickering, chapter 2.
14. Pickering, chapter 3.
15. Stewart Custer, *The Truth About the King James Version Controversy* (Greenville: BJU Press, 1981), p. 13.
16. D. A. Carson and John D. Woodbridge, *Hermeneutics, Authority, and Canon* (Grand Rapids: Academie Books, 1986), p. 29-31.
17. D. A. Carson, "Preface" to *Biblical Interpretation and the Church*, (Exeter: Paternoster Press, 1984), p. 9.
18. D. A. Carson, *The Inclusive-Language Debate* (Grand Rapids: Baker, 1998), p. 10. Moreover, speaking of his views on translations, he says "lest I be dismissed out of hand as another modernist, I protest strenuously that when I sign the thoroughly conservative Articles of Faith . . . , I do so without the slightest reservation" (See *The King James Version Debate*, p. 10).
19. Carson explained his unpublished view of conjectural emendation in an

interview. He allows the possibility of emendation based on Old Testament examples and cites a former emendation in Isaiah 53 that became an actual variant when it was found among the Dead Sea Scrolls.

20. Pickering, p. 79.
21. Pickering, p. 51 for artificial groupings; pp. 53-54 for Aland's quote.
22. Pickering, p. 57. Also, on page 55, he points out that codex D is classed as Western but when compared with chief representatives of each type it disagrees more with the Western than any other!
23. Harry A. Sturz, *The Byzantine Text-Type and New Testament Textual Criticism* (Nashville: Thomas Nelson, 1984), pp. 95-96.
24. Sturz, pp. 127-28.
25. Sturz, pp. 129-30.
26. Sturz, p. 228 notes that there are 170 variants in the Byzantine supported both by papyri and the Alexandrian type but opposed by the Western type. These are listed in Table 5 (pp. 223-27).

Questions

1. Explain the Majority Text and distinguish it from the Textus Receptus.

2. What distinguishes conservative Eclecticism from other types of eclecticism?

3. Why are the distinctions above important?

4. Explain the Independent Text Type Theory.

5. What are the main contributions to textual criticism of the Majority text view? of conservative eclecticism? of Independent Text Types?

6. What is the foremost objection to the Majority Text view? to Conservative Eclecticism? to the Independent Text Type Theory?

7. Match each scholar to one of the theories in this chapter.

    a. Alan Cairns
    b. D. A. Carson
    c. Stewart Custer
    d. Zane Hodges
    e. Wilbur Pickering
    f. Harry Sturz

8. Identify the theory that describes normal transmission of Scripture as follows.

    a. Copyists were more careful than copyists of other texts.
    b. Frequency and types of errors are comparable to other texts.

9. How does the Majority Text view explain the oldest manuscripts?

10. How does conservative eclecticism explain the mass of manuscripts?

CHAPTER 8

EXTREME VIEWS

Besides the three refinements discussed in Chapter 7, some other views have also developed out of the controversies between Burgon and Westcott and Hort.

Radical Eclecticism

Eclecticism has a number of different meanings in the writings of different scholars. The textual scholar, Eldon J. Epp tackled this terminological problem applying it to refer to one of three methods of textual criticism:

(1) choosing a variant reading based on the best indications from both external and internal evidence considered together,
(2) a choice based on internal evidence (see above) alone, and
(3) an analysis that leans more toward external evidence (see above).

Bruce Metzger applied the term unapprovingly to men like **G. D. Kilpatrick** and **J. K. Elliott**, who apply method (2). As we have seen, Metzger himself promotes a critical text obtained by method (1), which is quite different from the practices of those he criticized. Gordon D. Fee, also promoting method (1), prefers the term "rigorous" eclectics for Kilpatrick and Elliott and "reasoned" eclectics for the more balanced approach of most modern scholars. The consensus of opinion among those who define eclecticism is that most modern scholars who use the term do so as eclectic "generalists." In this way, varying opinions regarding internal evidence are kept in check by the more objective data from the manuscripts themselves.

Position

Kilpatrick and Elliott, the foremost radical eclectics, apply the principles of internal evidence solely. This position results in five distinctives that set them apart from both the critical and conservative schools of eclecticism.

First, they reject the text types. They argue that since the history of each manuscript is untraceable, the groupings into types are artificial, superficial, and ultimately meaningless. Appeals to such types carry no weight as evidence.

Second, since groupings are considered irrelevant, the external evidence is useless. Whether a manuscript dates to the fourth or tenth century, or whether it comes from Egypt or Italy is nothing more than trivia if such details do not help to group manuscripts in the marshalling of evidence. Likewise, whether a reading is common or rare is inconsequential since it cannot be known whether the true reading survived in one copy or many. Note that such scholars stand alone in rejecting all external evidence against all six of the other views of textual criticism. For these scholars, the only way to tell which reading is correct is to check the internal evidence of the context, author's style, and similar considerations.

Third, any manuscript may preserve the original reading. Since the history cannot be traced, it may be possible that a single manuscript preserves the true reading in a given passage. Kilpatrick and Elliott often favor a single manuscript's reading against all the other manuscripts. This is indeed eclecticism in the extreme.

Fourth, to go further, every source of readings is fair game. Theoretically, the original may be preserved in a quotation by one of the Church Fathers rather than a manuscript. In fact, it may have been lost in Greek altogether and be preserved only in the translation from some Old Syriac, Armenian, or Ethiopic version.

Finally, carrying this thinking to its end, a strictly conjectural reading may be adopted on the basis that it might exist in a manuscript not yet discovered! Now at this point, any textual researcher, cut free from all restrictions but his own imagination could come up with virtually any reading that pleased him.

Contributions

The main contribution of radical eclecticism is its studies related to the internal evidence (second distinctive). Being interested in the author's style, such scholars provide detailed studies of the styles of the human authors of the New Testament. Such studies contribute to knowledge of language and background of the books, and thus aid interpretation. However, the studies do not limit or determine what the writer would or could have said and is at best quite a subjective criterion for identifying the autographic text.

The rejection of text types by radical eclecticism (first distinctive) is logically neither a strength or weakness. However, it does serve a strengthening role within eclecticism since it reminds those who use text types that it is a theory and to use it with caution.

Likewise the view (third distinctive) that the true reading can theoretically be preserved in a solitary manuscript serves as a caution to Majority Text scholars. The Majority Text claims statistical support for its superiority[1], but statistics applied to real instances will have exceptions. For instance, suppose that 100 babies are born at your local hospital annually and that one in a hundred babies dies of typhoid each year in America. Your best prediction for any given baby born at that hospital is that he will not die of typhoid (since it is so rare). While one probably will die statistically (that you predicted would live), if you single out a local baby for typhoid death prediction, you would only gain a second wrong prediction to your credit. Refraining from singling out one as likely to die of typhoid cuts your errors by half. Of course, two or three babies could die (since the statistic is only an average), but your successful predictions will be greater by refraining from attempts to identify that one percent. Predicting the majority behavior unilaterally is the safest policy, but not flawless. The Majority Text position argues that it is statistically ill-advised to repeatedly and frequently reject the majority odds of being correct. However, this does not mean that the Majority text is never in error where a single manuscript has the original reading. Thus, the recognition that original readings may occur in isolation is a distinctive of radical eclecticism that highlights an oft-neglected point in the Majority Text position. This point should encourage caution in statements of Majority Text scholars.

Objections

The theory of radical eclecticism rejects the existence of text types (first distinctive) as do Majority Text scholars (for different reasons). However, although the other distinctives of radical eclecticism appear to follow from the first, Majority Text scholars draw completely different conclusions. This means that the other four distinctives of radical eclecticism do not follow necessarily from the denial of the text type hypothesis and are additional hypotheses which require separate justification. Careful analysis shows that the distinctives ignore the doctrine of the preservation of Scripture. These practices of radical eclecticism contradict clear biblical doctrines and are completely unacceptable to Bible believers.

As noted earlier, all scholars should acknowledge that it is at least possible for a single manuscript to preserve the original reading (distinctive 2). However, when this truth is invoked repeatedly to justify adoption of unique readings, Christians of various views grow increasingly uncomfortable.

Radical eclectic scholars may adopt distinctive readings from versions (Coptic, Old Latin, Syriac, etc.) and not based on any Greek manuscript (fourth distinctive). In such cases, back translation becomes necessary to reconstruct the wording of the Greek, and we approach the situation where no one can know the precise word though we can know the translated meaning. This puts a heavier strain upon the doctrine of preservation especially if such readings are frequently adopted.

Radical eclectic scholars can countenance numerous conjectural emendations in the New Testament (fifth distinctive). This conflicts with the biblical view of preservation. In Chapter 6, we showed that conjectural emendation is not a legitimate practice in the textual criticism of the Bible. However, if Metzger and Aland are culpable for applying it once, then so much more the frequent and wholesale practice of it must be roundly condemned. As we have shown in Chapters 2-4, God has preserved His Word, and there is no need for guessing what He said in numerous passages.[2]

Internal Evidence Issues

It has been noted by many that relying solely on internal evidence (second distinctive) results in the subjective handling of Scripture. Not surprisingly, no two radical eclectic scholars agree on readings. Adopting readings from manuscripts, the Fathers, versions, and their own creative conjectures usually results in wild variation. Such subjectivity is an obvious weakness denounced by scholars of all other positions.

However, at first glance, rejection of external evidence (second distinctive) may not seem offensive. Both eclectic and non-eclectic scholars tend to think that some things (but not others) dismissed by the radical eclectics are in their favor. The deemphasis of manuscript age and location details (which correlate with types) may seem good to Majority Text advocates. Likewise, the dismissal of the counting of manuscripts supporting a given variant may seem good to Eclectic scholars. However, both points defy orthodox Christian views of preservation. Consider the following.

Christians need not hide from facts. The God of truth created all and rules all. What he created and what he providentially allows is both comprehensible in light of His Word and consistent with it. Ignoring or dismissing evidence about the details of manuscripts is neither scientific nor honest. Ideally, the original reading would be found in all manuscripts. That is, if all were copied perfectly, the oldest manuscripts, the most manuscripts, manuscripts from every part of the ancient world, and manuscripts from every century of Christendom would agree precisely and point harmoniously to a common source—the autograph. If we fail to attend to all these types of details, we will forget that such agreement typifies the overwhelming majority of the New Testament text! Remember that variants are exceptions rather than the rule and all manuscripts are copies of copies of copies of the same inspired documents.

While we may lament that the copying was imperfect and we may focus on different aspects to try to resolve the minor tensions remaining, the ideal should be kept in mind. In Chapters 2-4, we argued that age, number, and distribution are all important evidences of preservation. While these lines of evidence conflict in the small number of passages over which textual critics pour, no textual critic should ever denigrate any of the three. It is possible to argue that one is more important than another for resolving those conflicts without calling any unimportant. All are important evidences of God's providential preservation of Scripture.

The radical eclectic scholar has relinquished all three simultaneously. He can look at a passage in which every manuscript and version agrees precisely and still offer a conjectural emendation. He sees no divine guide in the preservation of Scripture. He treats Scripture as he would an ancient book extant in only two manuscripts and for which some reconstruction is needed. He considers this Book no higher than any other human book. Such subjective treatment of God's Word is substantially different from previous textual positions, and it is the only one clearly identifiable as error. Nor is preservation the only doctrine from which many radical eclectic scholars stray.

Reminders

In the previous chapter we noted that Pickering (promoting the Majority Text) tended to lump all eclectic scholars together. The unfairness of this should now be very clear. Pickering correctly complains that scholars like Kilpatrick and Elliott frequently choose between variants strictly on internal considerations, which is too subjective, and that they indulge in conjectural emendation, which amounts to a scholarly caprice unacceptable with the Word of God. Unfortunately, having depicted the worst aspects of radical eclecticism, Pickering tries to portray these as the inevitable outcome of Westcott and Hort's textual methodologies. The impression is that modern textual criticism is left to the whims of men like Kilpatrick and Elliott and that this deplorable condition is the fault of Westcott and Hort who started the whole matter of eclecticism. In reality Hort pointed textual research in the direction of such eclecticism only with caution. He warned stringently of its dangers. He prophesied eloquently the need to rely heavily on external evidence rather than on the more subjective internal evidence.[3]

Moreover, we have argued that distinctions must be maintained in fairness to those holding various views. Most critical and conservative textual scholars condemn conjectural emendation just as Pickering does: Metzger, Aland, Epp, Kenyon, K. W. Clark, and A. F. J. Klijn. While you may recall that Metzger and Aland include one instance of it, this is not the same as is done by radical eclectic scholars. Certainly none of these scholars reject all external evidence as the radical eclectics do.

Finally, in fairness to radical eclectic scholars, it should be noted that they do not all resort to distinctive readings and invoke conjectural emendation to the same degree. It is at least theoretically possible for a Christian scholar to embrace radical eclecticism and ignore external evidence yet without adopting any conjectural emendations of the text.

KJV Only

Of the many possible manuscripts and versions, few have ever been promoted as perfect. We have already seen that no manuscript has ever been promoted as perfect (though Sinaiticus and Vaticanus came as close as any). Of versions, the Vulgate is the primary example historically. Today, however, the King James Version has come to hold such a position in some circles, contrary to what Christians have always believed about the Bible.

The term **KJV Only** is as confusing as the term eclecticism. Anyone may have a personal preference for the King James Version (also called KJV, Authorized Version, or A.V.). However, KJV Only advocates extol the KJV alone, and their arguments claim more than a preference for a version. They set forth a theory of God's providential preservation of Scripture. Translation issues will be addressed in future chapters, but the KJV Only position belongs with theories of textual criticism because its advocates promote a theory of preservation and transmission that replaces the corresponding views of other textual theories. Thus, this view bears on textual matters to the extent that it determines the textual views of its advocates.

The KJV Only position, then, goes beyond preference and stands outside theories of manuscript evidence. Most KJV Only advocates believe that the King James Version is the only English translation that can be called God's inspired Word. This means that the inspiration and preservation views surrounding it must exceed the inspiration which can be accorded to any other honest translation of the Word of God.

How did such a position develop? In 1930, Benjamin G. Wilkinson published the first defense of the KJV Only position, though it was not widely read.[4] In 1955, J. J. Ray, a missionary and Bible teacher, published a popular book[5] in response to growing confusion about the rampant multiplication of English versions of Scripture. His book reflected the rising tide of concern which Bible-believing fundamentalists all over the world began to feel. He tied his defense of the Word of God to issues surrounding the King James Version. In 1970 David Otis Fuller published the first of his three paperback collections of works defending the King James Only position and attacking the Westcott-Hort text. Today, the leading advocate of this view is **D. A. Waite**, who has written an entire volume attacking Westcott and Hort personally.[6]

These men, strongly committed to the inspiration and authority of God's Word, condemn the Westcott-Hort text and admit for use nothing but the King James Version (or possibly the TR). J. J. Ray asserted that we are faced with two Bibles, one produced by God and a competing one produced by Satan. The claim alarmed many devoted Bible-believing fundamentalists, who trusted Ray's thesis that all the Bible versions except the KJV must be firmly resisted by Bible believers. Unfortunately, his claims amount to a cry of "wolf." Such false alarms (1) distract from the real and frequently more serious dangers, and (2) inevitably brings division between those who recognize its false nature and those who do not.

Some scholars dismiss all these writers as reactionaries or propogandists. While this accusation may characterize some of these writers, **Philip Mauro** serves as the clearest exception. Mauro is a KJV advocate as vociferous as Burgon, but remains balanced, acknowledges the facts, and makes valuable contributions to the arena of textual debate.[7]

Position

Adherents to the KJV Only view hold to the logic of faith and make the same four applications as did Hills (see Chapter 6). They argue that God has preserved Scripture by making it the dominant text in every age, that believers can recognize the true text, that competing texts and text types are satanic, and that God has blessed only the pure text. Thus, all other versions and textual theories are at best unwitting tools in the demonic plot to undermine God's chosen version in English.[8] Donald A. Waite blatantly accuses Westcott and Hort of being "the prime movers in the construction of the elaborate-yet fictitious-system of New Testament Textual Criticism, the inventors of a doctored Greek text."[9]

While the King James Only position shares the logic of faith with the Textus Receptus view, it differs in that it fails to acknowledge translation error or differences between the traditional text and the KJV. Textus Receptus advocates such as Hills acknowledge that the KJV differs from the TR at several points and address those passages separately and at length to discern whether they are errors of copyists or original inspired text preserved through sources such as the Vulgate. However, KJV Only advocates, such as J. J. Ray, quote Hills and recommend his book but never summarize his treatment of differences between the TR and the

KJV. Ray downplays the differences. The logic of faith and God's blessing on the Traditional Text suffice as proof for him with or without the TR. Ray rejects any possibility of error or divergence of the KJV from the Traditional Text.

The logic of faith sees God's providence superintending the traditional texts to bless the KJV as the primary Bible of English-speaking Christendom for almost four centuries.[10] Thus, the KJV should be considered correct even where it varies from the TR. The fact that KJV has gone through revisions is a slight problem, so they single out the 1611 edition as the final court of appeal. While Hills always stresses the TR[11], Ray rarely mentions the TR without a qualifying clause such as "which gave us the KJV of 1611."[12]

Thus, KJV Only advocates may often quote Burgon, Hills, and even Pickering but only as they are useful toward their own goals.[13] Majority Text advocates will acknowledge a few copyist's errors in the KJV (as the KJV translators themselves admitted) and do not make the logic of faith a central point. TR advocates will spend much time defending the TR. They will either acknowledge a few translation errors from the TR or justify the KJV's divergence from the TR at those few points on other grounds. KJV Only advocates may borrow Majority or TR arguments but with constant application to the KJV without mentioning that a few passages exist to which such arguments will not apply.

Most King James Only writers make lengthy comparisons of other versions to the KJV.[14] Such lists are perhaps the clearest indication of the KJV Only position, since only its advocates make the KJV rather than the Greek a primary standard of comparison.

A few KJV Only writers go considerably further. Some assert that no one is saved unless led to Christ using a King James Bible,[15] or that foreign versions are not the Word of God unless translated from the KJV rather than from Greek manuscripts. The best known of all KJV Only promoters, **Peter Ruckman,** is probably also the most extreme. The term **Ruckmanism** has come into use to describe this extreme form of KJV Onlyism. Ruckman has said that wherever the KJV differs from the Greek manuscripts, the KJV is correct and the Greek is wrong and that "Mistakes in the A.V. 1611 are advanced revelation!"[16] In other words, he viewed the translators as getting direct revelation from God concerning the correct translation, which offers such a degree of accuracy that the KJV can resolve textual issues among the Greek manuscripts.

Contributions

While not even offering manuscript evidence or textual theory (other than what Textus Receptus or Majority text advocates had already offered) to advance their views, some proponents of the KJV-Only position have contributed to the larger discussion by raising some real and substantial issues that need addressing.

First of all, KJV Only advocates have, by their very insistence on the preeminence of the King James version, thereby emphasized that translations of the Word of God are in fact no less than *the* Word of God. Textual theorists have tended to allow this important consideration to settle into obscurity by their constant emphasis upon the manuscripts and text types. But it is a consideration that deserves top priority in a day when the thought of divine revelation is mocked by the media. For this reason, the King James translators themselves, in their preface to the reader (see chapter 10), placed highest emphasis upon this fact.

Second, the KJV Only position has attracted a large following due to its simplicity. Many fundamentalists, especially those lacking training in Bible colleges, Christian universities, or seminaries, would rather avoid troubling contentions about their "final authority," the Bible. They naturally prefer to leave these matters to pastors and seminary professors. They simply desire assurance that their Bible is indeed the Word of God and that they can trust it. Claims about "more accurate" translations or "better" manuscripts imply that something is inaccurate or lacking in the King James version, which conflicts with their longstanding faith that the KJV *is* the Word of God. The claims, then, raise questions that they feel unequipped to answer and appear to be direct attacks upon the King James version, and by logical extension, the Bible itself. Combined with the fact that even non-KJV-Only pastors caution Christians against bad translations (such as RSV, see chapters 11-12), they may grow suspect of all other versions. For these reasons, some laymen and pastors within fundamentalism cleave to the simplicity and security inherent in the KJV Only position.[17] This again evidences the unfortunate paucity of writing and teaching on textual matters demonstrating that other textual positions are consistent with Scripture.

Third, some KJV Only proponents raise the question as to whether laymen ought to be dependent upon (sometimes liberal) Greek scholars as to what is or is not the most accurate text and translation of the Bible.[18] After all, Jesus tells us that God sent His Holy Spirit to guide believers into all truth (John 16:13). Such reasoning ignores the fact that God gave pastors and teachers to His church as well as the Holy Spirit. Having the Holy Spirit will not substitute for learning languages like Greek and Hebrew. True, God does not expect every believer to learn these matters. But we ought to thank Him that He placed in some such gifts for the edifying of His church. To frivolously condemn scholarship condemns also Erasmus, the scholar who provided the Greek New Testament for the scholar Martin Luther to translate into German and the scholars of the King James version to translate into our KJV Bible. We are, in a sense, dependent on these scholars if we choose to be, but anyone who cares to may free himself of that dependence by doing exactly what the scholars themselves did. He can apply himself diligently to the hard work of learning the languages and the history and studying textual matters for himself.

If he does not choose to do so, he has no right to complain about the scholars. In fact, though, we are not in the position of being forced to trust ungodly liberal scholars. There are many godly men among textual scholars who help to warn God's people of errors from the ungodly ones.[19]

Objections

Four objections can be raised against the KJV Only position, and two more apply to the most extreme proponents. First, the KJV Only position misapplies the logic of faith idea to polarize versions and manuscripts into those from God and those from the devil. Westcott and Hort are vilified as the source of all modern theories and versions. We have previously critiqued this non-sequitur in detail (see Chapter 6), showing how it misrepresents eclecticism.

Second, J. J. Ray asserts that "the Bible has been providentially preserved for us in the Greek Textus Receptus, from which the King James Bible was translated in 1611. Any version of the Bible that does not agree with this text, is certainly founded upon corrupt manuscripts."[20] This premise enables him to evaluate other versions by comparing them side by side with the KJV and merely listing differences. Yet such writers denounce Hort for judging the TR as corrupt as compared with Vaticanus.[21] The practice is the same, only the base of comparison differs. Neither has biblical support for the selection of base. Assuming that a manuscript is the standard and making comparisons to show how other versions have strayed is circular reasoning. Mauro acknowledges "that the sum of all the variant readings taken together does not give ground for the slightest doubt as to any of the fundamental points of faith and doctrine."[22]

Third, the fact that God has blessed a version so long proves nothing beyond the fact that God has blessed His Word. God has

historically blessed various texts, even when there have been some
substantive disagreements between them. The Greek text of the
Old Testament (Septuagint) varies from the Hebrew Masoretic
text. At times the King James Version follows the Hebrew text in
the Old Testament, but where the New Testament quotes the Old
it reflects the Septuagint. In spite of such biblical examples, J. J.
Ray denounced Jerome's Latin Vulgate.[23] However, if any version
has ever been "received," it was the Vulgate which enjoyed use by
virtually all of western Christendom for over a thousand years.

Fourth, KJV Only writers incorrectly insist that Scripture
demands the method of preservation they describe. J. J. Ray cites
Psalm 12:6-7, "The words of God are pure words . . . thou shalt
PRESERVE THEM EVERY ONE from this generation for ever"
[emphasis his]. He concludes from this passage that "The Bible
God wrote has been providentially preserved for us in the Greek
Textus Receptus, from which the King James Bible was translated
in 1611."[24] Even if we concede that God's promise here is to preserve
His words,[25] it does not follow that only the Textus Receptus and
King James Version preserve God's words. The psalmist, writing
in Hebrew can hardly have specified which text or version preserves
the original wording. God's promise of preservation is disturbed
neither by Greek manuscripts nor by faithful translations—or else
the King James itself could not have been prepared. God promised
to (preserved) them but did not specify any particular manuscript
or version. It is one thing to argue the fact of preservation from
Scripture, but it is quite another to extrapolate the means.

The final objections apply only to the most extreme branch of
KJV Onlyism. Those who argue that in 1611 God guided the
KJV translators to produce an inspired translation trod theologically
dangerous ground. For one thing, such an act would require
apostolic-type miracles (a point granted by some but by no means
all modern Christians). Further, God revealed Scripture to the
apostles with their knowledge in contrast to the KJV translators

who specifically disavowed having such help from God (read their own words in Chapter 10). Moreover, if receiving Christ requires a KJV, how did people receive Christ before 1611? And if there were other authoritive Bibles before 1611, and the KJV became the authoritative wording at that time, then has God's Word changed?

Furthermore, the branch that holds to a conspiracy theory unfairly lumps the three schools of eclecticism together. Others, such as Ruckman[26], even lump Hodges and Farstad (Majority text) into the so-called "Alexandrian Cult" of eclecticism. James R. White exposes Riplinger's arguments that suppresses the other side of the evidence to make her weak argument sound stronger[27]. Likewise, Ruckman's lumping of Majority text and eclectic groups is an obvious straw man that would be accepted by neither side. Such deplorable conduct should find no place among Christians for whom truth is to be preeminent.

Ruckman accuses textual critics of tampering with Scripture, when he says "those who knew it [Greek], altered it to suit themselves"[28]. Recall, however, that only the radical eclectics resort to regular conjectural emendations on their own whim. All other textual scholars follow existing readings without altering them. The accusation, then, misrepresents critical and conservative eclectic scholars by lumping them with the radical eclectic scholars. In light of this the following admission by Philip Mauro is significant.[29]

> But no two of these thousands of manuscripts are exactly alike; and every discrepancy raises a distinct question requiring separate investigation and separate decision. While, however, the precise reading of thousands of passages is affected by these differences, it must not be supposed that there is any uncertainty whatever as to the teaching and testimony of the New Testament in its entirety. The consoling facts in

that regard are: (1) that the vast majority of the variant readings are so slight (a mere question of a single letter, or an accent, or a prefix, or a case ending) as not to raise any question at all concerning the true sense of the passage; and (2) that the sum of all the variant readings taken together does not give ground for the slightest doubt as to any of the fundamental points of faith and doctrine. In other words, the very worst text that could be constructed from the abundant materials available would not disturb any of the great truths of the Christian faith.

Such an amazing admission by a KJV Only advocate takes the wind out of the sails of the conspiratorialists. If the most liberal of the critical eclectic scholars set out to begin an anti-KJV conspiracy group and consistently chose the worst possible reading from his alternatives, no doctrinal changes would result. It is a tribute to His marvelous providential preservation that God has so prepared Scripture, that even if such alarmists were correct about conspirators against the text, they would not be significant!

Reminders

In general, the KJV Only position, then, displays serious weaknesses but need not be heretical. Just as Christians may disagree over interpretation of spiritual gifts or Calvinist-Arminian issues, they may accept various views on textual criticism. Some who hold to the KJV Only view remain "quietly convinced" and do not make it a test of fellowship. They are cautious in their statements and avoid undermining the unchangeableness of God's Word.

While the exact inspired-English wording sounds comforting, God expects study, comparing thoughts and preaching with Scripture, and even comparing Scripture with Scripture. Such demands ensure that Christians get the tenor of Scripture and will not be ensnared by some copyist's error or translators quirk, which

God knew would come when he committed his Word to human care. Would the AV 1611 be any easier to understand or apply if we did not need to check its weak translation spots? Not at all. We would still have to study 1611 dictionaries to correctly understand obsolete terms and more importantly words that have changed meaning, and we would also still have difficult passages to consider. In fact, the textual differences between the Textus Receptus and the Westcott-Hort text cause less confusion for the average layman than, for example, differences between the Old Testament books of Kings and Chronicles. In other words, it is no harder for a layman to resolve the variants between differing text types than to do the same thing with the apparent numerical discrepancies between Kings and Chronicles in the same text type. While resolutions for differences in Kings and Chronicles exist,[30] it requires more study and effort to resolve them.

The various KJV Only views on the preservation of Scripture do not contradict Scripture, but neither are they proved from Scripture. As with all human interpretations, Christians are free to adopt such theories consistent with Scripture but have no right to treat their interpretations as equal with Scripture. Christ Himself rebuked the Pharisees for treating their own traditions as equal with Scripture to undermine what Scripture said.

Unfortunately, some KJV Only advocates, in their zeal to promote their own view as the only correct one, castigate all other views as false. Some go so far as to accuse those who disagree of heresy or doctrinal error. However, by so doing they themselves are committing the heresy of divisive factionalism as condemned in 1 Corinthians 11:18-19 (see also 1:10, 3:3, Gal. 5:10). Peter Ruckman is a prime example of such factionalism, and his outrageous slander and vitriolic railing have even embarrassed some who agree with him. More reasonable KJV Only advocates see the issues in their proper scope and context and separate from Ruckman's heresy.[31]

On the other side, those who hold to eclectic positions often fail to distinguish those who promote either the Textus Receptus or the Majority Text from KJV Only positions. For instance, James R. White says that the King James Only position actually encompasses five groups[32]. However, his first three groups include Majority Text and Textus Receptus scholars. These men do not identify themselves with the KJV Only movement and do promote well-known positions clearly differentiated from KJV Only. Some of them prefer the KJV as the best *existing* English version, but also recognize the need for a better one. Though White presents their views briefly and fairly, including them in his book simply adds to the already muddied waters that confuse these positions. As Pickering unfairly lumped the eclectic positions, White falls into the common pitfall of unfairly grouping the non-eclectic positions.

Conclusion

The positions in this chapter can be held by good Christians. However, the extreme forms constitute heresy. Christians must avoid heresy by holding fast to sound doctrine. They must resist the drift away from the fundamental doctrines of the faith that has carried away many scholars. In warfare, soldiers attack enemies—not the fallen. The enemies in the Christian's spiritual battle are theological liberals outside the church such as Kilpatrick and divisive wolves inside the church such as Ruckman.

KJV Only proponents must temper their tendency toward strife over a minor issue. Those who truly care for God's Word should focus on preaching passages from the Bible instead of using God's pulpit to teach their personal opinions about the English Bible. Christians espousing the KJV Only view should protect themselves against the charge of heresy by not majoring on minor issues.

Endnotes

1. Wilbur N. Pickering, *The Identity of the New Testament Text* (Nashville: Thomas Nelson, 1980), pp. 44-48. See also Alan Cairns, p. 380.
2. J. A. Bengel, the Father of N.T. Textual Criticism, said "No *conjecture* is ever of any consideration to be listened to." See *Gnomon of the New Testament*, vol. I, p. 14.
3. "But in dealing with this kind of evidence equally competent critics often arrive at contradictory conclusions as to the same variations. Nor indeed are the assumptions involved in Intrinsic Evidence of Readings to be implicitly trusted." Westcott and Hort, *Introduction*, p. 21.
4. Benjamin G. Wilkinson, "Our Authorized Bible Vindicated," 1930 reprinted in *Which Bible* by David Otis Fuller (Grand Rapids: Grand Rapids International Publications, 1970, 1971), pp. 93-235 with foreward about the author (pp. 91-92). Wilkinson would have been read primarily by those in his Seventh Day Adventist circles.
5. Jasper James Ray, *God Wrote Only One Bible* (Junction City, Oregon: Eye Opener Publishers, 1955, 1976).
6. D. A. Waite, *The Theological Heresies of Westcott and Hort* (Collingswood, N. J.: The Bible for Today, 1978).
7. See Philip Mauro, "Which Version?" in David Otis Fuller, *True or False* (Grand Rapids: Grand Rapids International Publications, 1973, 1978), pp. 56-122.
8. Ray, pp. 15, 17.
9. D. A. Waite, *Theological Heresies*, p. 1. Some writers carry this attack further and try to argue that even Hodge and Warfield (see Chapter 1) fell victim to a changing view of the text that came from apostate European schools. For the details on their speculations see "B. B. Warfield, Common Sense Philosophy and Biblical Criticism" by Theodore P. Letis (*American Presbyterians*, Fall 1991, pp. 175-189) and *A Testimony Founded For Ever* by James H. Sightler (Greenville: Sightler Pubs., 1999).
10. Wilkinson sets forth the logic of faith to polarize versions and later praises the KJV as the author of "vastly more missionary enterprises than any other version" (reprinted in Fuller, *Which Bible?*, pp. 104-5, 234). It is impossible to determine whether missionaries were moved by inspired

text common to all versions of Scripture or by something peculiar to the KJV. The former seems more likely since Matthew 28:19-20 is in every good translation.

11. The final chapter title in Hills' *Believing Bible Study* is "The Textus Receptus and the Common Faith" (no KJV mention). Even his defenses of the KJV are TR based, see pp. 196-215.

12. Ray, see pp. 27, 28, 30, 70, 88, 93, 94, 96, 100, 104, 106 for qualifying clauses. Also, see pp. 32, 105 [2x], 116 for KJV linked to the TR by "and."

13. D. A. Waite for instance has monographs (see bibliography) on both the Textus Receptus and the Majority Text. The former simply draws on Burgon as ammunition against KJV competition. The latter quotes Zane Hodges and Alfred Martin to the same end. Dr. Waite makes no critique of either and ignores points of disagreement. His largest and more recent work, *The King James Version Defended; A four-fold superiority: Texts, Translators, Technique, Theology*, attests his true position and suggests that the former works were simply to attack eclecticism rather than to elaborate his position.

14. Ray critiques 44 versions by comparing them to the KJV at 162 passages. This occupies one quarter of his book (pp. 36-70). Of course, none of the passages used involve differences between the TR and KJV. By listing the number of divergences from the KJV/TR, he implies that the NASB is twice as bad as the Douay Bible of the Catholics! The RSV gets his worst rating (158 divergences), so he promptly lists another 31 diverging passages (pp. 78-83).

15. James B. Williams claims to have heard such a statement on a radio broadcast. See the book he edited entitled *From the Mind of God to the Mind of Man* (Greenville: Ambassador-Emerald International, 1999), p. 5.

16. Ruckman, *The Christian's Handbook of Manuscript Evidence* (Pensacola, Florida: Pensacola Bible Press, 1970), p. 126. Ruckmanism thrives on inverted logic such as correcting Greek manuscripts from an English version produced from their progeny some ten centuries later.

17. When we add to this the fact that some focus their ministry on stirring up textual and translation controversies among fundamentalists, it is not surprising that we have such a tragic schism over these issues.

18. James R. White presents this question as typical in such discussions (p.

247) and also quotes Ruckman, who attacks Greek scholars on this basis (p. 110).

19. Unfortunately, some of those who make the loudest clamor against scholarship offer in its place only their own opinions. In many instances, they themselves have no expertise in textual matters and offer stones for bread.

20. Ray, p. 106. On the next page he promotes Hills' *Believing Bible Study,* which makes similar claims (see Chapter 6).

21. A. F. Hort, p. 211. See footnote 3 in Chapter 7 for quote and discussion.

22. Mauro, "Which Version?" in Fuller, *True or False?* p. 62.

23. Ray, pp. 97-102. He traces the Received Text of the New Testament from the original Greek, through the Syriac Peshitta and the Old Latin, to Erasmus and the KJV. The Vulgate, which he bypasses, was not just used by Catholics but also by men like Wycliffe, who even translated the Bible into English from it.

24. Ray, p. 106. For a similarly emphasized quotation of the passage in Psalm 12 and a similar conclusion drawn, see D. A. Waite, *Defending the King James Bible,* pp. 6, 17.

25. Many commentators believe that "Thou shalt preserve them" actually refers to the afflicted and poor (v. 6) rather than the Scripture. See Franz Delitzsch, *Psalms* in Commentary on the Old Testament, vol. 5 translated by Francis Bolton (Grand Rapids: Eerdmans, 1990 reprint), pp. 195-97.

26. Ruckman, *Custer's Last Stand* (Pensacola, Florida: Pensacola Baptist Bookstore, 1981), p. 4.

27. James R. White, pp. 95-109.

28. Ruckman, *Handbook,* p. 138.

29. Mauro, "Which Version?" in Fuller, *True or False,* p. 62.

30. Gleason L. Archer, *Encyclopedia of Bible Difficulties* (Grand Rapids: Zondervan, 1982), pp. 221-22.

31. David W. Cloud is representative of KJV Only advocates who have repudiated Ruckmanism. See his article "Is the KJV Advanced Revelation," *O Timothy,* volume 12, issue 5, 1995, pages 1-5. The article presents a detailed critique and repudiation of Ruckman's position on advanced revelation. Cloud is the editor of this monthly magazine, a publication of Bible Baptist Church in Oak Harbor, Washigton, where he pastors. He

has also exposed Gail A. Riplinger's errors in *New Age Bible Versions: A Critique* (Oak Harbor, WA: Way of Life Literature, 1994, 1998).
32. White, pp. 1-4.

Questions

1. Name two proponents of radical eclecticism.

2. Name five distinctives of radical eclecticism.

3. Which distinctive of radical eclecticism is clearly heretical and why?

4. What positive contribution has radical eclecticism made?

5. Name three KJV Only advocates and identify the most balanced.

6. Identify the primary contribution of the KJV Only position.

7. Name two weaknesses of the King James Only position.

8. What extreme branch of the KJV Only view is heretical and why?

9. Why is it important that non-eclectic writers distinguish critical and conservative eclecticism from radical eclecticism?

10. Why is it important that eclectic writers distinguish the Textus Receptus and Majority Text positions from KJV Onlyism.

CHAPTER 9

COMPARING THEORIES

You have now surveyed seven modern views of textual criticism. Strengths and weaknesses have been mentioned for each view in passing, but some of the modifications in the theories address only minor weaknesses while leaving major issues unaddressed. The purpose of this chapter is to summarize briefly the central views of each of the seven theories and the major strength and weakness of each.

It should at least be clear that all theories have some weaknesses. None of the scholars were divinely inspired to know exactly how manuscripts were copied and preserved. To resolve the complex issues fully would require the omniscience of God. For humans, theories must be evaluated on the same grounds used to evaluate scientific theories or to isolate faulty parts in a car. Some background on these criteria will be useful.

Criteria of Comparison

All theories must be evaluated first for consistency with Scripture. Of the seven tests for evaluating theories, being scriptural is foundational. If a theory fails the test of harmony with Scripture it is unbiblical, and depending on the severity of the failure, may be heretical. However, all of the seven modern theories of textual criticism pass this test. We have already noted that none of the modern views are necessarily heretical. This foundational criterion is the only one that all seven theories can pass without qualification.

The seven criteria for evaluating theories follow. Any theory of textual criticism must satisfy these tests.

1. Biblical—it must not contradict Scripture but display harmony with it, especially with regard to inspiration and preservation.
2. Coherent—it must not contradict itself.
3. Adequate—it must explain all the facts.
4. Consistent—it must not contradict known principles.
5. Accurate—it must fit the facts precisely.
6. Simple—it must not require many revisions and modifications to patch holes.
7. Fruitful—it must help as a tool in interpretation and must guide useful research.

After being in harmony with Scripture, theories must also satisfy the other six criteria in order of importance. For instance, what good is a very simple theory if it contradicts itself? The modern theories of textual criticism all meet the second and third most important criteria for a good theory. A theory must be coherent (not contradicting itself) and adequate to explain the facts. As the modern theories have been refined and developed from the historical views, any inconsistencies have been removed and inadequate aspects have been resolved. This does not mean that some scholars of one position may not accuse another position of self-contradiction, but this is usually because the scholar is critiquing the other position from his own set of assumptions rather than evaluating the theory in context. Thus, evaluation of modern theories requires both care and comparison on the final four criteria.

Next, textual theories should be consistent with other known laws, and they should be simple (not multiplying assumptions needlessly). Finally, previous criteria being met, textual theories should be both precise and fruitful (predicting other facts or opening useful lines of research).[1]

Christian scholars have held to each of the seven modern theories of textual criticism presented in the last three chapters. Views of textual criticism do not determine salvation, spirituality, or orthodoxy. The Bible does not speak directly to this issue; if it did, there would not be so much disagreement among sincere Bible believers. These views are theories, and we must distinguish the facts from the theories which propose to account for them. Like any theory, each theory has strengths and weaknesses and must be evaluated. Failure on any point other than harmony with Scripture is not a doctrinal matter. An incoherent or inadequate theory can be accused of stupidity, but not heresy. A theory that conflicts with some historical or scientific knowledge or is imprecise and inaccurate may be simple-minded, but it is not on that account unorthodox. An unnecessarily complex theory may be convoluted but is not therefore anti-Christian; while an unfruitful theory is probably useless but may not be unbiblical.

Recall that views promoting each text type are conceivable; however, no writer promotes a text type today. The Alexandrian type once promoted as Neutral is now supported indirectly based on other criteria. Likewise the Byzantine type is promoted indirectly by several views based on other criteria. The Western type is promoted only by some who see the Latin Vulgate as the best text but may appeal to papal decrees rather than textual evidence. The Caesarean type has never been promoted since it is not even defined in most New Testament books. The reader may profit from studying why each text type fails as theory in itself by identifying the most important criterion that the view failed to meet. Evaluating types (or individual manuscripts) as theories is beyond the scope of this book, and we will turn to evaluating the modern theories.

Critiquing the seven modern theories

First, concerning coherence. Four views provide a single objective criterion for identifying the reading most likely to be original: KJV only, Textus Receptus, Majority, and Independent Text Types. While the various Eclectic views involve more subjectivity in weighing evidence, all have expressed their methods without self-contradiction.

Second, each of the seven views is adequate. No matter what view you take, there will be facts that are difficult to explain. Still each theory has provided explanations for even the most difficult facts.

The summary below attempts to provide capsule reviews of the seven modern views. The views are arranged roughly in order from radical liberal to dogmatic traditional. It is worth repeating that the issues here are theoretical rather than theological. None of these views necessarily involves heresy; the issues involve interpretation of historical evidence.

Radical Eclecticism

DEFINITION: The original reading is the phrase or wording that the human author would most likely have used.

DISCUSSION: This view permits both external and internal evidence. By stressing stylistic and cultural criteria, it sets no limits on subjective evaluations or conjectural emendation.

METHODS: Select the reading consistent with author's style and scribal tendencies.

RESULTING TEXT: No printed version exists.

PROPONENTS: G. D. Kilpatrick, J. K. Elliott

SOURCE: *New Testament Textual Criticism: A Concise Guide* by David Alan Black (1999), p. 37.

STRENGTHS: provides thorough studies of styles of biblical writers.

WEAKNESSES: very subjective, permits textual revisions based on possible readings of undiscovered manuscripts or on the style of the author. May ignore all manuscript evidence.

Critical Eclecticism

DEFINITION: The original reading is most likely that supported by both external and internal evidence.

DISCUSSION: This view promotes critical evaluation of all evidence. On these grounds conjectural emendation may be exercised in rare cases in which no extant readings have convincing support from external evidence.

METHODS: Select the reading consistent with reliability of manuscripts, scribal tendencies, and style of the biblical author.

RESULTING TEXT: *Greek New Testament* (Stuttgart: United Bible Societies, 1983)

PROPONENTS: Bruce M. Metzger, Kurt Aland, Gordon D. Fee

SOURCE: *The Text of the New Testament* (1968)

STRENGTHS: seeks to evaluate all lines of evidence.

WEAKNESSES: may (rarely) prefer a conjectural emendation to every Greek manuscript, doubts preservation of any emended passage, subjective enough for some key disagreements among authors.

Conservative Eclecticism

DEFINITION: The original reading is most likely that supported by external evidence.

DISCUSSION: This view stresses external evidence to maintain objectivity and rejects the use of conjectural emendation as unnecessary in the light of the large mass of textual evidence.

METHODS: Select the reading of the most reliable manuscripts in light of scribal tendencies.

RESULTING TEXT: close to the UBS, the main difference is the lack of the conjecture

PROPONENTS: D. A. Carson, Stewart Custer

SOURCE: *The Truth about the KJV Controversy* (1981)

STRENGTHS: recognizes preservation of original text in existing manuscripts, acknowledges value of objective results, values the oldest manuscripts, studies scribal tendencies.

WEAKNESSES: must theorize to account for agreement of majority of manuscripts whenever the majority is not followed.

Independent Text Types

DEFINITION: The original reading is most likely preserved in the majority of the text types.

DISCUSSION: This view developed in reaction to Westcott and

Hort who considered Western manuscript evidence, but never Byzantine. It acknowledges all the text-types as representing valuable testimony to the original text.

METHODS: Each text type votes as an independent witness. Readings with the most votes wins.

RESULTING TEXT: only sample issues are published in source below

PROPONENT: Harry A. Sturz

SOURCE: *The Byzantine Text-Type and New Testament Textual Criticism* (1984)

STRENGTHS: Simple, objective, considers all Greek manuscript evidence, values both the oldest and the mass of manuscripts.

WEAKNESSES: Shares weaknesses of Eclecticism when the Majority Text is rejected, but shares weaknesses of the Majority position when the oldest manuscripts are rejected.

Majority Text

DEFINITION: The original reading is most likely reflected by the reading contained in a majority of manuscripts (regardless of text type).

DISCUSSION: Perceives the vast numbers of Greek manuscripts as evidence of God's preservation of the exact wording (not just the Bible in general). It does acknowledge the value of the early manuscripts for refuting liberal chronology, though it views some of these manuscripts as sloppy copies.

METHODS: Select the reading supported by the most manuscripts.

RESULTING TEXT: *The Greek New Testament according to the Majority Text* (New York: Thomas Nelson Pub., 1982)

PROPONENTS: Wilbur N. Pickering, Zane Hodges, Alan Cairns

SOURCE: *Identity of the New Testament Text* (1977)

STRENGTHS: Simple, objective, considers all Greek manuscript evidence, does not accept weakly supported TR passages like the Comma Johanneum since it is not in the majority of manuscripts.

WEAKNESSES: Must theorize to account for the variations from the majority among the older manuscripts.

Textus Receptus

DEFINITION: The original reading is to be found in Erasmus's edition of the Greek New Testament (based on manuscipts providentially provided by God to prepare the way for the KJV).

DISCUSSION: This view perceives God's providence overruling the problems which Erasmus himself admitted in his edition of the Greek text. The mass of manuscripts shows general preservation of most of the wording, but the view asserts that God guided Erasmus to use the specific manuscripts that he used to preserve the best text.

METHODS: Identifies original readings by checking Erasmus's text.

RESULTING TEXT: *Textus Receptus* (London: Trinitarian Bible Society, 1977)

PROPONENT: Edward F. Hills, Alfred Martin

SOURCE: *The King James Version Defended* (1956)

STRENGTHS: Simple objective criterion while still accepting the Greek as authoritative. Stresses preservation.

WEAKNESSES: Ignores all Greek manuscript evidence at several places (Comma Johanneum) and much evidence elsewhere; equates preservation with Greek texts that became popular ignoring early low popularity and formerly popular texts.

KJV Only

DEFINITION: The inspired text is precisely that found in the English translation known as the King James Version.

DISCUSSION: God guided the translation process so fully that debate over the Greek manuscripts can be resolved by comparisons to the English. This view sees God's providence overruling the weaknesses that the translators of the KJV perceived in their own work.

METHODS: Identifies the proper reading from the English KJV.

RESULTING TEXT: *King James Version,* 1611.

PROPONENTS: Philip Mauro, Benjamin Wilkinson, J. J. Ray, Peter S. Ruckman, D. A. Waite, David Otis Fuller, and others

SOURCE: *Christian's Handbook of Manuscript Evidence* (1970)

STRENGTHS: Simplest view for English speakers, objective criterion.

WEAKNESSES: Rejects importance of the original Greek of the autographs; ignores manuscript evidence; treats the translation as the original document; accepts commonly recognized interpolations such as the Comma Johanneum in spite of evidence; pre-KJV and foreign languages weakly addressed; ignores Christ's example of using both original Hebrew and a translation (Septuagint).

In summary, it should be noted that the Majority text, the Textus Receptus, and King James Only positions all appeal to Byzantine manuscripts but must be distinguished from a Byzantine text type theory. Some of these positions do not even acknowledge the existence of text types. A Byzantine theory would reject other types. The Majority text accepts each reading based on the majority of all manuscripts regardless of type and can theoretically differ from the Byzantine. Likewise, the TR usually reflects the Byzantine but being based on only a few manuscripts, it is not always or necessarily representative of the Byzantine (or even the Majority). Likewise the King James Only position is distinct from all of these in spite of following a translation that generally has Byzantine support.

In the same way the various types of Eclecticism should be sharply distinguished from one another and from the Alexandrian type. All Eclectic positions can and do select non-Alexandrian readings, though perhaps rarely. Radical Eclecticism denies the value of text types and a traceable manuscript history. Critical Eclecticism is more objective but still permits conjectural emendation. Conservative Eclecticism recognizes that the text of Scripture is preserved in total in the mass of manuscripts.

The theory of Independent Text Types deserves additional comment since it is Eclectic in method but largely Byzantine in result. Sturz accepts the reading of any text type if it is supported by a second text type. This provides a "widespread text"[2] always supported by at least two types, and shares the strengths of both the Eclectic and Majority positions when he accepts a reading supported by the Byzantine and Alexandrian types (with or without Western support). However, if he adopts an Alexandrian reading with Western support, he must explain how the majority of manuscripts came to be in error in that passage. If he accepts a Byzantine reading with Western support, he must explain why none of the most ancient manuscripts contain it. In other words, the same tension exists but it has been shifted from a general issue characteristic of the text to a reading-by-reading issue.

Theories of Textual Transmission		
theory	advantage	disadvantage
radical eclecticism	most flexible view for scholarly creativity	very subjective and quick to revise text
critical eclecticism	takes less liberty with Word of God while retaining place for scholarly insight	writers fail to stress inspiration; permits occasional conjectural emendation
conservative eclecticism	support of oldest manuscripts	majority of manuscripts must be explained
independent text types	support from oldest and most manuscripts	same problems but on individual variant basis
majority text	support of most manuscripts	lack of very ancient manuscripts must be explained
textus receptus	acknowledges value of studying Greek while retaining simple view of preservation	must apply logic of faith to Erasmus' text even where it differs from most manuscripts
KJV only	simplest expression of preservation	requires miraculous intervention for each copyist and translator

It is our view that Radical Eclecticism has the most serious problem. We have maintained that there are several possible views concerning the method of preservation. However, the subjective and wildly differing conclusions of Radical Eclectics show that their methods cannot identify the autographic text. In fact, the methods leave doubt as to whether the true wording can be known at all. This conflicts with the principle of preservation by anyone's definition. The problem here is at the level of consistency with a known principle (preservation).

The King James Only position fails the test of accuracy. The position that only one text can be current (traditional) at a time is simply inaccurate when compared to Christ's example of quoting both Hebrew and Septuagint. We do not call this inadequate (though some would) since replies are possible, but the position fails the criterion of accuracy since it does not predict the Lord's example but has to squirm around it. Similarly, the view of preservation by miraculous guidance of copyists, editors like Erasmus, and translators fails on accuracy since it requires God to do this without their knowledge (see next chapter). Even if one disagrees with this evaluation, one must admit that many extra assumptions are necessary to resolve these issues which causes problems at the next level, that of simplicity.

The Critical Eclectic and Textus Receptus positions also have problems satisfying the accuracy and simplicity criteria. Both views must justify passages not preserved in any Greek manuscript (the conjectural emendation in the critical text and the Latin back-translation of the end of Revelation in the Textus Receptus). Again we do not call the views inadequate but suggest that they can deal with such facts at worst inaccurately and at best by complicating the theory with unneeded assumptions.

Finally, the three other views have weaknesses but each offers a viable solution. The adequate explanation is consistent with known principles and is accurate. Each offers a minimum number of assumptions for handling the conflicting evidence. All three theories have been very fruitful. Of course, the theory that best satisfies all criteria is most likely to be correct. However, we will not attempt to single out the best theory. The final evaluation of these three theories depends largely on which assumptions seem most reasonable to the reader. From each perspective the other theories are flawed and fail one of the tests. It is only when evaluated in context that each satisfies all criteria.

In summary, all seven modern theories are orthodox and viable.

The three middle theories are more defensible as theories and are offered to the readers for mature consideration. We also wish to plead for courtesy among those of differing views concerning terminology.

Loaded Terms

In light of the multitude of theories, it should be clear that certain terms are emotionally "loaded". When a writer or preacher refers to the wording "in the Greek," a lay audience will take his word for this not recognizing that some choice among textual variants may have been made. When the variants are trivial and not germane to the point being made, no dishonesty has been perpetrated. Occasionally, however, the phrase is used as a scholarly sounding camouflage to make error sound true or to make a controversial point sound certain.

More importantly, the common phrase, **best manuscripts,** is a mere value judgment. No writers ever mean the best looking manuscript but rather refer to those manuscripts that they deem to best reflect the originals. The phrase is typical of Eclectic scholars, who intend it to mean "in the oldest manuscripts" (as Hort) or "in the reading least influenced by scribal errors" (as Aland) or even "in the manuscripts that I think reflect typical Pauline word choice and grammar" (as Kilpatrick). However, when used by scholars with other views it can mean "in most manuscripts" (as Pickering) or "in the traditional manuscripts" (as Hills). Readers should recognize that the phrase has meaning only in the context of the textual theory of the speaker, author, or preacher.

Endnotes

1. For more on the seven criteria for evaluating theories and examples of their use in science, see Chapter 8 "Complex Inductive Evidence" in *Better Thinking and Reasoning* by Ron Tagliapietra (Greenville: BJU Press, 1995), pp. 95-106.

2. Black, David Alan, *New Testament Textual Criticism: A Concise Guide* (Grand Rapids: Baker Book House, 1994), p. 40.

Questions

1. Match the following names with the view they taught. Aland, Carson, Custer, Elliott, Hills, Hodges, Kilpatrick, Mauro, Metzger, Pickering, Ruckman, Sturz.

2. Which criteria for evaluating theories are met by all seven modern views of textual criticism?

3. Evaluate a theory that promotes a strict acceptance of the Western text type based on the criteria for evaluating theories.

4. Which of the seven modern theories is subjective and fails the test of consistency? Which principle does it conflict with?

5. Which of the seven modern theories is least accurate? What evidence does it handle imprecisely?

6. Identify two other views that do not pass the tests of a good theory.

7. Which theory seems best to you and why?

8. Explain the failures of the remaining views. Can you guess how a proponent of either view would respond to your criticism?

9. What phrase could Eclectic scholars easily avoid so as to give less cause for offense among their brothers in Christ?

10. What views could avoid appeals to the logic of faith or miraculous intervention so as not to condemn their brothers as unspiritual?

UNIT III
Translation of Scripture

You now have the necessary background to understand issues concerning Bible translations. You have seen that God has preserved His Word and that issues concerning the ancient Greek manuscripts seldom affect meaning. This means that substantial differences between English versions must be caused by something else.

Indeed, even if everyone agreed precisely on the wording of the original Greek, there would still be a multitude of versions. People disagree on many principles of translation, such as whether to maintain a formal or casual style or whether word choice should be limited for an eighth grade reading level or for an adult. The following chapters will probe the issues concerning theories and practices of translators (chapter 11) and also provide some suggestions for selecting a translation (chapter 12).

However, we would like first to let the translators of the King James Version speak for themselves (chapter 10). The KJV has played a role even in textual criticism as the reader has already seen. However, some people say things about the King James Version contrary to what the translators themselves claimed. We have already made references to the views of this translation team, but we think it is important for the reader to see for himself what the translators thought. This will provide a good background for the final chapters.

The translators set out their ideas in the preface, entitled "The Translators to the Reader," for their 1611 edition of the King James Version. This preface is rarely printed today, so few Christians have had the opportunity to read it. Most people who have a King James Bible have an edition much more recent than 1611. The English of 1611 is difficult for the modern reader because of changes in word meaning, and a proper understanding of their preface would require looking up many words in the Old English Dictionary in order to see what the word meant almost four centuries ago. For this reason, we print the original preface followed by an updated version of it prepared by Dr. Randy Leedy of the Bible faculty at Bob Jones University. Of course, we encourage you to read as much of the original as you are comfortable with, but the simplest option is to read the update and occasionally compare it with the original to see how he did. The subheadings have also been inserted for ease of reference.

CHAPTER 10

THE TRANSLATORS TO THE READER[1]

Introduction Commending King James

Innovation Always Resisted

Zeal to promote the common good, whether it be by devising any thing ourselves, or revising that which hath been laboured by others, deserveth certainly much respect and esteem, but yet findeth but cold entertainment in the world. It is welcomed with suspicion instead of love, and with emulation instead of thanks: and if there be any hole left for cavil to enter, (and cavil, if it do not find an hole, will make one) it is sure to be misconstrued, and in danger to be condemned. This will easily be granted by as many as know story, or have any experience. For was there ever any thing projected, that savoured any way of newness or renewing, but the same endured many a storm of gainsaying or opposition? A man would think that civility, wholesome laws, learning and eloquence, synods, and Churchmaintenance, (that we speak of no more things of this kind) should be as safe as a sanctuary, and out of shot, as they say, that no man would lift up his heel, no, nor dog move his tongue against the motioners of them. For by the first we are distinguished from brute beasts led with sensuality: by the second we are bridled and restrained from outrageous behaviour, and from doing of injuries, whether by fraud or by violence: by the third we are enabled to inform and reform others by the light and feeling that we have attained unto ourselves: briefly, by the fourth, being brought together to a parley face to face, we sooner compose our differences, than by writings, which are endless: and lastly, that the Church be sufficiently provided for is so agreeable to good reason and conscience, that those mothers are holden to be less cruel, that kill their children as soon as they are born, than those nursing fathers and mothers, (wheresoever they be) that withdraw from them who hang upon their breasts (and upon whose breasts again themselves do hang to receive the spiritual and sincere milk of the word) livelihood and support fit for their estates. Thus it is apparent, that these things which we speak of are of most necessary use, and therefore that none, either without absurdity can speak against them, or without note of wickedness can spurn against them.

Yet for all that, the learned know, that certain worthy men have been brought to untimely death for none other fault, but for seeking to reduce their countrymen to good order and discipline: And that in some Commonweals it was made a capital crime, once to motion the making of a new law for the abrogating of an old, though the same were most pernicious: And that certain, which would be counted pillars of the State, and patterns of virtue and prudence, could not be brought for a long time to give way to good letters and refined speech; but bare themselves as averse from them, as from rocks or boxes of poison: And fourthly, that he was no babe, but a great Clerk, that gave forth, (and in writing to remain to posterity) in passion peradventure, but yet he gave forth, That he had not seen any profit to come by any synod or meeting of the Clergy, but rather the contrary: And lastly, against Churchmaintenance and allowance, in such sort as the ambassadors and messengers of the great King of kings should be furnished, it is not unknown what a fiction or fable (so it is esteemed, and for no better by the reporter himself, though superstitious) was devised: namely, That at such time as the professors and teachers of

Christianity in the Church of Rome, then a true Church, were liberally endowed, a voice forsooth was heard from heaven, saying, Now is poison poured down into the Church, etc. Thus not only as oft as we speak, as one saith, but also as oft as we do any thing of note or consequence, we subject ourselves to every one's censure, and happy is he that is least tossed upon tongues; for utterly to escape the snatch of them it is impossible.

Resistance to Innovation Always Aimed at the Most Important People

If any man conceit, that this is the lot and portion of the meaner sort only, and that Princes are privileged by their high estate, he is deceived. As *the sword devoureth as well one as another,* as it is in Samuel; nay, as the great commander charged his soldiers in a certain battle to strike at no part of the enemy, but at the face; and as the king of Syria commanded his chief captains *to fight neither with small nor great, save only against the king of Israel:* so it is too true, that envy striketh most spitefully at the fairest, and the chiefest. David was a worthy prince, and no man to be compared to him for his first deeds; and yet for as worthy an act as ever he did, even for bringing back the ark of God in solemnity, he was scorned and scoffed at by his own wife. Solomon was greater than David, though not in virtue, yet in power; and by his power and wisdom he built a temple to the Lord, such an one as was the glory of the land of Israel, and the wonder of the whole world. But was that his magnificence liked of by all? We doubt of it. Otherwise why do they lay it in his son's dish, and call unto him for easing of the burden? *Make,* say they, *the grievous servitude of thy father, and his sore yoke, lighter.* Belike he had charged them with some levies, and troubled them with some carriages: hereupon they raise up a tragedy, and wish in their heart the temple had never been built. So hard a thing it is to please all, even when we please God best, and do seek to approve ourselves to every one's conscience.

If we will descend to latter times, we shall find many the like examples of such kind, or rather unkind, acceptance. The first Roman Emperor did never do a more pleasing deed to the learned, nor more profitable to posterity, for conserving the record of times in true supputation, than when he corrected the Calendar, and ordered the year according to the course of the sun: and yet this was imputed to him for novelty and arrogancy, and procured to him great obloquy. So the first Christened Emperor (at the least wise, that openly professed the faith himself, and allowed others to do the like,) for strengthening the empire at his great charges, and providing for the Church, as he did, got for his labour the name *Pupillus*, as who would say, a wasteful Prince, that had need of a guardian or overseer. So the best Christened Emperor, for the love that he bare unto peace, thereby to enrich both himself and his subjects, and because he did not seek war, but find it, was judged to be no man at arms, (though indeed he excelled in feats of chivalry, and shewed so much when he was provoked,) and condemned for giving himself to his ease, and to his pleasure. To be short, the most learned Emperor of former times, (at the least, the greatest politician,) what thanks had he for cutting off the superfluities of the laws, and digesting them into some order and method? This, that he hath been blotted by some to be an Epitomist, that is, one that extinguished worthy whole volumes, to bring his abridgements into request. This is the measure that hath been rendered to excellent Princes in former times, *cum bene facerent, male audire,* for their good deeds to be evil spoken of. Neither is there any likelihood that envy and malignity died and were buried with the ancient. No, no, the reproof of Moses taketh hold of most ages; *Ye are risen up in your fathers' stead, an increase of sinful men. What is that that hath been done? that which shall be done: and there is no new thing under the sun,* saith the wise man. And St. Stephen, *As your fathers did, so do ye.*

King James's Firmness of Purpose

This, and more to this purpose, his Majesty that now reigneth (and long, and long, may he reign, and his offspring forever, *Himself, and children, and children's children always!*) knew full well, according to the singular wisdom given unto him by God, and the rare learning and experience that he hath attained unto; namely, That whosoever attempteth any thing for the publick, (especially if it pertain to religion, and to the opening and clearing of the word of God,) the same setteth himself upon a stage to be glouted upon by every evil eye; yea, he casteth himself headlong upon pikes, to be gored by every sharp tongue. For he that meddleth with men's religion in any part meddleth with their custom, nay, with their freehold; and though they find no content in that which they have, yet they cannot abide to hear of altering. Notwithstanding his royal heart was not daunted or discouraged for this or that colour, but stood resolute, *as a statue immoveable, and an anvil not easily to be beaten into plates,* as one saith; he knew who had chosen him to be a soldier, or rather a captain; and being assured that the course which he intended made much for the glory of God, and the building up of his Church, he would not suffer it to be broken off for whatsoever speeches or practices. It doth certainly belong unto kings, yea, it doth specially belong unto them, to have care of religion, yea, to know it aright, yea, to profess it zealously, yea, to promote it to the uttermost of their power. This is their glory before all nations which mean well, and this will bring unto them a far more excellent weight of glory in the day of the Lord Jesus. For the Scriptures saith not in vain, *Them that honour me I will honour:* neither was it a vain word that Eusebius delivered long ago, That piety toward God was the weapon, and the only weapon, that both preserved Constantine's person, and avenged him of his enemies.

Divine Power of Scripture

Scripture's Power Inherent in its Character

But now what piety without truth? What truth, what saving truth, without the word of God? What word of God, whereof we may be sure, without the Scriptures? The Scriptures we are commanded to search, *John* v. 39. *Isai.* viii. 20. They are commended that searched and studied them, *Acts* xvii. 11, and vii. 28, 29. They are reproved that were unskilful in them, or slow to believe them, *Matth.* xxii. 29. *Luke* xxiv. 25. They can make us wise unto salvation, *2 Tim.* iii. 15. If we be ignorant, they will instruct us; if out of the way, they will bring us home; if out of order, they will reform us; if in heaviness, comfort us; if dull, quicken us; if cold, inflame us. *Tolle, lege; tolle, lege;* Take up and read, take up and read the Scriptures, (for unto them was the direction) it was said unto St. Augustine by a supernatural voice. *Whatsoever is in the Scriptures, believe me,* saith the same St. Augustine, *is high and divine; there is verily truth, and a doctrine most fit for the refreshing and renewing of men's minds, and truly so tempered, that every one may draw from thence that which is sufficient for him, if he come to draw with a devout and pious mind, as true religion requireth.* Thus St. Augustine. And St. Hierome, *Ama Scripturas, et amabit te sapientia,* etc. Love the Scriptures, and wisdom will love thee. And St. Cyrill against Julian, *Even boys that are bred up in the Scriptures become most religious,* etc. But what mention we three or four uses of the Scripture, whereas whatsoever is to be believed, or practised, or hoped for, is contained in them? or three or four sentences of the Fathers, since whosoever is worthy the name of a Father, from Christ's time downward, hath likewise written not only of the riches, but also of the perfection of the Scripture? *I adore the fulness of the Scripture,* saith Tertullian against Hermogenes. And again, to Apelles an heretic of the like stamp he saith, *I do not admit that which thou bringest in* (or concludest) *of thine own* (head or store, *de tuo)* without Scripture. So St. Justin Martyr before him; *We must know by all means* (saith he) *that it is not lawful* (or possible) *to learn* (any thing) *of God or of right piety, save only out of the Prophets, who teach us by divine inspiration.* So St. Basil after Tertullian, *It is a manifest falling away from the faith, and a fault of presumption, either to reject any of those things that are written, or to bring in* (upon the head of them, ἐπεισαγεῖν) *any of those things that are* not written. We omit to cite to the same effect St. Cyrill Bishop of Jerusalem in his 4. *Catech.* St. Hierome against Helvidius,

St. Augustine in his third book against the letters of Petilian, and in very many other places of his works. Also we forbear to descend to later Fathers, because we will not weary the reader. The Scriptures then being acknowledged to be so full and so perfect, how can we excuse ourselves of negligence, if we do not study them? of curiosity, if we be not content with them? Men talk much of εἱρεσιώνη how many sweet and goodly things it had hanging on it; of the Philosopher's stone, that it turneth copper into gold; of *Cornucopia*, that it had all things necessary for food in it; of *Panaces* the herb, that it was good for all diseases; of *Catholicon* the drug, that it is instead of all purges; of Vulcan's armour, that it was an armour of proof against all thrusts and all blows, etc. Well, that which they falsely or vainly attributed to these things for bodily good, we may justly and with full measure ascribe unto the Scripture for spiritual. It is not only an armour, but also a whole armoury of weapons, both offensive and defensive; whereby we may save ourselves, and put the enemy to flight. It is not an herb, but a tree, or rather a whole paradise of trees of life, which bring forth fruit every month, and the fruit thereof is for meat, and the leaves for medicine. It is not a pot of *Manna*, or a cruse of oil, which were for memory only, or for a meal's meat or two, but, as it were, a shower of heavenly bread sufficient for a whole host, be it never so great, and, as it were, a whole cellar full of oil vessels; whereby all our necessities may be provided for, and our debts discharged. In a word, it is a panary of wholesome food against fenowed traditions; a physician's shop (as St. Basil calls it) of preservatives against poisoned heresies; a pandect of profitable laws against rebellious spirits; a treasury of most costly jewels against beggarly rudiments; finally, a fountain of most pure water springing up unto everlasting life. And what marvel? the original thereof being from heaven, not from earth; the author being God, not man; the inditer, the Holy Spirit, not the wit of the Apostles or Prophets; the penmen, such as were sanctified from the womb, and endued with a principal portion of God's Spirit; the matter, verity, piety, purity, uprightness; the form, God's word, God's testimony, God's oracles, the word of truth, the word of salvation, etc.; the effects, light of understanding, stableness of persuasion, repentance from dead works, newness of life, holiness, peace, joy in the Holy Ghost; lastly, the end and reward of the study thereof, fellowship with the saints, participation of the heavenly nature, fruition of an inheritance immortal, undefiled, and that never shall fade away. Happy is the man that delighteth in the Scripture, and thrice happy that meditateth in it day and night.

Scripture's Power Conveyed Through Translations

But how shall men meditate in that which they cannot understand? How shall they understand that which is kept close in an unknown tongue? as it is written, *Except I know the power of the voice, I shall be to him that speaketh a barbarian, and he that speaketh shall be a barbarian to me.* The apostle excepteth no tongue; not Hebrew the ancientest, not Greek the most copious, not Latin the finest. Nature taught a natural man to confess, that all of us in those tongues which we do not understand are plainly deaf; we may turn the deaf ear unto them. The Scythian counted the Athenian, whom he did not understand, barbarous: so the Roman did the Syrian, and the Jew: (even St. Hierome himself calleth the Hebrew tongue barbarous; belike, because it was strange to so many:) so the Emperor of Constantinople calleth the Latin tongue barbarous, though Pope Nicolas do storm at it: so the Jews long before Christ called all other nations *Lognasim,* which is little better than barbarous. Therefore as one complaineth that always in the Senate of Rome there was one or other that called for an interpreter; so lest the Church be driven to the like exigent, it is necessary to have translations in a readiness. Translation it is that openeth the window, to let in the light; that breaketh the shell, that we may eat the kernel; that putteth aside the curtain, that we may look into the most holy place; that removeth the cover of the well, that we may come by the water; even as Jacob rolled away the stone from the mouth of the well, by which means the flocks of Laban were watered.

Indeed without translation into the vulgar tongue, the unlearned are but like children at Jacob's well (which was deep) without a bucket or something to draw with: or as that person mentioned by Esay, to whom when a sealed book was delivered with this motion, *Read this, I pray thee,* he was fain to make this answer, *I cannot, for it is sealed.*

History of Bible Translations

Greek Translations

While God would be known only in Jacob, and have his name great in Israel, and in none other place; while the dew lay on Gideon's fleece only, and all the earth besides was dry; then for one and the same people, which spake all of them the language of Canaan, that is, Hebrew, one and the same original in Hebrew was sufficient. But when the fulness of time drew near, that the Sun of righteousness, the Son of God, should come into the world, whom God ordained to be a reconciliation through faith in his blood, not of the Jew only, but also of the Greek, yea, of all them that were scattered abroad; then, lo, it pleased the Lord to stir up the spirit of a Greek prince, (Greek for descent and language) even of Ptolemy Philadelph king of Egypt, to procure the translating of the book of God out of Hebrew into Greek. This is the translation of the *Seventy* interpreters, commonly so called, which prepared the way for our Saviour among the Gentiles by written preaching, as St. John Baptist did among the Jews by vocal. For the Grecians, being desirous of learning, were not wont to suffer books of worth to lie moulding in kings' libraries, but had many of their servants, ready scribes, to copy them out, and so they were dispersed and made common. Again, the Greek tongue was well known and made familiar to most inhabitants in Asia by reason of the conquests that there the Grecians had made, as also by the colonies which thither they had sent. For the same causes also it was well understood in many places of Europe, yea, and of Africk too. Therefore the word of God, being set forth in Greek, becometh hereby like a candle set upon a candlestick, which giveth light to all that are in the house; or like a proclamation sounded forth in the market-place, which most men presently take knowledge of; and therefore that language was fittest to contain the Scriptures, both for the first preachers of the gospel to appeal unto for witness, and for the learners also of those times to make search and trial by. It is certain, that that translation was not so sound and so perfect, but that it needed in many places correction; and who had been so sufficient for this work as the Apostles or apostolick men? Yet it seemed good to the Holy Ghost and to them to take that which they found, (the same being for the greatest part true and sufficient) rather than by making a new, in that new world and green age of the Church, to expose themselves to many exceptions and cavillations, as though they made a translation to serve their own turn; and therefore bearing witness to themselves, their witness not to be regarded. This may be supposed to be some cause, why the translation of the *Seventy* was allowed to pass for current. Notwithstanding, though it was commended generally, yet it did not fully content the learned, no not of the Jews. For not long after Christ, Aquila fell in hand with a new translation, and after him Theodotion, and after him Symmachus: yea, there was a fifth, and a sixth edition, the authors whereof were not known. These with the *Seventy* made up the *Hexapla,* and were worthily and to great purpose compiled together by Origen. Howbeit the edition of the *Seventy* went away with the credit, and therefore not only was placed in the midst by Origen, (for the worth and excellency thereof above the rest, as Epiphanius gathereth) but also was used by the Greek Fathers for the ground and foundation of their commentaries. Yea, Epiphanius above-named doth attribute so much unto it, that he holdeth the authors thereof not only for interpreters, but also for prophets in some respect; and Justinian the Emperor, injoining the Jews his subjects to use especially the translation of the *Seventy,* rendereth this reason thereof, Because they were, as it were, enlightened with prophetical grace. Yet for all that, as the Egyptians are said of the Prophet to be men and not God, and their horses flesh and not spirit: so it is evident (and St. Hierome affirmeth as much) that the *Seventy* were interpreters, they were not prophets. They did many things well, as learned men; but yet as men they stumbled and fell, one while through oversight, another while through ignorance; yea, sometimes they may be noted to add to the original, and sometimes to take from it; which made the Apostles to leave them many times, when they left the Hebrew, and to deliver the sense thereof according to the truth of the word, as the Spirit gave them utterance. This may suffice touching the *Greek* translations of the Old Testament.

Latin Translations

There were also within a few hundred years after Christ translations many into the *Latin* tongue; for this tongue also was very fit to convey the Law and the Gospel by, because in those times very many countries of the West, yea, of the South, East, and North, spake or understood Latin, being made provinces to the Romans. But now the Latin translations were too many to be all good; for they were infinite: (*Latini interpretes nullo modo numerari possunt,* saith St. Augustine.) Again, they were not out of the *Hebrew* fountain, (we speak of the Latin translations of the Old Testament) but out of the Greek stream; therefore the Greek being not altogether clear, the Latin derived from it must needs be muddy. This moved St. Hierome, a most learned Father, and the best linguist without controversy of his age, or of any other that went before him, to undertake the translating of the Old Testament out of the very fountains themselves; which he performed with that evidence of great learning, judgment, industry, and faithfulness, that he hath for ever bound the Church unto him in a special remembrance and thankfulness.

Other Translations

Now though the Church were thus furnished with Greek and Latin translations, even before the faith of Christ was generally embraced in the Empire: (for the learned know, that even in St. Hierome's time the Consul of Rome and his wife were both Ethnicks, and about the same time the greatest part of the Senate also) yet for all that the godly learned were not content to have the Scriptures in the language which themselves understood, Greek and Latin, (as the good lepers were not content to fare well themselves, but acquainted their neighbours with the store that God had sent, that they also might provide for themselves,) but also for the behoof and edifying of the unlearned, which hungered and thirsted after righteousness, and had souls to be saved as well as they, they provided translations into the vulgar for their countrymen, insomuch that most nations under heaven did shortly after their conversion hear Christ speaking unto them in their mother tongue, not by the voice of their minister only, but also by the written word translated. If any doubt hereof, he may be satisfied by examples enough, if enough will serve the turn. First, St. Hierome saith, *Multarum gentium linguis Scriptura ante translata docet falsa esse quæ addita sunt*, etc., that is, *The Scripture being translated before in the languages of many nations doth shew that those things that were added* (by Lucian or Hesychius) *are false.* So St. Hierome in that place. The same Hierome elsewhere affirmeth that he, the time was, had set forth the translation of the *Seventy, suæ linguæ hominibus*; that is, for his countrymen of Dalmatia. Which words not only Erasmus doth understand to purport, that St. Hierome translated the Scripture into the Dalmatian tongue; but also Sixtus Senensis, and Alphonsus a Castro, (that we speak of no more) men not to be excepted against by them of Rome, do ingenuously confess as much. So St. Chrysostome, that lived in St. Hierome's time, giveth evidence with him: *The doctrine of St. John* (saith he) *did not in such sort* (as the Philosophers' did) *vanish away: but the Syrians, Egyptians, Indians, Persians, Ethiopians, and infinite other nations, being barbarous people, translated it into their (mother) tongue, and have learned to be (true) Philosophers,* he meaneth Christians. To this may be added *Theodoret*, as next unto him both for antiquity, and for learning. His words be these, *Every country that is under the sun is full of these words*, (of the Apostles and Prophets;) *and the Hebrew tongue* (he meaneth the Scriptures in the *Hebrew* tongue) *is turned not only into the language of the Grecians, but also of the Romans, and Egyptians, and Persians, and Indians, and Armenians, and Scythians, and Sauromatians, and, briefly, into all the languages that any nation useth.* So he. In like manner Ulpilas is reported by Paulus Diaconus and Isidore, and before them by Sozomen, to have translated the Scriptures into the *Gothick* tongue: John Bishop of Sevil, by Vasseus, to have turned them into *Arabick* about the year of our Lord 717: Beda, by Cistertiensis, to have turned a great part of them into Saxon: Efnard, by Trithemius, to have abridged the *French* Psalter (as Beda had done the *Hebrew)* about the year 800; King Alured, by the said Cistertiensis, to have turned the Psalter into *Saxon:* Methodius, by Aventinus, (printed at Ingolstad) to have turned the Scriptures into *Sclavonian:* Valdo Bishop of Frising, by Beatus Rhenanus, to have caused about that time the Gospels to be translated into *Dutch* rhyme, yet extant in the library of Corbinian: Valdus, by divers, to have turned them himself, or to have gotten them turned into *French,* about the year 1160: Charles the Fifth of that name, surnamed *The wise,* to have caused them to be turned into *French* about 200 years after Valdus' time; of which translation there be many copies yet extant, as witnesseth Beroaldus. Much about that time, even in our King Richard the Second's days, John Trevisa translated them into English, and many English Bibles in written hand are yet to be seen with divers; translated, as it is very probable, in that age. So the Syrian translation of the New Testament is in most learned men's libraries, of Widminstadius' setting forth; and the Psalter in Arabick is with many, of Augustinus Nebiensis' setting forth. So Postel affirmeth, that in his travel he saw the Gospels in the Ethiopian tongue: And Ambrose Thesius allegeth the Psalter of the Indians, which he testifieth to have been set forth by Potken in Syrian characters. So that to have the Scriptures in the mother tongue is not a quaint conceit lately taken up, either by the Lord Cromwell in England, or by the Lord Radevile in Polony, or by the Lord Ungnadius in the Emperor's dominion, but hath been thought upon, and put in practice of old, even from the first times of the conversion of any nation; no doubt, because it was esteemed most profitable to cause faith to grow in men's hearts the sooner, and to make them to be able to say with the words of the Psalm, *As we have heard, so we have seen.*

Roman Catholic Resistance

Now the church of Rome would seem at the length to bear a motherly affection toward her children, and to allow them the Scriptures in the mother tongue; but indeed it is a gift, not deserving to be called a gift, an unprofitable gift: they must first get a licence in writing before they may use them; and to get that, they must approve themselves to their Confessor, that is, to be such as are, if not frozen in the dregs, yet sowered with the leaven of their superstition. Howbeit it seemed too much to Clement the Eighth, that there should be any licence granted to have them in the vulgar tongue, and therefore he overruleth and frustrateth the grant of Pius the Fourth. So much are they afraid of the light of the Scripture, (*Lucifugæ Scripturarum,* as Tertullian speaketh) that they will not trust the people with it, no not as it is set forth by their own sworn men, no not with the licence of their own Bishops and Inquisitors. Yea, so unwilling they are to communicate the Scriptures to the people's understanding in any sort, that they are not ashamed to confess, that we forced them to translate it into English against their wills. This seemeth to argue a bad cause, or a bad conscience, or both. Sure we are, that it is not he that hath good gold, that is afraid to bring it to the touchstone, but he that hath the counterfeit; neither is it the true man that shunneth the light, but the malefactor, lest his deeds should be reproved; neither is it the plain dealing merchant that is unwilling to have the weights, or the meteyard, brought in place, but he that useth deceit. But we will let them alone for this fault, and return to translation.

Defense of the Authorized Version Against Objections

Objections Listed

Many men's mouths have been opened a good while (and yet are not stopped) with speeches about the translation so long in hand, or rather perusals of translations made before: and ask what may be the reason, what the necessity of the employment. Hath the church been deceived, say they, all this while? Hath her sweet bread been mingled with leaven, her silver with dross, her wine with water, her milk with lime? (*lacte gypsum male miscetur,* saith St. Irenee.) We hoped that we had been in the right way, that we had had the oracles of God delivered unto us, and that though all the world had cause to be offended, and to complain, yet that we had none. Hath the nurse holden out the breast, and nothing but wind in it? hath the bread been delivered by the Fathers of the Church, and the same proved to be *lapidosus,* as Seneca speaketh? What is it to handle the word of God deceitfully, if this be not? Thus certain brethren. Also the adversaries of Judah and Jerusalem, like Sanballat in Nehemiah, mock, as we hear, both at the work and workmen, saying, *What do these weak Jews, etc.? will they make the stones whole again out of the heaps of dust which are burnt? although they build, yet if a fox go up, he shall even break down their stony wall.* Was their translation good before? Why do they now mend it? Was it not good? Why then was it obtruded to the people? Yea, why did the Catholicks (meaning Popish Romanists) always go in jeopardy for refusing to hear it? Nay, if it must be translated into English, Catholicks are fittest to do it. They have learning, and they know when a thing is well, they can *manum de tabula.*

Protestant Objections Answered

We will answer them both briefly: and the former, being brethren, thus with St. Hierome, *Damnamus veteres? Minime, sed post priorum studia in domo Domini quod possumus laboramus.* That is, *Do we condemn the ancient? In no case: but after the endeavours of them that were before us, we take the best pains we can in the house of God.* As if he said, Being provoked by the example of the learned that lived before my time, I have thought it my duty to assay, whether my talent in the knowledge of the tongues may be profitable in any measure to God's Church, lest I should seem to have laboured in them in vain, and lest I should be thought to glory in men (although ancient) above that which was in them. Thus St. Hierome may be thought to speak.

And to the same effect say we, that we are so far off from condemning any of their labours that travelled before us in this kind, either in this land, or beyond sea, either in King Henry's time, or King Edward's, (if there were any translation, or correction of a translation, in his time) or Queen Elizabeth's of ever renowned memory, that we acknowledge them to have been raised up of God for the building and furnishing of his Church, and that they deserve to be had of us and of posterity in everlasting remembrance. The judgment of Aristotle is worthy and well known: *If Timotheus had not been, we had not had such sweet musick: but if Phrynis* (Timotheus' master) *had not been, we had not had Timotheus.* Therefore blessed be they, and most honoured be their name, that break the ice, and give the onset upon that which helpeth forward to the saving of souls. Now what can be more available thereto, than to deliver God's book unto God's people in a tongue which they understand? Since of an hidden treasure, and of a fountain that is sealed, there is no profit, as Ptolemy Philadelph wrote to the Rabbins or masters of the Jews, as witnesseth Epiphanius: and as St. Augustine saith, *A man had rather be with his dog than with a stranger* (whose tongue is strange unto him). Yet for all that, as nothing is begun and perfected at the same time, and the latter thoughts are thought to be the wiser, so if we building upon their foundation that went before us, and being holpen by their labours, do endeavour to make that better which they left so good; no man, we are sure, hath cause to mislike us; they, we persuade ourselves, if they were alive, would thank us. The vintage of Abiezer, that strake the stroke: yet the gleaning of grapes of Ephraim was not to be despised. See Judges viii. 2. Joash the king of Israel did not satisfy himself till he had smitten the ground three times; and yet he offended the Prophet for giving over then. Aquila, of whom we spake before, translated the Bible as carefully and as skilfully as he could; and yet he thought good to go over it again, and then it got the credit with the Jews, to be called κατ' ἀκρίβειαν, that is, accurately done, as St. Hierome witnesseth. How many books of profane learning have been gone over again and again, by the same translators, by others? Of one and the same book of Aristotle's Ethicks there are extant not so few as six or seven several translations. Now if this cost may be bestowed upon the gourd, which affordeth us a little shade, and which to day flourisheth, but to morrow is cut down; what may we bestow, nay, what ought we not to bestow, upon the vine, the fruit whereof maketh glad the conscience of man, and the stem whereof abideth for ever? And this is the word of God, which we translate. *What is the chaff to the wheat? saith the Lord. Tanti vitreum, quanti verum margaritum!* (saith Tertullian.) If a toy of glass be of that reckoning with us, how ought we to value the true pearl! Therefore let no man's eye be evil, because his Majesty's is good; neither let any be grieved, that we have a Prince that seeketh the increase of the spiritual wealth of Israel: (let Sanballats and Tobiahs do so, which therefore do bear their just reproof;) but let us rather bless God from the ground of our heart for working this religious care in him to have the translations of the Bible maturely considered of and examined. For by this means it cometh to pass, that whatsoever is sound already, (and all is sound for substance in one or other of our editions, and the worst of ours far better than their authentick vulgar) the same will shine as gold more brightly, being rubbed and polished; also, if any thing be halting, or superfluous, or not so agreeable to the original, the same may be corrected, and the truth set in place. And what can the King command to be done, that will bring him more true honour than this? And wherein could they that have been set a work approve their duty to the King, yea, their obedience to God, and love to his Saints, more, than by yielding their service, and all that is within them, for the furnishing of the work? But besides all this, they were the principal motives of it, and therefore ought least to quarrel it. For the very historical truth is, that upon the importunate petitions of the Puritanes at his Majesty's coming to this crown, the conference at Hampton-court having been appointed for hearing their complaints, when by force of reason they were put from all other grounds, they had recourse at the last to this shift, that they could not with good conscience subscribe to the communion book, since it maintained the Bible as it was there translated, which was, as they said, a most corrupted translation. And although this was judged to be but a very poor and empty shift, yet even hereupon did his Majesty begin to bethink himself of the good that might ensue by a new translation, and presently after gave order for this translation which is now presented unto thee. Thus much to satisfy our scrupulous brethren.

Catholic Objections Answered

No translation is unworthy to be called the Word of God.

Now to the latter we answer, That we do not deny, nay, we affirm and avow, that the very meanest translation of the Bible in English, set forth by men of our profession, (for we have seen none of their's of the whole Bible as yet) containeth the word of God, nay, is the word of God: as the King's speech which he uttered in Parliament, being translated into French, Dutch, Italian, and Latin, is still the King's speech, though it be not interpreted by every translator with the like grace, nor peradventure so fitly for phrase, nor so expressly for sense, everywhere. For it is confessed, that things are to take their denomination of the greater part; and a natural man could say, *Verum ubi multa nitent in carmine, non ego paucis offendar maculis, etc.* A man may be counted a virtuous man, though he have made many slips in his life, (else there were none virtuous, for *in many things we offend all,*) also a comely man and lovely, though he have some warts upon his hand; yea, not only freckles upon his face, but also scars. No cause therefore why the word translated should be denied to be the word, or forbidden to be current, notwithstanding that some imperfections and blemishes may be noted in the setting forth of it. For what ever was perfect under the sun, where Apostles or apostolick men, that is, men endued with an extraordinary measure of God's Spirit, and privileged with the privilege of infallibility, had not their hand? The Romanists therefore in refusing to hear, and daring to burn the word translated, did no less than despite the Spirit of grace, from whom originally it proceeded, and whose sense and meaning, as well as man's weakness would enable, it did express. Judge by an example or two.

Plutarch writeth, that after that Rome had been burnt by the Gauls, they fell soon to build it again: but doing it in haste, they did not cast the streets, nor proportion the houses, in such comely fashion, as had been most sightly and convenient. Was Catiline therefore an honest man, or a good patriot, that sought to bring it to a combustion? or Nero a good Prince, that did indeed set it on fire? So by the story of Ezra and the prophecy of Haggai it may be gathered, that the temple built by Zerubbabel after the return from Babylon was by no means to be compared to the former built by Solomon: for they that remembered the former wept when they considered the latter. Notwithstanding might this latter either have been abhorred and forsaken by the Jews, or profaned by the Greeks? The like we are to think of translations. The translation of the *Seventy* dissenteth from the Original in many places, neither doth it come near it for perspicuity, gravity, majesty. Yet which of the Apostles did condemn it? Condemn it? Nay, they used it, (as it is apparent, and as St. Hierome and most learned men do confess;) which they would not have done, nor by their example of using it so grace and commend it to the Church, if it had been unworthy the appellation and name of the word of God.

The value of a translation does not depend on the
translator's theological convictions.

And whereas they urge for their second defence of their vilifying and abusing of the English Bibles, or some pieces thereof, which they meet with, for that hereticks forsooth were the authors of the translations: (hereticks they call us by the same right that they call themselves catholicks, both being wrong:) we marvel what divinity taught them so. We are sure Tertullian was of another mind: *Ex personis probamus fidem, an ex fide personas?* Do we try men's faith by their persons? We should try their persons by their faith. Also St. Augustine was of another mind: for he, lighting upon certain rules made by Tychonius a Donatist for the better understanding of the word, was not ashamed to make use of them, yea, to insert them into his own book, with giving commendation to them so far forth as they were worthy to be commended, as is to be seen in St. Augustine's third book *De Doctr. Christ.* To be short, Origen, and the whole Church of God for certain hundred years, were of another mind: for they were so far from treading under foot (much more from burning) the translation of Aquila a proselyte, that is, one that had turned Jew, of Symmachus, and Theodotion both Ebionites, that is, most vile hereticks, that they joined them together with the Hebrew original, and the translation of the *Seventy* (as hath been before signified out of Epiphanius) and set them forth openly to be considered of and perused by all. But we weary the unlearned, who need not know so much; and trouble the learned, who know it already.

Catholics Revise Their Work No Less than Protestants.

Yet before we end, we must answer a third cavil and objection of their's against us, for altering and amending our translations so oft; wherein truly they deal hardly and strangely with us. For to whom ever was it imputed for a fault (by such as were wise,) to go over that which he had done, and to amend it where he saw cause? St. Augustine was not afraid to exhort St. Hierome to a *Palinodia* or recantation. The same St. Augustine was not ashamed to retractate, we might say, revoke, many things that had passed him, and doth even glory that he seeth his infirmities. If we will be sons of the truth, we must consider what it speaketh, and trample upon our own credit, yea, and upon other men's too, if either be any way an hinderance to it. This to the cause. Then to the persons we say, that of all men they ought to be most silent in this case. For what varieties have they, and what alterations have they made, not only of their service books, portesses, and breviaries, but also of their Latin translation? The service book supposed to be made by St. Ambrose, *(Officium Ambrosianum)* was a great while in special use and request: but Pope Adrian, calling a council with the aid of Charles the Emperor, abolished it, yea, burnt it, and commanded the service book of St. Gregory universally to be used. Well, *Officium Gregorianum* gets by this means to be in credit; but doth it continue without change or altering? No, the very Roman service was of two fashions; the new fashion, and the old, the one used in one Church, and the other in another; as is to be seen in Pamelius a Romanist, his preface before *Micrologus*. The same Pamelius reporteth out of Radulphus de Rivo, that about the year of our Lord 1277 Pope Nicolas the third removed out of the churches of Rome the more ancient books (of service,) and brought into use the missals of the Friers Minorites, and commanded them to be observed there; insomuch that about an hundred years after, when the above named Radulphus happened to be at Rome, he found all the books to be new, of the new stamp. Neither was there this chopping and changing in the more ancient times only, but also of late. Pius Quintus himself confesseth, that every bishoprick almost had a peculiar kind of service, most unlike to that which others had; which moved him to abolish all other breviaries, though never so ancient, and privileged and published by Bishops in their Dioceses, and to establish and ratify that only which was of his own setting forth in the year 1568. Now when the Father of their church, who gladly would heal the sore of the daughter of his people softly and slightly, and make the best of it, findeth so great fault with them for their odds, and jarring; we hope the children have no great cause to vaunt of their uniformity. But the difference that appeareth between our translations, and our often correcting of them, is the thing that we are specially charged with; let us see therefore whether they themselves be without fault this way, (if it be to be counted a fault, to correct) and whether they be fit men to throw stones at us: *O tandem major parcas insane minori:* They that are less sound themselves ought not to object infirmities to others. If we should tell them, that Valla, Stapulensis, Erasmus, and Vives, found fault with their vulgar translation, and consequently wished the same to be mended, or a new one to be made; they would answer peradventure, that we produced their enemies for witnesses against them; albeit they were in no other sort enemies, than as St. Paul was to the Galatians, for telling them the truth; and it were to be wished, that they had dared to tell it them plainlier and oftner. But what will they say to this, That Pope Leo the Tenth allowed Erasmus' translation of the new Testament, so much different from the vulgar, by his apostolic letter and bull? That the same Leo exhorted Pagnine to translate the whole Bible, and bare whatsoever charges was necessary for the work? Surely, as the apostle reasoneth to the Hebrews, that *if the former Law and Testament had been sufficient, there had been no need of the latter:* so we may say, that if the old vulgar had been at all points allowable, to small purpose had labour and charges been undergone about framing of a new. If they say, it was one Pope's private opinion, and that he consulted only himself; then we are able to go further with them, and to aver, that more of their chief men of all sorts, even their own Trent champions, Paiva and Vega, and their own inquisitor Hieronymus ab Oleastro, and their own Bishop Isidorus Clarius, and their own Cardinal Thomas a vio Cajetan, do either make new translations themselves, or follow new ones of other men's making, or note the vulgar interpreter for halting, none of them fear to dissent from him, nor yet to except against him. And call they this an uniform tenor of text and judgment about the text, so many of their worthies disclaiming the new received conceit? Nay, we will yet come nearer the quick. Doth not their Paris edition differ from the Lovain, and Hentenius's from them both, and yet all of them allowed by authority? Nay, doth not Sixtus Quintus confess, that certain Catholicks (he meaneth certain of his own side) were in such an humour of translating the Scriptures into Latin, that Satan taking occasion by them, though they thought of no such matter, did strive what he could, out of so uncertain and manifold a variety of translations, so to mingle all things, that nothing might seem to be left certain and firm in them, etc.? Nay further did not the same Sixtus ordain by an inviolable decree, and that with the counsel and consent of his Cardinals, that the Latin edition of the Old and New Testament, which the council of Trent would have to be authentick, is the same without controversy which he then set forth, being diligently corrected and printed in the printing-house of Vatican? Thus Sixtus in his preface before his Bible. And yet Clement the Eighth, his immediate successor to account of, publisheth another edition of the Bible, containing in it infinite differences from that of Sixtus, and many of them weighty and material; and yet this must be authentick by all means. What is to have the faith of our glorious Lord Jesus Christ with yea and nay, if this be not? Again, what is sweet harmony and consent, if this be? Therefore, as Demaratus of Corinth advised a great King, before he talked of the dissensions among the Grecians, to compose his domestick broils; (for at that time his queen and his son and heir were at deadly feud with him) so all the while that our adversaries do make so many and so various editions themselves, and do jar so much about the worth and authority of them, they can with no shew of equity challenge us for changing and correcting.

Purposes and Procedures Underlying the Authorized Version

Improvement upon Existing Good Translations

But it is high time to leave them, and to shew in brief what we proposed to ourselves, and what course we held, in this our perusal and survey of the Bible. Truly, good Christian Reader, we never thought from the beginning that we should need to make a new translation, nor yet to make of a bad one a good one; (for then the imputation of Sixtus had been true in some sort, that our people had been fed with gall of dragons instead of wine, with wheal instead of milk;) but to make a good one better, or out of many good ones one principal good one, not justly to be excepted against; that hath been our endeavour, that our mark. To that purpose there were many chosen, that were greater in other men's eyes than in their own, and that sought the truth rather than their own praise. Again, they came, or were thought to come, to the work, not *exercendi causa*, (as one saith) but *exercitati*, that is, learned, not to learn; for the chief overseer and ἐργοδιώκτης under his Majesty, to whom not only we, but also our whole Church was much bound, knew by his wisdom, which thing also Nazianzen taught so long ago, that it is a preposterous order to teach first, and to learn after; that τὸ ἐν πίθῳ κεραμίαν μανθάνειν, to learn and practise together, is neither commendable for the workman, nor safe for the work. Therefore such were thought upon, as could say modestly with

St. Hierome, *Et Hebræum sermonem ex parte didicimus, et in Latino pene ab ipsis incunabilis, etc. detriti sumus; Both we have learned the Hebrew tongue in part, and in the Latin we have been exercised almost from our very cradle.* St. Hierome maketh no mention of the Greek tongue, wherein yet he did excel; because he translated not the Old Testament out of Greek, but out of Hebrew. And in what sort did these assemble? In the trust of their own knowledge, or of their sharpness of wit, or deepness of judgment, as it were in an arm of flesh? At no hand. They trusted in Him that hath the key of David, opening, and no man shutting; they prayed to the Lord, the Father of our Lord, to the effect that St. Augustine did; *O let thy Scriptures be my pure delight; let me not be deceived in them, neither let me deceive by them.* In this confidence, and with this devotion, did they assemble together; not too many, lest one should trouble another; and yet many, lest many things haply might escape them. If you ask what they had before them; truly it was the Hebrew text of the Old Testament, the Greek of the New. These are the two golden pipes, or rather conduits, wherethrough the olive branches empty themselves into the gold. St. Augustine calleth them precedent, or original, tongues; St. Hierome, fountains. The same St. Hierome affirmeth, and Gratian hath not spared to put it into his decree, That *as the credit of the old books (he meaneth of the Old Testament) is to be tried by the Hebrew volumes; so of the new by the Greek tongue,* he meaneth by the original Greek. If truth be to be tried by these tongues, then whence should a translation be made, but out of them? These tongues therefore, (the Scriptures, we say, in those tongues) we set before us to translate, being the tongues wherein God was pleased to speak to his Church by his Prophets and Apostles. Neither did we run over the work with that posting haste that the *Septuagint* did, if that be true which is reported of them, that they finished it in seventy two days; neither were we barred or hindered from going over it again, having once done it, like St. Hierome, if that be true which himself reporteth, that he could no sooner write any thing, but presently it was caught from him, and published, and he could not have leave to mend it: neither, to be short, were we the first that fell in hand with translating the Scripture into English, and consequently destitute of former helps, as it is written of Origen, that he was the first in a manner, that put his hand to write commentaries upon the Scriptures, and therefore no marvel if he overshot himself many times. None of these things: The work hath not been huddled up in seventy two days, but hath costs the workmen, as light as it seemeth, the pains of twice seven times seventy two days, and more. Matters of such weight and consequence are to be speeded with maturity: for in a business of moment a man feareth not the blame of convenient slackness. Neither did we think much to consult the translators or commentators, Chaldee, Hebrew, Syrian, Greek, or Latin; no, nor the Spanish, French, Italian, or Dutch; neither did we disdain to revise that which we had done, and to bring back to the anvil that which we had hammered: but having and using as great helps as were needful, and fearing no reproach for slowness, or coveting praise for expedition, we have at length, through the good hand of the Lord upon us, brought the work to that pass that you see.

Marginal Notes on Alternate Readings

Some peradventure would have no variety of senses to be set in the margin, lest the authority of the Scriptures for deciding of controversies by that shew of uncertainty should somewhat be shaken. But we hold their judgment not to be so sound in this point. For though, *whatsoever things are necessary are manifest,* as St. Chrysostome saith; and, as St. Augustine, *in those things that are plainly set down in the Scriptures all such matters are found, that concern faith, hope, and charity:* Yet for all that it cannot be dissembled, that partly to exercise and whet our wits, partly to wean the curious from lothing of them for their every where plainness, partly also to stir up our devotion to crave the assistance of God's Spirit by prayer, and lastly, that we might be forward to seek aid of our brethren by conference, and never scorn those that be not in all respects so complete as they should be, being to seek in many things ourselves, it hath pleased God in his Divine Providence here and there to scatter words and sentences of that difficulty and doubtfulness, not in doctrinal points that concern salvation, (for in such it hath been vouched that the Scriptures are plain,) but in matters of less moment, that fearfulness would better beseem us than confidence, and if we will resolve, to resolve upon modesty with St. Augustine, (though not in this same case altogether, yet upon the same ground) *Melius est dubitare de occultis, quam litigare de incertis:* It is better to make doubt of those things which are secret, than to strive about those things that are uncertain. There be many words in the Scriptures, which be never found there but once, (having neither brother nor neighbor, as the Hebrews speak) so that we cannot be holpen by conference of places. Again, there be many rare names of certain birds, beasts, and precious stones, etc., concerning which the Hebrews themselves are so divided among themselves for judgment, that they may seem to have defined this or that, rather because they would say something, than because they were sure of that which they said, as St. Hierome somewhere saith of the *Septuagint.* Now, in such a case, doth not a margin do well to admonish the Reader to seek further, and not to conclude or dogmatize upon this or that peremptorily? For as it is a fault of incredulity, to doubt of those things that are evident; so to determine of such things as the Spirit of God hath left (even in the judgment of the judicious) questionable, can be no less than presumption. Therefore, as St. Augustine saith, that variety of translations is profitable for the finding out of the sense of the Scriptures: so diversity of signification and sense in the margin, where the text is not so clear, must needs do good; yea, is necessary, as we are persuaded. We know that Sixtus Quintus expressly forbiddeth that any variety of readings of their vulgar edition should be put in the margin; (which though it be not altogether the same thing to that we have in hand, yet it looketh that way;) but we think he hath not all of his own side his favourers for this conceit. They that are wise had rather have their judgments at liberty in differences of readings, than to be captivated to the one, when it may be the other. If they were sure that their high priest had all laws shut up in his breast, as Paul the Second bragged, and that he were as free from error by special privilege, as the dictators of Rome were made by law inviolable, it were another matter; then his word were an oracle, his opinion a decision. But the eyes of the world are now open, God be thanked, and have been a great while; they find that he is subject to the same affections and infirmities that others be, that his skin is penetrable; and therefore so much as he proveth, not as much as he claimeth, they grant and embrace.

Variety in Word Choice

Another thing we think good to admonish thee of, gentle Reader, that we have not tied ourselves to an uniformity of phrasing, or to an identity of words, as some peradventure would wish that we had done, because they observe, that some learned men somewhere have been as exact as they could that way. Truly, that we might not vary from the sense of that which we had translated before, if the word signified the same thing in both places, (for there be some words that be not of the same sense every where,) we were especially careful, and made a conscience, according to our duty. But that we should express the same notion in the same particular word; as for example, if we translate the Hebrew or Greek word once by *purpose,* never to call it *intent;* if one where *journeying,* never *travelling;* if one where *think,* never *suppose;* if one where *pain,* never *ache;* if one where *joy,* never *gladness,* &c. Thus to mince the matter, we thought to savour more of curiosity than wisdom, and that rather it would breed scorn in the atheist, than bring profit to the godly reader. For is the kingdom of God become words or syllables? Why should we be in bondage to them, if we may be free? use one precisely, when we may use another no less fit as commodiously? A godly Father, in the primitive time, shewed himself greatly moved, that one of newfangledness called κραββάτον, σκίμπους, though the difference be little or none; and another reporteth, that he was much abused for turning *cucurbita* (to which reading the people had been used) into *hedera.* Now, if this happen in better times, and upon so small occasions, we might justly fear hard censure, if generally we should make verbal and unnecessary changings. We might also be charged (by scoffers) with some unequal dealing towards a great number of good English words. For, as it is written of a certain great Philosopher, that he should say, that those logs were happy that were made images to be worshipped; for their fellows, as good as they, lay for blocks behind the fire: so if we should say, as it were, unto certain words, Stand up higher, have a place in the Bible always; and to others of like quality, Get you hence, be banished for ever; we might be taxed peradventure with St. James's words, namely, *To be partial in ourselves, and judges of evil thoughts.* Add hereunto that niceness in words was always counted the next step to trifling; and so was to be curious about names too; also that we cannot follow a better pattern for elocution than God himself; therefore he using divers words in his holy writ, and indifferently for one thing in nature: we, if we will not be superstitious, may use the same liberty in our English versions out of the Hebrew and Greek, for that copy or store that he hath given us. Lastly, we have on the one side avoided the scrupulosity of the Puritanes, who leave the old Ecclesiastical words, and betake them to other, as when they put *washing* for *baptism,* and *congregation* instead of *Church:* as also on the other side, we have shunned the obscurity of the Papists, in their *azymes, tunike, rational, holocausts, prepuce, pasche,* and a number of such like, whereof their late translation is full, and that of purpose to darken the sense, that since they must needs translate the Bible, yet, by the language thereof, it may be kept from being understood. But we desire that the Scripture may speak like itself, as in the language of Canaan, that it may be understood even of the very vulgar.

Concluding Warning Against Rejection and Neglect

Many other things we might give thee warning of, gentle Reader, if we had not exceeded the measure of a preface already. It remaineth that we commend thee to God, and to the Spirit of his grace, which is able to build further than we can ask or think. He removeth the scales from our eyes, the vail from our hearts, opening our wits that we may understand his word, enlarging our hearts, yea, correcting our affections, that we may love it above gold and silver, yea, that we may love it to the end. Ye are brought unto fountains of living water which ye digged not; do not cast earth into them, with the Philistines, neither prefer broken pits before them, with the wicked Jews. Others have laboured, and you may enter into their labours. O receive not so great things in vain: O despise not so great salvation. Be not like swine to tread under foot so precious things. Say not to our Saviour with the Gergesites, Depart out of our coasts; neither yet with Esau sell your birthright for a mess of pottage. If light be come into the world, love not darkness more than light: if food, if clothing, be offered, go not naked, starve not yourselves. Remember the advice of Nazianzene, *It is a grievous thing* (or dangerous) *to neglect a great fair, and to seek to make markets afterwards:* also the encouragement of St. Chrysostome, *It is altogether impossible, that he that is sober* (and watchful) *should at any time be neglected:* lastly, the admonition and menacing of St. Augustine, *They that despise God's will inviting them, shall feel God's will taking vengeance of them.* It is a fearful thing to fall into the hands of the living God; but a blessed thing it is, and will bring us to everlasting blessedness in the end, when God speaketh unto us, to hearken; when he setteth his word before us, to read it; when he stretcheth out his hand and calleth, to answer, here am I, here are we to do thy will, O God. The Lord work a care and conscience in us to know him and serve him, that we may be acknowledged of him at the appearing of our Lord JESUS CHRIST, to whom with the Holy Ghost be all praise and thanksgiving. Amen.

The Translators to the Reader

Introduction Commending King James

Innovation Always Resisted

Zeal to promote the benefit of society, whether by producing something new or by improving that which already exists, certainly deserves much respect and esteem; nevertheless, the world grants it no better than an icy reception. Such zeal is greeted with suspicion rather than love, and with jealousy rather than thanks. If a benefactor of mankind leaves any point open to frivolous objection (and when no such opening exists the objectors will always make one), he is sure to be misrepresented, and he runs the risk of being condemned. Anyone who either knows history or has experience will quickly recognize this truth. Has anything new or improved ever been introduced without provoking storms of controversy? One would think that the ideals of civility, good government, education and communication, orderly assemblies for the administration of church affairs, and provision for the clergy (along with many other such things) would be so far beyond objection that no man would raise a hand nor would a dog move its tongue against those desiring to promote them. After all, civility distinguishes us from brute beasts who know nothing beyond their appetites. Good government bridles us and restrains us from offensive behavior and from injuring one another, whether by fraud or by violence. Education and communication enable us to inform and reform others by the knowledge and sensitivity we ourselves have gained, and ecclesiastical assemblies bring us together face to face so that we settle our differences sooner than we could do by writing books, which multiply themselves to infinity. Finally, provision for the clergy commends itself irresistibly to common sense and to conscience, for those who would deprive their pastors (from whom, ironically, they themselves receive their spiritual sustenance) are like a mother who, even worse than killing her child at the moment of birth, starves him to death over time. It is apparent, then, that these things of which we speak are most necessary and, therefore, that nobody can speak against them without absurdity or kick at them without branding himself an evil man.

In spite of all this, the learned know that certain worthy men have been brought to untimely death for no other fault than that of promoting civility by seeking to bring their countrymen to good order and discipline, that in some nations it was made a capital crime to introduce legislation nullifying an existing law, however harmful the existing law may have been, and that even some who wished to be known as pillars of the State and patterns of virtue and wisdom resisted for a long time pleas for temperate language in writing and in speech, as though wholesome words were like rocks at sea or boxes of poison. On the fourth point, it was no child but rather a great cleric who said (in writing, even, for the benefit of future generations) that he had not seen any good to come from any ecclesiastical assembly, but rather the contrary. He said it in passion, perhaps, but he said it just the same. Finally, it is widely known what a myth was invented against adequate provision for the clergy. At the time when the professors and teachers of Christianity in the church of Rome (which was then a true church) received generous wages, a voice was purportedly heard from heaven, saying, "Now is poison poured down into the Church . . . . " That this is nothing more than a fable is admitted even by the one who originated it, superstitious as he was, but the point remains that even the virtue of generosity toward ministers of the church has aroused vigorous resentment. So not only whenever we speak, as someone said, but also whenever we do anything noteworthy or significant, we subject ourselves to everyone's censure. To be only lightly tortured by tongues is the best one can hope for; to completely escape their snapping is impossible.

Resistance to Innovation Always Aimed at the Most Important People

Now if somebody imagines that this kind of thing happens only to unimportant people, and that kings are exempted by their high position, he is deceived. Just as "the sword devoureth as well one as another," as it says in Samuel, and, more to the point, as the great commander ordered his soldiers in a certain battle to strike at no part of the enemy except the face, and as the king of Syria commanded his chief captains to "fight neither with small nor great, save only with the king of Israel," so it is all too true, that envy strikes most spitefully at those of greatest beauty and at those of highest rank. David was an excellent king, whose early reign, at least, is peerless. Nevertheless one of the best things he ever did, bringing back the ark of God in dignity, earned him the scorn and scoffing of his own wife. Solomon was greater yet than David (in power though not in virtue), and by his power and wisdom he built for the Lord a temple so magnificent that it became not only Israel's glory but the wonder of the whole world. But did everyone appreciate his achievement? We doubt it. The contrary attitude manifests itself in the people's demand of his son: "Make the grievous servitude of thy father, and his sore yoke, lighter." Very likely he had burdened them with some taxes and tariffs, and the people had mounted a complaint and wished in their hearts that the temple had never been built. All this shows how difficult it is to please everyone, even when we please God most of all and seek to approve ourselves to everyone's conscience.

If we come down to later times, we will find many similar examples of this kind, or rather unkind, acceptance. The first Roman Emperor did nothing more pleasing to the scholars nor more beneficial to posterity, for maintaining historical records in proper chronology, than correcting the calendar and establishing the solar year. Yet this act brought him charges of novelty and arrogance, and he endured much abuse for it. Similarly the first Christian Emperor (first, at least, to profess the faith openly and allow others to do likewise), for strengthening the empire at great personal expense and for providing for the Church as he did, received as his thanks the epithet *Pupillus,* meaning a wasteful prince who needed a guardian to protect him from himself. Likewise the best of the Christian Emperors was viewed as a poor soldier and condemned for giving himself to ease and pleasure, all because he loved peace and went to war only when forced to do so. Those who viewed him so seemed ignorant that his aim was the prosperity not only of himself but also of his subjects and that he had proved himself quite formidable when provoked to combat. And what thanks did that most learned Emperor of former times (at least the greatest politician) receive for eliminating unnecessary laws and reducing the legal code to systematic order? His thanks was to be dubbed by some as an Epitomist, that is, one who destroyed whole volumes of excellent worth in order to create demand for his abridgements. This is the appreciation that has been rendered to excellent rulers in ages past, that their good deeds should be evil spoken of. Of course, neither envy nor hatefulness died and was buried with the ancient. No, no! Moses' reproof applies to nearly every generation: "Ye are risen up in your fathers' stead, an increase of sinful men." "What is it that hath been done? that which shall be done: and there is no new thing under the sun," the wise man says. Saint Stephen speaks likewise: "As your fathers did, so do ye."

King James's Firmness of Purpose

All this and more is well known to his Majesty that now reigns (and long, and long, may he reign, and his descendants forever, "Himself and children, and children's children always!"). His God-given wisdom along with his own rare attainments in learning and experience have taught him that whoever attempts anything for the public (especially if it touches on religion and deals with interpreting and explaining the Word of God) exposes himself as an object of every ill intent; indeed, he throws himself headfirst into the swords and spears, to be gored by every sharp tongue. For he that in any way touches the people's religion touches their custom, indeed, their personal domain, and even though they are discontent with the religion they have, yet they cannot bear the thought of change. Nevertheless his royal heart was not daunted or discouraged because of one blustering argument or another, but he stood resolute, "as a statue immoveable, and an anvil not easily to be beaten into plates," as somebody said. He knew who had chosen him to be a soldier, or rather a captain, and being certain that what he intended to do would greatly glorify God and build up His Church, he would not allow those plans to be thwarted by any of the speeches and schemes raised up against him. It is certainly the responsibility of kings (in fact, it is *especially* their responsibility) to pay attention to religion: to know it rightly, profess it zealously, and to promote it to the fullest extent of their ability. This is their glory before all well-meaning nations, and this will bring unto them a far more excellent weight of glory in the day of the Lord Jesus. For the Scriptures say not in vain, "Them that honour me I will honour"; neither was it a vain statement that Eusebius made long ago, that piety toward God was the weapon, in fact the *only* weapon, that both preserved Constantine's life and avenged him of his enemies.

Divine Power of Scripture

Scripture's Power Inherent in its Character

What piety is there, though, without truth? What truth, what saving truth is there without the Word of God? What Word of God is there, of which we may be certain, without the Bible? It is the Bible that we are commanded to search (John 5:39; Isa. 8:20). Those who searched and studied the Scriptures are commended (Acts 17:11; 8:28-29). Those who were unskillful in them, or slow to believe them, were rebuked (Matt. 22:29; Luke 24:25). The Scriptures can make us wise unto salvation (II Tim. 3:15). If we should be ignorant, they will instruct us; if lost, they will bring us home; if out of order, they will correct us; if sorrowful, comfort us; if sluggish, invigorate us; if cold, inflame us. *Tolle, lege; tolle, lege;* "Take up and read, take up and read" the Scriptures (for the command referred to the Bible), it was said unto Augustine by a supernatural voice. "Whatsoever is in the Scriptures, believe me," said the same Augustine, "is high and divine; there is verily truth, and a doctrine most fit for the refreshing and renewing of men's minds, and truly so tempered, that every one may draw from thence that which is sufficient for him, if he come to draw with a devout and pious mind, as true religion requireth." This is what Augustine said. And Jerome said, "Love the Scriptures, and wisdom will love thee." And Cyril said, against Julian, "Even boys that are bred up in the Scriptures become most religious . . . . " But why bother mentioning three or four uses of Scripture when they contain everything that we must believe, practice, and hope for? Or why quote three or four sentences from the Fathers, when everyone worthy of that title, from the time of Christ on, has written of both the riches and the perfection of the Scriptures? "I adore the fulness of the Scripture," said Tertullian against Hermogenes. And again, to Apelles, a heretic of the same sort, he said "I do not admit that which thou bringest in" (or concludest) "of thine own" (thinking or learning) apart from Scripture. Justin Martyr, earlier than Tertullian, speaks the same way: "We must know by all means," he says, "that it is not lawful" (or possible) "to learn" (anything) "of God or of right piety, save only out of the Prophets, who teach us by divine inspiration." And, after Tertullian, Basil also speaks the same way: "It is a manifest falling away from the faith, and a fault of presumption, either to reject any of those things that are written, or to bring in" (contrary to them) "any of those things that are" not written. We will refrain from citing to the same effect Cyril, Bishop of Jerusalem, in his fourth Catechism; Jerome against Helvidius; Augustine in his third book against the letters of Petilian and in numerous other places in his works. We will also refrain from descending to the later Fathers, in order not to weary the reader. Since the Scriptures are acknowledged to be so full and so perfect, how can we excuse our negligence if we do not study them, or our excessive curiosity if we are not content with them? Men exclaim about Iresine, how many sweet and pleasant things it had hanging on it; about the Philosopher's stone, that it turns copper into gold; about Cornucopia, that it contains all things necessary for food; about Panacea the herb, that it cures all diseases; about Catholicon the drug, that it purges the body of every harmful fluid; about Vulcan's armor, that it could not be penetrated by any thrust or blow, and so forth. Very well; what they falsely or vainly attributed to these things for physical good, we may properly and fully ascribe to the Scripture for spiritual good. It is not only an armor, but also a whole armory of weapons, both offensive and defensive, by which we may save ourselves and put the enemy to flight. It is not an herb, but a tree, indeed a whole paradise of trees of life, which bring forth fruit every month, whose fruit is good for food and whose leaves are good for medicine. It is not a pot of Manna or a jar of oil, which were good only for a remembrance (in the case of the Manna) or for a meal or two (in the case of the oil). Rather, the Scripture is, so to speak, a shower of heavenly bread sufficient for a whole multitude, no matter how great, and a whole cellar filled with barrels of oil by which all our needs may be met and, by selling some, our debts repaid. In a word, it is a pantry of wholesome food in exchange for moldy traditions, a pharmacy of antidotes to poisonous heresies, a compendium of sound legislation to restrain rebellious spirits, a treasury of most costly jewels rather than common rocks, and, finally, a fountain of purest water springing up unto eternal life. And should we be surprised? The Scriptures come from heaven, not from earth; the Author is God, not man; the composer is the Holy Spirit, not the intelligence of the apostles or prophets; the penmen had been set apart from the womb and filled with a special measure of God's Spirit; the subject matter is truth, piety, purity and uprightness; the form is God's Word, God's testimony, God's oracles, the word of truth, of salvation, and so forth. The Scripture grants enlightenment of mind, stability of conviction, repentance from dead works, newness of life, holiness, peace and joy in the Holy Spirit, and the goal and reward of studying it is fellowship with the saints, sharing in the divine nature, and the possession of "an inheritance immortal, undefiled, and that shall never fade away." Happy is the man that delights in the Scripture, and three times happy is the man who meditates in it day and night.

Scripture's Power Conveyed Through Translations

But how can men meditate on what they cannot understand? And how will they understand what is kept secret in a foreign language? as it is written, "Except I know the power of the voice, I shall be to him that speaketh a barbarian, and he that speaketh shall be a barbarian to me." The apostle makes no exceptions for any language; not for Hebrew, the most ancient, nor for Greek, with its vast vocabulary, nor for Latin, the most precise. Nature teaches a natural man to admit the obvious: in relation to languages which we do not know, we are deaf, and turning a deaf ear toward them is no fault. The Scythian thought the Athenian, whom he did not understand, a barbarian; the Roman thought the same of the Syrian and the Jew (even Jerome himself calls the Hebrew language barbarous, probably because it was foreign to so many); the Emperor of Constantinople took the same view toward the Latin tongue, despite the anger of Pope Nicholas at the insult. In the same way the Jews long before Christ called all other nations *Lognasim*, which is little better than barbarous. Therefore, just as someone complained that in the Senate of Rome somebody or another was always calling for an interpreter, so the Church, in order to avoid being driven to a similar extremity, must always have translations of the Bible readily available. Translation is the thing that opens the window to let in the light; it breaks the shell that we may eat the kernel; it draws aside the curtain that we may look into the most holy place; it uncovers the well and gives access to the water, just as Jacob rolled away the stone from the mouth of the well, enabling Laban's flocks to drink. In fact, in the absence of a translation into common language, the uneducated are no better off than children at Jacob's well (which was deep), having no bucket or anything with which to draw water. They are just the same as the one mentioned by Isaiah, who, when a sealed book was delivered to him with the request, "Read this, I pray thee," had to answer, "I cannot, for it is sealed."

History of Bible Translations

Greek Translations

When God wished to be known only in Jacob and to have his name great in Israel alone, while the dew lay only on Gideon's fleece and the rest of the ground was dry, then for a single people who all spoke the language of Canaan, that is, Hebrew, a single original in Hebrew was sufficient. But the time was coming when the Sun of righteousness, the Son of God, would come into the world, the one ordained by God to bring salvation by faith in his blood not to the Jews only, but also to the Greeks, and indeed to all who were scattered abroad. When this fulness of time drew near, behold, the Lord was pleased to stir up the spirit of a Greek prince (Greek by descent and language), Ptolemy Philadelph, king of Egypt, to have the book of God translated from Hebrew into Greek. This is the translation of the "Seventy" interpreters, commonly so called [known more widely today as the *Septuagint,* which is Latin for *seventy*], which prepared the way for our Savior among the Gentiles by written preaching, as John the Baptist did among the Jews with his voice. This happened because the Greeks, who esteemed education highly, were not content to allow valuable books to lie molding in kings' libraries. Rather, they put many of their servants, skilled scribes, to work at copying out such books in order to disseminate them widely. In addition, the Greek language was well known to most of the population of Asia as a result of the conquests made by the Greeks and the colonists they had sent abroad. For the same reasons Greek was also widely understood in much of Europe and even of Africa. So then the Word of God, translated into Greek, by that means becomes like a candle set on a candlestick, giving light to all that are in the house, or like a proclamation cried out in the marketplace, which most people immediately hear about. For this reason the Greek language was best vehicle for the Scriptures, to provide a witness both for the first preachers of the gospel to appeal to and also for the first hearers to consult in order to verify what they heard and to learn yet more. It is certain that the Septuagint was in some respects an unsound and imperfect translation, needing correction in many places. Who would have been as qualified for this work as the Apostles or their companions? Yet it seemed good to the Holy Spirit and to them to use the Bible commonly available (which was essentially true and sufficient) rather to make a new translation, an act which, in that new world and in that tender age of the Church, would have exposed them to much argument and opposition. To have made a new translation at that time would have appeared self-serving and, by putting the Apostles in the position of bearing witness to themselves, would have discredited their testimony. We may suppose that such reasons prompted the apostles' choice to approve the Septuagint for regular use. Nevertheless, though it was generally accepted, it did not fully satisfy the theologians, not even the Jewish ones. Not long after Christ, Aquila produced a new translation, and after him Theodotion did the same, and after him Symmachus; indeed, there was a fifth and a sixth translation, the authors of which are unknown. All these together made up the Hexapla, a work skillfully and usefully compiled by Origen. Yet the Septuagint remained dominant and for that reason not only was given the central position in Origen's Hexapla (because it was the best, as Epiphanius understands it) but also was used by the Greek Fathers as the basis for their commentaries on Scripture. Indeed, the just-mentioned Epiphanius thought so highly of it that he viewed its authors not only as translators but also as prophets to some extent, and Justinian the Emperor, giving a reason for commanding his Jewish subjects to use the Septuagint above the other translations, says that the Seventy were, so to speak, enlightened with prophetic grace. Even so, just as the Egyptians are said by the Prophet to be men and not God, and their horses to be flesh and not spirit, even so it is evident (and Jerome affirms as much) that the Seventy were translators, not prophets. They did many things well, as *scholarly* men, but yet as *men* they stumbled and fell, here through oversight and there through ignorance. Sometimes they observably added to the original while other times they omitted things; for this reason the Apostles often abandoned the Septuagint, where it abandoned the Hebrew, and proclaimed the meaning of the original according to the truth of the word, as the Spirit enabled them. This is enough said about the Greek translations of the Old Testament.

Latin Translations

Within a few centuries of the life of Christ, many Latin translations of the Bible were also made. This language was also well suited for disseminating the Law and the gospel, being understood throughout a great portion of the Roman empire, especially in the West. The Latin translations, though, were very numerous (Augustine says there is no way to count them all), and not all of them were good. Furthermore, because the Latin Old Testament was translated from the Greek instead of the Hebrew (comparable to drinking from a stream instead of its fountain), any muddiness in the Greek taints the Latin as well. This situation prompted Jerome, a most learned Father, and without a doubt the best linguist who had ever lived, to undertake a translation of the Old Testament out of the original Hebrew. He accomplished this task with such a display of scholarship, discernment, diligence, and accuracy that the Church of every succeeding generation owes him a debt of special remembrance and gratitude.

Other Translations

So it was that the Church was supplied with Greek and Latin translations, even before the Christian faith was generally embraced in the Empire (for the educated know that, even in Jerome's time, the Consul of Rome and his wife were both pagans, as were the majority of the Senate). Nevertheless, educated Christians were not content to have the Scriptures in languages which they alone could understand, just as the good lepers were not content to enjoy a good meal themselves, but informed their neighbors about the abundance of food God had provided, that they might share the benefit. In the same way, educated Christians provided translations into native languages in order to benefit and edify their less educated countrymen, who hungered and thirsted after righteousness and whose souls needed saving as much as those of the learned. As a result, most nations of the earth, shortly after their conversion, could hear Christ speaking to them in their native languages, not only by the voice of the preacher but also by the written word translated. If anyone doubts what we say, there are enough examples to satisfy him, if any number at all will do the job. First, Jerome says, "The Scripture being translated before in the languages of many nations shows that those things that were added [by the heretics Lucian or Hesychius] are false." This is Jerome's teaching in one passage. The same Jerome elsewhere affirms that, at one time, he had set forth the Septuagint "for the people of his own language," that is, for his countrymen of Dalmatia. That these words mean that Jerome translated the Scripture into the Dalmatian language was frankly admitted not only by Erasmus but also by Sixtus of Siena and by Alphonsus a Castro (to name but two), men with whom Catholics do not argue. Chrysostom, a contemporary of Jerome, gives further evidence, saying, "The doctrine of John did not in such sort [i.e., as the that of the philosophers did] vanish away, but the Syrians, Egyptians, Indians, Persians, Ethiopians, and infinite other nations, being barbarous people, translated it into their mother tongue and have learned to be true philosophers" (he means that they became Christians). To this we may add Theodoret, who comes just after Jerome both in time and in learning. These are his words: "Every country that is under the sun is full of these words [those of the apostles and prophets], and the Hebrew tongue [i.e., the Hebrew Scriptures] is turned not only into the language of the Greeks, but also of the Romans and Egyptians and Persians and Indians and Armenians and Scythians and Samaritans and, briefly, into all the languages that any nation uses." This is Theodoret's teaching. Similarly Ulfilas is reported by Paul the Deacon and Isidore, and before them by Sozomen, to have translated the Scriptures into Gothic; John, Bishop of Sevil, is said by Vasseus to have translated them into Arabic around A.D. 717; Bede is said by Cistertiensis to have translated much of them into Saxon. According to Trithemius, Efnard abridged the French Psalter (as Bede had done the Hebrew) about the year 800; King Alfred is said by the same Cistertiensis, to have translated the Psalter into Saxon; Methodius is said by Aventinus (printed at Ingolstadt) to have translated the Scriptures into Slavonic in about 900. Valdo, Bishop of Freising, is said by Beatus Rhenanus to have caused the gospels to be translated into Dutch rhyme at about the same time; this work may yet be found in the library of Corbinian. Several witnesses testify that Peter Waldo either himself translated or prompted someone else to translate the Bible into French about the year 1160; Charles V, surnamed "The Wise," is said to have sponsored another French translation about 200 years later, of which many copies still exist, according to Beroalde. At just about that time, in the days of our King Richard II, John Trevisa translated the Scriptures into English, and many handwritten English Bibles are still in use here and there, very likely translated during that period. Also the Syriac translation of the New Testament, published by Widmanstadt, is in the libraries of most scholars, and the Psalter in Arabic, translated by

Augustinus Nebiensis, is common. Postel affirms that in his travels he saw the gospels in Ethiopian, and Ambrose Thesius claims that the Indians have the Psalter, set forth by Potken using the Syriac alphabet. We conclude, then, that having the Scriptures in the language of the people is not a strange notion recently conceived, either by Lord Cromwell in England or by Lord Radziwill in Poland, or by Lord Ungnadius in Germany. Rather, it has been carefully considered and carried out since long ago, since the earliest conversion of any nation. It has been done, no doubt, because it was viewed as most beneficial in order to speed the growth of faith in men's hearts and to bring them to the point where they could say with the Psalmist, "As we have heard, so we have seen."

Roman Catholic Resistance

Now the church of Rome gives the appearance of finally having come to show a motherly affection toward her children by allowing them the Scriptures in the mother tongue. But it is a gift undeserving to be called a gift, a worthless gift. Before a Catholic may use the Scriptures, he must first get permission in writing, and to get that permission, he must prove himself qualified to the priest who hears his confessions. And the only ones qualifed are those who, if not frozen in the dregs, are at least fermented by the leaven of Catholic superstition. Nevertheless Clement VIII was unwilling to grant any permission to have the Scriptures in common language, and therefore he overruled and nullified the permission of Pius IV. The Catholics are so afraid of the light of the Scripture ("shunners of the light of the Scriptures," as Tertullian puts it) that they will not trust the people with it, not even as it is translated by their own sworn men, not even with the permission of their own bishops and inquisitors. In fact, they are so unwilling to communicate the Scriptures to people's understanding in any way that they shamelessly admit that we forced them to translate them into English against their wills. This confession seems to indicate that they have either a bad case or a bad conscience, or both. We are sure that it is not the person with good gold who is afraid to bring it to the touchstone, but the one with the counterfeit; not the honorable man who shuns the light, but the criminal; not the honest merchant who is unwilling to have his weights and measures tested, but the deceitful. But we will leave them alone for this fault and return to the matter of translation.

Defense of the Authorized Version Against Objections

Objections Listed

Many men have been talking for a long time (and have not yet been silenced), complaining about the translation (or rather the study of previous translations) so long in production. They ask why this is being done, why this work is necessary. "Has the church been deceived all this time?" they ask. "Has her sweet bread been mixed with leaven, her silver with dross, her wine with water, her milk with lime?" ("Lime mixes poorly with milk," said Irenaeus.) "We hoped that we were on the right road, that we had received the oracles of God, and that, though the rest of the world might have reason to be offended and to complain, we had none. Has the nursing mother offered her breast with nothing but wind in it? Have the Fathers of the Church given us bread that proves to be full of stones, as Seneca says? What does it mean to handle the Word of God deceitfully, if these men are not doing it?" This is how certain brethren are talking. We also hear some mocking, adversaries of God's work like Sanballat in Nehemiah, saying, "What do these weak Jews . . . ? Will they make the stones whole again out of the heaps of dust which are burnt? Although they build, yet if a fox go up, he shall even break down their stony wall." These mockers say, "Was their translation good before? Why are they now correcting it? Was it not good? Why then was it foisted upon the people? Indeed, why have the Roman Catholics always jeopardized their souls by refusing to hear it? Really, if it must be translated into English, the Catholics are best suited to do it. They are scholars; they know when something has been done well, and they know to leave well enough alone.

Protestant Objections Answered

We will answer both these groups briefly. The first group, since they are our brethren, we will answer with the words of Jerome: "Do we condemn the ancient? Certainly not; but, with an eye to the efforts of those who were before us in the house of God, we labor to the fullest extent of our ability." It is as though he said, "Being provoked by the example of the scholars who lived before me, I have considered it my duty to try to make my linguistic skills at least somewhat useful to God's church, lest my work in the languages should seem to be in vain and lest I should appear to glory in men above what they deserve, ancient and venerable as they may be." This is Jerome's attitude.

To the same effect we maintain that we in no way condemn any of the labors of those who preceded us in this sort of work, either in this land, or beyond the sea, either in King Henry's time or King Edward's (if there was any translation or revision in his time) or in the time of Queen Elizabeth of ever renowned memory. So far from condemning them, we in fact acknowledge that they were raised up by God to build and to provide for his Church and that they deserve to be held always in remembrance by us and by our children. The declaration of Aristotle is well known and worth considering: "Without Timotheus we would not have had such sweet music, but without Phrynis (Timotheus's teacher) we would not have had Timotheus." Therefore, those who break the ice and put into motion things that yield progress toward the saving of souls deserve our blessing and honor. Now what can be more effective toward that goal than to deliver God's book to God's people in a language which they understand? After all, a hidden treasure or a sealed fountain has no value (as Ptolemy Philadelph wrote to the Rabbis, or Jewish teachers, according to Epiphanius), and, as Augustine said, "A man would rather be with his dog than with someone who does not speak his language." We must also consider that nothing is begun and perfected at the same time and that later thoughts are thought to be wiser than earlier ones. So we are sure that nobody has any reason to disapprove of us for building upon the foundation laid by others and, with the help of their labors, improving upon what they did so well. Indeed, we feel sure that they, if they were still alive, would thank us. The vintage of Abiezer surpassed all rivals; nevertheless the gleaning of grapes of Ephraim was nothing to be despised (Judges 8:2). Joash the king of Israel was not satisfied until he had struck the ground three times; nevertheless he angered the prophet for stopping at that. Aquila, whom we mentioned earlier, translated the Bible as carefully and as skilfully as he could, yet he thought it good to go over it again; only then did the Jews sanction it as "accurately done," as Jerome witnesses. How many books of secular learning have been revised again and again, both by the same translators and by others? The single book of Aristotle's Ethics exists in no fewer than six or seven different translations. Now if this effort may be expended upon the gourd, which gives a little shade, flourishing today and being cut down tomorrow, what effort may we expend, indeed, what effort ought we *not* to expend upon the vine whose fruit makes man's conscience glad and whose stem abides forever? This vine, of course, is the Word of God, which we translate. "What is the chaff [worth in comparison] to the wheat? saith the Lord." "If glass is so precious, how much more so a genuine pearl!" said Tertullian. If a glass bauble is of such value to us, how ought we to value the true pearl! Therefore let no man resent his Majesty's generosity, and let no one be grieved that we have a King who seeks the increase of the spiritual wealth of Israel. Let Sanballats and Tobiahs do so, who therefore bear the rebuke they deserve, but let us rather thank God from the bottom of our heart for creating in our King this religious concern to have the translations of the Bible reviewed and examined with full and careful deliberation. For by this means it comes about that whatever is already sound (and all is substantially sound in at least one of the Protestant editions, the worst of which is far better than the Romanists' authorized English version) will, like gold, shine more brightly because of the rubbing and polishing. And if anything should be found awkward or unwarranted or out of keeping with the original, it may be corrected, and truth may take the place of error. What can the King command to be done that will bring him more true honor than this? And how could those who have been appointed to the task better demonstrate their duty to the King, even more, their obedience to God and love for His saints, than by offering their service, with all that is in them, for the carrying out of the work? But besides all this, these complainers were the main promoters of the translation; therefore they ought least to oppose it. Consider the facts of history. When his Majesty came to the throne, a conference was appointed at Hampton Court to hear the grievances of the Puritans, who earnestly requested a new translation of the Bible. When forced by reason to abandon every other basis for this request, they finally contrived the claim that they could not with good conscience subscribe to the *Book of Common Prayer*, because it confirms and preserves the Bible translation it contains, which, according to them, is full of mistakes. Even though this argument was judged to be a very poor and empty one, still, at that point his Majesty began to consider the good that might result from a new translation, and soon he gave order for this translation, which is now presented to you. We can hope that these facts will satisfy our brethren whose consciences are troubled by our work.

Catholic Objections Answered

No translation is unworthy to be called the Word of God.

To the second group, the mockers, we give this answer. We do not deny, in fact, we solemnly affirm that the very poorest translation of the Bible into English, set forth by men of Protestant conviction (for we have not yet seen a Catholic translation of the whole Bible) contains the Word of God; no, *is* the Word of God. This is just the same as the fact that a speech of the King in Parliament, when translated into French, Dutch, Italian, and Latin, is still the King's speech, even if it is not interpreted by each translator with equal refinement or perhaps with such stylistic beauty or such clarity of meaning in every passage. For it is commonly recognized that things are to be evaluated according to their overall character, and an ordinary man could say, as Horace has it, "Truly, when the splendors in a song are many, I will not complain about a few imperfections . . . . " A man may be considered virtuous in spite of having made many mistakes in his life (otherwise no one would be virtuous, for "in many things we offend all"), or he may be considered handsome and attractive in spite of having some warts on his hand or some freckles or even scars on his face. There is no reason, then, why a Scripture translation should be denied to be Scripture or be forbidden publication, even though some imperfections and blemishes may be apparent in the production of it. For what has ever been perfect under the sun, except where apostles or apostolic men (that is, men filled with an extraordinary measure of God's Spirit and privileged with infallibility) were involved? The Romanists, then, by refusing to hear and daring to burn translations of Scripture, did nothing less than insult the Spirit of grace, from whom the Scripture originally proceeded and whose sense and meaning, as well as human weakness would permit, the translations did express.

Consider an example or two. Plutarch writes that, after Rome had been burnt by the Gauls, they soon began to rebuild the city. But, in their haste, they did not lay out the streets or proportion the houses in the most attractive and convenient possible manner. Was Catiline then demonstrating honesty or patriotism when he tried to set the city on fire? Or was Nero a good prince for succeeding in burning it down? In the same way, we may gather from the story of Ezra and the prophecy of Haggai, that the temple built by Zerubbabel after the return from Babylon was not at all comparable to the former one, built by Solomon, for those who remembered the former temple wept when they looked upon the latter. Should Zerubbabel's temple then have been either forsaken by the Jews or profaned by the Greeks? We should take the same view toward translations. The Septuagint differs from the original Hebrew in many places, and it comes nowhere near it with respect to clarity, dignity, and majesty. Yet which of the apostles condemned it? Condemn it? No, indeed! They used it (as is obvious, and as Jerome and most Bible scholars agree), something they would not have done, nor would they have set an example that honored it and commended it to the church, if it had been unworthy to be called the Word of God.

The value of a translation does not depend on the translator's theological convictions.

Now the Catholics' second defense for vilifying and abusing the English translations of the Bible (or of some portion of it) which they encounter is that the translators were, of all things, heretics (they call us heretics for the same reason that they call themselves Catholics, and they are wrong on both counts). This claim astonishes us, and we wonder what kind of theology taught them to think like this! We are sure that Tertullian thought otherwise, "Do we approve men's beliefs based on their place in the world, or do we approve their place in the world based on their beliefs?" Certainly we should do the latter. Augustine thought otherwise, for when he came across a helpful set of rules for interpreting the Bible, rules authored by a Donatist named Tychonius, he was not ashamed to make use of them. In fact, he put them into his own book, commending them to the extent that they deserved commendation; they are in his third book "Of the Teachings of Christ." To keep things brief, Origin and the whole Church of God for several hundred years thought otherwise, for consider how they treated the Greek translation of Aquila, a proselyte to Judaism, and those of Symmachus and Theodotion, both of whom were Ebionites, adherents to a vile heresy. Far from treading these translations under foot, let alone from burning them, they put them together with the original Hebrew and the Septuagint (as the earlier mention of Epiphanius suggested) and published them openly to be examined and studied by everyone. But we are wearing out the unlearned, who do not need to know so much, and annoying the learned, who know it already.

Catholics Revise Their Work No Less than Protestants.

Nevertheless, before we stop we must answer a third complaint and objection of the Catholics against us, that we revise and correct our translations so often. In this matter they treat us harshly and strangely indeed. For who was ever charged with a fault (by the wise, that is) for going over what he had done and correcting it where he saw good reason to do so? Augustine was not afraid to exhort Jerome to a *palinodia,* that is, a recantation. The same Augustine was not ashamed to retract, or perhaps more accurate, to revoke, many things that he had earlier approved, and he even takes pride in the fact that he can recognize his faults. If we wish to be sons of the truth, we must give heed to what the truth says, and we must trample upon our own reputation, and even upon that of other men, if either should in any way present a hindrance to it. This is our answer to the complaint itself. But to the persons we say, that, of all men, they ought to be most silent in this case. For what differences do they have, and what changes have they made, not only in their service books, hymnals, and breviaries, but also in their Latin translation? The service book reputed to have been produced by Ambrose (*Officium Ambrosianum*) was widely used and especially popular for a long time. But Pope Adrian, calling a council with the aid of Charles the Emperor, abolished it. In fact, he burned it, and he commanded the service book of Gregory to be used exclusively. Very well; *Officium Gregorianum* then becomes the standard, but does it continue without change or revision? No; the Roman service itself was of two kinds, the new and the old, and some churches used one while others used the other. Pamelius, a Catholic, reflects this situation in his preface to *Micrologus*. The same Pamelius reports that in about A.D. 1277, according to Radulphus de Rivo, Pope Nicholas III removed the more ancient service books from the churches of Rome and brought into use the missals of the Friars Minorites, commanding them to be used in that city. This change was so thorough that, when the above-named Radulphus happened to be at Rome about a hundred years later, he found all the service books to be of the new type. But do not suppose that this chopping and changing took place only in earlier ages; it has also happened recently. Pius V himself admits that nearly every diocese had a unique kind of service, quite different from the service of others. This situation prompted him to establish and authorize the breviary that he produced himself in 1568, abolishing all others with no regard to their antiquity or to the fact that they enjoyed official sanction and publication. Now when the Father of their Church, who would gladly heal the sore of the daughter of his people softly and slightly, and make the best of it, finds so much fault with the children for their differences and conflicts, we suspect that the children have no great reason to brag about their uniformity. But their particular charge against us is not that we have changed at all, but rather that the changes are substantial and that we make them so often. Let us see, then, whether our accusers themselves are faultless in this respect (if correcting may be considered a fault) and whether they are fit to throw stones at us. Somebody wrote, "O greater madman, may you come, at last, to spare a less," which is to say that those who are less sound themselves ought not to make accusations about the infirmities of others. If we should tell them that Valla, Stapulensis, Erasmus, and Vives found fault with the Latin Vulgate and consequently wanted it to be either revised or replaced with a new translation, they would answer, perhaps, that we have called their enemies as witnesses against them. (We observe, though, that they were enemies only in the sense in which Paul was the Galatians' enemy, for telling them the truth; they would have done well to tell it to them more clearly and more often!) But what will they say to the fact that Pope Leo X, by his apostolic letter and bull, approved Erasmus' translation of the New Testament, even though it was so much different from the Vulgate? What will they say to the fact that the same Leo exhorted Pagnine to translate the whole Bible and that he bore all the expenses necessary for the work? Surely, just as the apostle argues to the Hebrews, that "If the former Law and Testament had been sufficient, there had been no need of the latter," so we may point out that if the Vulgate had been acceptable at every point, there would have been little reason to go to the work and expense of producing a new Latin Bible. Perhaps the Catholics would respond that this was simply the private opinion of one Pope, who consulted no one else on the matter. But we can go further and maintain that many of their most important men, of all sorts (including their champions at Trent, Paiva and Vega, their inquisitor Hieronymus ab Oleastro, their Bishop Isidorus Clarius, and their Cardinal Thomas a vio Cajetan), either make new translations themselves, or use new translations made by others, or point out the Vulgate's awkwardness. None of them fear to disagree with it or to contradict it. Do they call this a consistent state of the text itself and of opinion about the text, when so many of their leaders reject the currently popular notion? But, indeed, we will probe yet closer to the nerve. Does not their Paris edition differ from the Lovain, and that of Hentenius from both of those, and yet all of them have official approval? Indeed, does not Sixtus V maintain that certain Catholics (he means those on his own side) were so taken with the idea of translating the Scriptures into Latin that, although they had no such intent, Satan took advantage of them and did what he could to create such confusion out of so great a variety of translations that nothing in the Bible seemed to be left firm and certain? Yet further, did not the same Sixtus establish by an inviolable decree, supported by the advice and consent of his Cardinals, that the Latin version of the Old and New Testament which the council of Trent determined should be official is undeniably the one which he published at that time, carefully corrected and printed in the Vatican press? This is what Sixtus writes in the preface before his Bible. And yet Clement VIII, the very next Pope of any importance, publishes another version of the Bible, containing innumerable differences from that of Sixtus, many of which are weighty and substantial, and yet this must be the official version at any cost. What does it mean to "have the faith of our glorious Lord Jesus Christ with yea and nay," if this is not it? And what good is "sweet harmony and consent" if this is it? Therefore, as Demaratus of Corinth advised a great King to resolve his domestic quarrels before addressing the strife among the Greeks (for at that time his queen and his son were his mortal enemies), even so, until our enemies themselves stop making so many versions of the Bible with such great differences between them, and stop quarreling so much about the value and authority of these versions, they cannot fairly challenge us for revising and correcting.

Purposes and Procedures Underlying the Authorized Version

Improvement upon Existing Good Translations

But it is high time to change the subject from our enemies to a brief discussion of our own plans and procedures for examining and surveying the Bible. In all honesty, good Christian Reader, we have never intended, from the beginning, to make a new translation, or even to turn a bad one into a good one (for then the accusation of Sixtus would have been true to some degree, that our people had been fed with the bile of dragons instead of wine, with pus instead of milk). Rather, our intent has been to make a good translation better, or to combine many good ones into one foremost good one, a translation against which no one could object with any fairness; this has been the goal toward which we have labored. To that end there were many chosen who were greater in other men's esteem than in their own and who sought the truth rather than their own praise. Furthermore, they came to the work, not as men seeking to gain skill in the field, but as men highly skilled, or at least thought to be so. For the head overseer and supervisor under his Majesty, to whom not only we but also our whole Church was much indebted, knew in his wisdom what Nazianzen also taught so long ago, that to teach first and to learn later is to turn things backward, and that "to learn pottery by making a wine jar," that is, to build skill by undertaking a task requiring professional expertise, is neither commendable for the workman nor safe for the work. Therefore men were sought out who could say modestly with Jerome, "We have learned Hebrew in part, and we have also been exercised in the Latin language almost from our very cradle." (Jerome makes no mention of the Greek language, in which

he also excelled, because he did not translate the Old Testament from
the Greek but from the Hebrew.) And with what attitude did these
men come together? With confidence in their own knowledge or in
the exactness of their reasoning or in the depth of their understanding?
In other words, did they trust in the arm of flesh? They certainly did
not. They trusted in Him who has the key of David, who opens and
no man shuts; they prayed to the Lord, the father of our Lord, just
like Augustine did: "O let thy Scriptures be my pure delight; let me
not be deceived in them, neither let me deceive by them." With this
confidence and in this devotion they assembled together. There were
not too many of them, to minimize inconvenience and conflict, yet
there were many, to insure adequate attention to detail. Regarding
the texts they had in front of them, they had the Hebrew text of the
Old Testament and the Greek of the New. These are the two golden
pipes, or rather channels, through which the olive branches empty
themselves into the golden candlestick. Augustine calls them precedent,
or original languages; Jerome calls them fountains. The same Jerome
affirms, and Gratian did not refrain from putting it into his decree,
that "As the credit of the old books [he means the books of the Old
Testament] is to be tried by the Hebrew volumes, so of the new by
the Greek tongue [he means by the original Greek]." If truth is to be
tested by these languages, then from what other languages should a
translation be made? Therefore these are the Scripture texts we set
before us from which to translate, since they are the languages in
which God was pleased to speak to his Church by his Prophets and
Apostles. We have not run through our task with the wild haste that
characterized the Septuagint translators, if the tradition that they
finished their work in seventy-two days is true. Neither were we
forbidden or hindered from revising our first draft, in contrast to
Jerome, assuming that what he says is true, that as soon as he wrote
anything it was immediately snatched from him and published,
without his having a chance to revise it. Neither, to be short, were we
the first ones to undertake a translation of the Bible into English and
therefore destitute of previous examples, in contrast to Origen, of
whom it is written that he was in a sense the first one to attempt the

writing of commentaries on the Bible, and therefore it is no surprise if he made many mistakes. But none of these things characterized our work. The translation was not thrown together in seventy-two days; rather it has cost the laborers (as light as the labor seemed) the trouble of twice seven times seventy-two days, and more. Maturity is better than speed in carrying out matters of such importance and consequence, for a man engaged in a weighty project does not fear being blamed for taking an appropriate amount of time. We did not hesitate to consult other translations or commentaries, whether in Aramaic, Hebrew, Syriac, Greek, or Latin, or in the modern languages: Spanish, French, Italian, or Dutch. Neither did we think our work too good to revise, so we brought back to the anvil that which we had already hammered. So, availing ourselves of every help that we needed, and neither fearing reproach for slowness nor coveting praise for speed, we have finally, through the good hand of the Lord upon us, brought the work to the result that you see.

Marginal Notes on Alternate Readings

Some people perhaps wish to have no marginal notes giving alternate readings, fearing that such a display of uncertainty might to some extent shake the authority of the Scriptures for settling controversies. But we think their judgment is not entirely sound on this point. For, although "whatsoever things are necessary are manifest," as Chrysostom says, and, according to Augustine, "in those things that are plainly set down in the Scriptures all such matters are found, that concern faith, hope, and charity," nevertheless it cannot be denied that God has been pleased, in his divine providence, to scatter here and there words and sentences of such difficulty and uncertainty that we do better to respond to them with fearfulness than with confidence. Of course, we need not fear that such uncertainties affect doctrinal points concerning salvation, for we have already quoted authorities maintaining that the Scriptures are clear on these things; nevertheless in less important matters there are difficulties regarding which, if we wish to decide anything, we do best to decide to be moderate along with Augustine, who said (though not regarding exactly the same situation, yet using the same reasoning), "It is better to make doubt of those things which are secret than to strive about those things that are uncertain." It seems that God has put these uncertainties into the Scripture, partly to exercise and to sharpen our minds, partly to teach inquisitive people not to look down upon the Scripture as being so clear on every point that it contains no challenge, partly also to arouse our devotion to plead for the assistance of God's Spirit by prayer, and finally, that we might be eager to seek help from our brethren by conferring with them, and that we might never scorn those who in some areas do not fully measure up to what they should be, since we ourselves are deficient in many respects. There are many words in the Bible that appear only once (having neither brother nor neighbor, as the Hebrews say) so that we can get no help with their meaning by comparing contexts. Similarly, there are many rare names of certain birds, beasts, precious stones, and other things concerning which the opinion of the Hebrews themselves is so divided that they seem to have defined this or that more because they wished to say something than because they were sure of what they said, as Jerome somewhere says regarding the Septuagint. Now, in a case like that, is it not a good thing for a marginal note to warn the reader that further study is necessary and that he should not conclude or dogmatize closed-mindedly on this or that? For just as the doubting of things that are evident is the fault called unbelief, in the same way to claim certainty about things which the Spirit of God has left questionable, even in the judgment of competent judges, can be nothing less than presumption. Therefore, as Augustine says that a variety of translations helps one to discover the meaning of the Scriptures, just the same, marginal notations of various possibilities of significance and meaning must do good. Indeed, we are persuaded, they are necessary. We know that Sixtus V explicitly forbids any alternate readings from the Vulgate to be put in the margin (which, though it does not match our case exactly, yet it tends in the same direction), but we suspect that he does not have all the Catholics behind him regarding this position. Those who are wise would rather have freedom to decide among alternative readings than to be captive to one, when the other may be correct. If they were sure that their high priest had all laws under lock in his own breast, as Paul II bragged, and that his special privilege rendered his reliability as absolute as Roman law rendered a dictator's authority, it would be a different matter. In that case, his word would be a divine utterance, his opinion a decision. But the eyes of the world are now open, thank the Lord, and have been for a long time. People have discovered that he is subject to the same passions and infirmities that others are and that his skin is not impenetrable; therefore, they acknowledge and embrace what he can prove, not what he merely claims.

Variety in Word Choice

Another thing we think you need to know, gentle reader, is that we have not tied ourselves to a uniformity of phrasing or to a consistent equivalence of words, as some perhaps may wish we had done, observing that some scholarly men somewhere have been as exact as they could in that matter. Now in fact, in order to avoid varying from the sense of what we had translated earlier, if a word before us signified the same thing as in the earlier passage (for there are some words that do not mean the same thing in every context) we fulfilled our duty by being especially careful and conscientious. But we did not follow the notion that we should always express the same idea with the same particular word, as, for example, that once we translated a Hebrew or Greek word by "purpose" we should never call it "intent"; once we used "journeying" never "travelling"; once we used "think" never "suppose"; once we used "pain," never "ache"; once we used "gladness," never "joy," and so on. We thought that to reduce the matter of word choice to such a mechanical exercise would smack more of fastidiousness than wisdom and that it would do more to breed scorn in the atheist than to bring profit to the godly reader. After all, has the kingdom of God become words and syllables? Why should we be in bondage to them if we may be free? Why should we rigidly restrict ourselves to one word when we may profitably use another one that is no less fitting? A godly Father, in the early days of the Church, became very angry that an innovator called a *krabbaton* [the Greek word for a cot-like bed] a *skimpous,* though there is little or no difference, and another reports that he was greatly abused for changing *cucurbita* (the reading to which the people had been accustomed) to *hedera* [Latin plant names]. Now, if this happened in better times than ours, and over such small issues, we might justly fear severe rebuke if we were to make a large number of unnecessary changes in wording. We might also be charged (by scoffers) with treating a great number of good English words unfairly. For, as it is written about a certain great Philosopher, that, in his opinion the logs fashioned into images for worship were better off than their neighbors who, though equally good, lay as blocks behind the fire, even so if we should say, as it were, to certain words, "Stand up higher; we will use you regularly in the Bible," and to others of equal quality, "Get out of here; be banished forever," we might perhaps be labeled with the words of James, "to be partial in ourselves, and judges of evil thoughts." Consider further that to quibble about words has always been seen as just a step away from deception, and it is the same with fussiness over names. And there is no better example for us to follow in our literary style than God himself. Since in his holy Scriptures he freely uses a variety of words to stand for one idea, we, if we will not be over-scrupulous, may take the same liberty in our English translations from Hebrew and Greek, in view of the abundant supply that he has given us. Finally, we have on the one hand avoided the distrustfulness of the Puritans, who repudiate the old Ecclesiastical words in favor of others, as when they use "washing" in place of "baptism" and "congregation" in place of "church," and on the other hand we have shunned the obscurity of the Catholics with their "azumes," "tunike," "rational," "holocausts," "prepuce," "pasche," and many similar things, of which their recent translation is full. The Catholics have done this intentionally, in order to obscure the meaning so that, even though they are forced to translate the Bible, yet, by the language they use, they may keep it from being understood. But we desire that the Scripture may speak like itself, as in the language of Canaan, so that it may be understood even by the most common people.

Concluding Warning Against
Rejection and Neglect

We might give you warning of many other things, gentle Reader, if we had not already exceeded the limits of a preface. It remains only for us to commend you to God, and to the Spirit of his grace, which is able to build beyond what we can ask or think. He removes the scales from our eyes and the veil from our hearts, opening our minds that we may understand his word, enlarging our hearts and even correcting our emotions that we may love it more than gold and silver, and that we may love it to the end. You are brought to fountains that you did not have to dig; do not dump dirt into them, with the Philistines, and do not prefer broken pits over them, with the wicked Jews. Others have labored, and you may benefit from their labors. Oh, do not receive such great things in vain; oh, do not despise so great salvation! Do not be like pigs, treading under foot such precious things; neither be like dogs, tearing and abusing what is holy. Do not say to our Savior with the Gergasites, "Depart out of our coasts," and do not, with Esau, sell your birthright for a mess of pottage. If light has come into the world, do not love darkness more than light; if you are offered food and clothing, do not go naked and starve yourselves. Remember the advice of Nazianzene: "It is a grievous thing (or dangerous) to neglect a great fair, and to seek to make markets afterwards" and the encouragement of Chrysostom: "It is altogether impossible that he that is sober (and watchful) should at any time be neglected." Finally, heed the warning and threat of Augustine: "They that despise God's will inviting them shall feel God's will taking vengeance of them." It is a fearful thing to fall into the hands of the living God, but it is a blessed thing, and it will bring us to everlasting blessedness in the end, to listen when God speaks to us, to read his word when he sets it before us, and, when he stretches out his hand and calls, to answer, "Here am I, here are we to do thy will, O God." May the Lord create within us a concern and a conscience to know him and serve him, that we may be acknowledged by him at the appearing of our Lord JESUS CHRIST, to whom, with the Holy Spirit, may all praise and thanks be given. Amen.

Endnotes

[1] The Translators to the Reader: The Original Preface of the King James Version of 1611 Revisited. Erroll F. Rhoads and Liana Lupas, eds. New York: American Bible Society, 1997.

Questions

1. According to the KJV translators, why is Bible translation necessary?

2. What two translations do the KJV translators single out as especially important? Why?

3. According to the ancient writers quoted by the KJV translators, who first translated the Bible or portions of it into these languages?

     a. Arabic
     b. Dalmatian
     c. English
     d. French
     e. Gothic
     f. Saxon
     g. Slavonic

4. What body did the KJV translators condemn for its opposition to providing Scripture in the common tongues?

5. What three important principles of translations did the KJV translators discuss in response to their opponents?

6. What did the KJV translators emphasize as the basis of their translation?

7. How did they characterize their work in contrast to the Septuagint translators, Jerome, and Origen?

8. Explain why the KJV translators included possible alternate meanings of some words in marginal notes.

9. Give examples cited by the KJV translators for the situation in question 8.

10. What goal did the KJV translators attempt to achieve by avoiding the extremes of the Puritans and Catholics?

CHAPTER 11

TRANSLATION PRINCIPLES AND ISSUES

For a number of years now an increasingly large number of modern English translations of the New Testament have appeared that differ considerably from the time-honored-standard of the King James Version. These changes can result from any combination of four factors:

1. manuscript basis
2. language development
3. translation methods and goals
4. theological bias

The most controversial factor is the differing Greek text underlying modern versions of the New Testament. Almost without exception, modern translations reflect a text closer to the 1881 Greek text which Westcott and Hort edited than to the Textus Receptus, which Desiderius Erasmus edited in 1522. Since the Textus Receptus is the basis for our beloved King James Version, every English version based on the Westcott-Hort Greek text will naturally share differences from the KJV at these points.

In spite of all the uproar, our first five chapters stressed that these differences affect very few passages and never affect doctrine.

Why then do some versions seem so different than others? This chapter will explore the other three reasons given above.

Language Development

Some variations between translations trace directly to changes in meanings of English words since the seventeenth century. Every language develops (or decays) over the centuries so that some words and phrases become obsolete and are replaced with new ones.

Most of us have heard that the word *conversation* as used in the KJV means *conduct* or *lifestyle*. Did the KJV translators mess up? Not at all. If you check the *Old English Dictionary* to see what the word *conversation* meant in 1611, you will find that its meaning at that time included the manner of lifestyle. In following centuries, people quit using the term to refer to actions, and it has come to refer strictly to speech. It would be wrong to read words from one time period with meanings derived from another. One must read an author's words using the meanings he intended according to his time period.

In fact, you will be hard pressed to make any sense of this verse from an English version of 950 A.D. It is impossible to read the verse using modern meanings because the words are not part of English anymore.

> Sothlice, up sprungenre sunnan, hie adrugodon and forscruncon, for thaem the hie naefdon wyrtruman.

You might not recognize Matthew 13:6 as English, but it is from the Wessex Gospels, the oldest surviving translation of the Gospels in English. English has changed drastically in the intervening millennium.

As with the Wessex Gospels, there will also come a time when few will understand the KJV. Indeed, some day Elizabethan English will seem to be a foreign language, and only scholars who study its literature will understand it. In fact, even today, very few people who promote the KJV 1611 actually use it because it is already quite difficult to read. The current edition of the KJV dates from 1769 and is not as difficult (due to extensive spelling corrections and corrections of wording in at least eight passages).[1]

It is possible, then, for the translators of 1611 to have done a very good job of translation and yet for the wording to confuse modern readers. As already mentioned, a person today may read Hebrews 13:5-7 and think it is a command to speak wholesome words, when in reality the command encompasses all that we say and do. Using our modern knowledge of English to read Elizabethan English leaves us open to making mistakes in understanding the Word of God without even knowing it. This is why the KJV translators themselves stressed the importance of up-to-date translations. Refer back to their own words presented in Chapter 10.

As another example, the word *corn* in the KJV refers to grain in general and especially wheat. The word referred to grain in Elizabethan English and still has this meaning in England. However, in American English the word has changed its meaning to refer to Indian corn or maize. Maize is a New World crop and did not reach Europe before the time of Columbus. It was certainly unheard of in Bible times in the Middle East. The KJV translators used a proper and good translation that is still used in some modern versions in England, but it is easily misunderstood by Americans. When Americans use the word *corn*, they never mean wheat. This reflects a tendency for such words to narrow in meaning from general to specific over time in living languages (other examples include *prevent, study,* and *published*).

In other words, frequently differences between older versions and modern versions are superficial. When you see the words *conduct* and *grain* in a modern version instead of *conversation* and *corn*, there is no contradiction between that version and the KJV. Instead, the version is identifying the meaning intended by the KJV translators. Such issues are neither manuscript issues nor issues about how to translate a word, they are simply evidence of changing usage of English words.

Two responses to this are possible. One is to continue to use the time-tested and beautiful poetic language of the KJV and to simply keep in mind words like *conversation* and *corn* that have changed meaning. This may require investing in an *Old English Dictionary* to check before criticizing a modern version that seems to read differently. It is essential that we properly understand what God says in His Word. It is also not difficult since only a few dozen words have changed meaning. The other possible response is to obtain a more modern version. It is noteworthy that the King James translators themselves recommended this in their translators' preface (see chapter 10). Chapter 12 will address this issue in more detail.

What is Translating?

Greek manuscripts are not the main cause of differences among translations, and even language development accounts for only a few dozen differences. The primary reason for differences among versions is that the translators themselves hold to different philosophies of translation and use different methods to achieve different purposes in their translations. To understand these differences requires some grounding in the processes of translating. To begin with, consider some processes that fall short of translating.

Transliteration

Below are the words from the Greek **text** of 1 Thessalonians 1:8. They will look strange to anyone who has not studied Greek.

ἀφ' ὑμῶν γὰρ ἐξήχηται ὁ λόγος τοῦ κυρίου
οὐ μόνον ἐν τῇ Μακεδονίᾳ καὶ [ἐν τῇ] 'Αχαΐᾳ,
ἀλλ' [καὶ] ἐν παντὶ τόπῳ ἡ πίστις ὑμῶν ἡ πρὸς
τὸν θεὸν ἐξελήλυθεν, ὥστε μὴ χρείαν ἔχειν
ἡμᾶς λαλεῖν τι.

If we substitute letters from the English alphabet which
correspond to each of these Greek letters, we obtain a
transliteration (transfer of letters). The transliteration of the
text above follows.

aph' humōn gar exēchētai ho logos tou kuriou ou
monon en tē Makedonia kai en tē Achaia all' [kai] en panti
topō hē pistis humōn hē pros ton theon exelēluthen,
hōste mē chreian echein hē mas lalein ti.[2]

The transliteration looks much more like English, because you
can now sound out the **phonetic** sounds. However, it still carries
no meaning for the English reader.

You will find some words transliterated in the Bible such as
Talitha cumi in Mark 5:41. Christ spoke that phrase in Aramaic,
and Mark preserved the exact words rather than translating them.
Greeks who did not know Aramaic needed to have the letters
converted from Aramaic to their own Greek letters before they
could pronounce the word for themselves. Transliteration is used
in some isolated cases like this when the event carried so much
drama or significance that the writer considered it important to
preserve the original sounds (often with the translated meaning
following). Transliteration is helpful for Bible study to aid the use
of reference works that refer to the Greek when the reader lacks
knowledge of the original languages. Transliteration clearly falls far
short of translation.

Glosses

To make a text meaningful, a translator must convey more than the mere sounds and letters from one language to another. One step beyond transliterating a text is to gloss each word. A word used in one language as an equivalent for a word in another language is called a **gloss**. Instead of substituting letter for letter, glossing substitutes word for word. Consider the previous verse with a gloss written below each word.

ἀφ' ὑμῶν γὰρ ἐξήχηται   ὁ λόγος τοῦ
from you for out has been sounded the word of the

κυρίου οὐ μόνον ἐν τῇ Μακεδονίᾳ καὶ [ἐν τῇ] Ἀχαΐᾳ,
Lord not only in the Macedonia and [in the] Achaia,

ἀλλ' [καὶ] ἐν παντὶ τόπῳ ἡ πίστις ὑμῶν ἡ πρὸς
but [also] in every place the faith of you the toward

τὸν θεὸν ἐξελήλυθεν, ὥστε μὴ χρείαν ἔχειν
the God went out, so that not need to have

ἡμᾶς λαλεῖν τι.
us to speak anything.

Even though we replaced each word with its meaning, the sentence makes little sense in English. The process of glossing stresses **vocabulary,** or word meaning. Anyone who has studied a foreign language knows that there is more to understanding a language than simply substituting equivalent English words. Vocabulary is only one element of language.

Another aspect of language involves **grammar,** which denotes the system for producing sentences in a given language. Making a sentence requires understanding how to correctly combine parts of speech (nouns, verbs, etc.). While a person can speak without knowing which words are nouns and which are verbs, he cannot convey meaning without putting the right ones in the right places.

Proper grammar keeps us from saying, "I gave gifts to they." In this example, the form them is required rather than they because it is an indirect object. The word *they* is the proper form for a subject. Such differences in form "signal" an indirect object in English. This is also quite important in languages like Greek where each function of a noun requires a different ending, called an **inflection**, to exhibit proper grammar.

It should be clear from this example that what can be said with one word in one language may require two or more words in its translation to another language. The single Greek verb ἐξήχηται (exēchētai) was glossed by the words "out has been sounded." The prefix means *out*, and the inflection on the verb signals the past tense and passive voice among other things (it could be translated "*it* has been sounded out" if the subject had not been clarified later in the sentence). Similarly, the two English words "to them" would be required to translate the single noun αὐτοῖς (autois) with its correct inflection.

Consider the text again as we revise the glosses to more fully account for such points of grammar. Typical **interlinear** (referring to meanings *between the lines* of text) translations employ such glosses.

ἀφ' ὑμῶν γὰρ ἐξήχηται   ὁ λόγος τοῦ
From you for has been sounded forth the word of the

κυρίου οὐ μόνον ἐν τῇ Μακεδονίᾳ καὶ [ἐν τῇ] Ἀχαΐα,
Lord not only in   Macedonia and [in]   Achaia,

ἀλλ' [καὶ] ἐν παντὶ τόπῳ ἡ πίστις ὑμῶν ἡ πρὸς
but [also] in every place faith your toward

τὸν θεὸν ἐξελήλυθεν, ὥστε μὴ χρείαν ἔχειν
God went out, so that no need have

ἡμᾶς λαλεῖν τι.
we to speak anything.

This is much better, but it remains awkward. There is still more to language than vocabulary and grammar processes.

Translation

In English, we rely on word order rather than word form (inflection) to carry the meaning of the text. Thus the three words, "loved," "Carol," and "Joe," do not communicate to us until we place them into a certain order. The two sentences that can be formed differ significantly. We can make the words say, "Joe loved Carol" or "Carol loved Joe." In Greek, the sense of the sentence can be conveyed regardless of the word order since the inflected form of "Joe" and "Carol" will determine which is the subject and which the object. Paying careful attention to the order of words is the process of **syntax**. As indicated, Greek and English often employ a different syntax.

Returning to our text, we will now consider syntax as we gloss the words. Notice that the glosses are the same as used in the interlinear passage, but they are rearranged with normal English syntax. This produces a clear translation of the verse.

> For from you the Word of the Lord has been sounded forth
> not only in Macedonia and [in] Achaia, but in every place
> your faith toward God went out so that we have no need to
> speak anything.

Although this is a reasonably accurate translation, it is not the only possible one. Notice that the King James Version casts this verse into only a slightly more poetic form:

> For from you sounded out the word of the Lord not only in
> Macedonia and Achaia, but also in every place your faith to
> God-ward is spread abroad; so that we need not to speak
> anything. I Thessalonians 1:8, KJV

Translating from one language to another is a highly complex task, and views abound concerning how to best handle all the factors involved. These various translation views will be addressed next.

While transliteration, glosses, and interlinears are useful tools for translators, none qualify as a translation. A translator must consider vocabulary, grammar, and syntax. If any of these are ignored, the result is not a translation.

A **translation**, then, is a conversion of meaning (not just sounds) from one language into another in light of the vocabulary, grammar, and syntax of both languages.

Translation Issues

Bible translation offers even greater hurdles than translating from Spanish to English. People studying Spanish use a similar alphabet, and easily understand the culture which has much in common with modern America (history of Western civilization, modern technology, etc.). However, the Biblical languages lack these similarities to English. The Bible comes from the Middle East and requires the reader to understand its culture patterns, some of which are more similar to Oriental patterns than American. Further, it was written in ancient times, and the culture had no thought of modern technology.

Translators strive to convert the vocabulary, grammar, and syntax into English but must simultaneously make decisions regarding other issues as well. In spite of the complexities of languages, any detail of any language in any text can be translated (or at least explained). However, as Carson notes, "they cannot all be translated in the same way and in the same limited space as in the donor text."[3] Three key areas with which translators must wrestle in their task involve discourse, style, and cultural elements.

Discourse

We have seen that sentences must be translated as a whole unit. However, if each sentence is translated without attention to neighboring sentences and context, The paragraph may not make much sense. When the translator concerns himself with issues broader than a sentence (paragraph, chapter, entire book), he is considering **discourse**. Discourse involves the relationship of sentences to one another to convey a point.

The purpose of the discourse determines the **genre**. The Bible contains various types of discourse depending upon the purpose of the communication: historical narratives (Acts), poetry (Psalms), personal letters (Titus), open letters (Ephesians), and prophecy (Isaiah). We noticed earlier that some English sentences may be appropriate in poetry that would never be used in casual speech. In other words, the category of writing is relevant to every translator.

Discourse divides translations into three types: literal, idiomatic, or paraphrased. As we have shown, word-for-word literal glossing is not translation. Inflections may require additional words, while figures of speech will almost always require the use of different words. A **literal translation**, then, describes the attempt to convey a word-for-word meaning as closely as possible without obstructing communication. The advantage of a literal translation is that the personal views and interpretations of the translators affect the translation very little. Since the translators try to stay close to the wording of the text, and may use consistent glosses where contexts permit, they lack opportunity to explain or interpret what they think it means. The KJV and NASB are examples of this type of translation.

In contrast, **idiomatic** translations attempt to communicate the meaning in natural English.[4] This goal takes priority over the order and grammatical form of the individual words. Such translators are willing to restate the text to obtain more understandable English. Where a literal translation may not flow in natural English (hampered by concern for the syntax and vocabulary of Hebrew and Greek), the idiomatic translation restructures each sentence into normal English idiom. The disadvantage is that the translator has done some interpretation for the reader. Passages that God intended to be obscure or ambiguous are now clarified based on the translator's personal interpretation of what God meant. Still, the idiomatic translation follows the original on a sentence-by-sentence basis and cannot interpret large blocks at will. The *New International Version* (NIV) is an example of such a translation.

A **paraphrase**[5] attempts to preserve the meaning of the discourse as a whole rather than words or sentences. Its advantage is that the entire paragraph can be rendered to communicate the main thought to the desired audience—even a small child. Yet such a simplified explanation will certainly involve far more of the translator's interpretations and therefore strays the most from the original wording of the text. The *Living Bible* (LB) is an example of a paraphrase.

Style

Style involves such things as the difficulty of the words chosen by the author, the complexity and length of the sentences, and the number of figures of speech or references to other authors. The differences between reading Dr. Seuss, a typical newspaper, and an engine repair manual are substantial even though all are in English with the same grammar and syntax, and their vocabulary all comes from the same dictionary.

The human authors of Scripture also had different styles. Paul wrote in long sentences with allusions to other poets and philosophers. Luke, the doctor, wrote with even more scholarship than Paul. On the other hand, Peter and John wrote much more simply. That is why Peter said of Paul's writing that some things were hard to understand. Peter wrote in common speech like a news reporter, whereas Paul wrote more like a literature professor.

Every translator must select a style for his translation. The difficulty of Elizabethan English gives a sense of solemnity to the writings of Luke and Paul that may be quite appropriate but make

John and Peter, the fishermen, sound like scholars. No popular translation attempts to reproduce a style similar to the original. Instead translators usually select a style appropriate to a modern reader at a given grade level. Some try to translate at an eighth grade level, while some may try to communicate to small children.

Culture

The fourth source of differences in translations involves how the translator addresses the culture. For instance, in ancient times, much business was conducted at the gate of the city, which served as a combination of market and city council. When ancient peoples read that Lot sat in the gate of Sodom, they understood that he was prosperous and influential in the city. Americans lack this background knowledge and may falsely assume that Lot was simply loitering around the city gates.

The translator, understanding the cultural background, must decide whether to communicate that background in the translation. Some translators believe that anything understood by the original writer and readers should be communicated so that the modern reader can have the same understanding as the original readers did. D. A. Carson has pointed out the virtual impossibility of this task.[6]

Today's English Version (TEV, also called *Good News for Modern Man* or *Good News Bible*, GNB) translated by Robert Bratcher is an example of this type of translation. This version uses the word *Emperor* rather than *Caesar*, and translates the Hebrew idiom "as a backsliding heifer"(Hos. 4:16) with the English idiom "as stubborn as mules." Ancient coins, weights, and measures are all converted to modern units, and many religious terms such as propitiation and repentance are avoided by using an explanatory phrase instead. By such means the reader more easily understands and identifies with the action in the Biblical accounts.

Besides the incorporation of cultural information into the translation, the TEV incorporates both idiomatic translation and paraphrase. Its idiomatic translation of Acts 2:37 renders "pricked to the heart" with "deeply troubled." This is not a cultural issue but attempts to convey the meaning of the phrase in simple English. The TEV frequently rephrases rhetorical questions as direct statements and divides up long sentences for clarity.[7] It also condenses to form a paraphrase in Leviticus 19:32. Translated literally in the KJV, we read "Thou shall rise up before the hoary head, and honor the face of the old man," while the TEV simply says, "Show respect for old people and honor them."

Psalm 92:10b illustrates a complex interplay of the cultural and discourse issues in the TEV. The KJV reads literally: "You have poured fresh oil over me," while the TEV renders the phrase "You have blessed me with happiness." The pouring of fresh oil on a person is the act of anointing. This cultural practice was one sign of God's blessing, hence their idiomatic English avoids the technical religious terms. However, the addition of the phrase "with happiness" is a paraphrased interpretation of the translators.

Translation Philosphies

The principle of **cultural equivalence** promoted use of the "closest 'natural' equivalent to the statement of the text."[8] The term *natural* refers to the way a bilingual person would translate. It suggests that the best choice in translating a word is one that signifies the same object when the object serves the same function in both cultures.

Eugene A. Nida, who first stated this principle, recognized that the ideal is often unattainable. He offered guidelines for attaining the closest equivalence possible. If an object is unknown in a culture or if it serves such a different purpose as to make the meaning misleading, the translator should select one of three alternatives: use a different object with a similar function, describe the object or function, or adopt a foreign term. He provides detailed directions concerning when each option is appropriate and how best to implement it.[9] He implies that the use of foreign terms should be a last resort, and would therefore support use of modern units of measure and currency as well as articles of clothing and food in place of the ancient ones.

On the other hand, Nida condemned use of cultural equivalents when not absolutely necessary. He recommended use of foreign words rather than import a name for God (which may make God seem foreign). He also preferred the foreign term to a cultural equivalent for a term like *sheep* that is central to Old Testament practice and New Testament symbolism.[10]

As we shall presently see, the translators of several modern versions extended Nida's principle to practices he would condemn. They wished to convey culture in order that today's reader may respond in the same way that the original readers did. Making the ancient culture come alive in modern terms in this way is called **dynamic equivalence**.[11] To attain this goal, translators employ idiomatic translation, paraphrase, and cultural parallels. Translators who hold to this view may interchange "white as wool" with "white as snow" when preparing a translation for a West African jungle tribe on the grounds that the readers would not understand snow. Likewise a translator in a tribe that raises pigs rather than sheep may substitute the one stock animal for the other.

Henry A. Osborn represents a more conservative philosophy of translation. He promotes a literal philosophy. For instance, he argues that justify must be translated by a word that means "to make straight, correct, or right" rather than one meaning "to make clean," so as not to confuse it with *sanctify*. Likewise, where the Greek has separate words for *sign, wonder,* and *power*, it will not do to translate *sign* with a word having one of the other meanings.[12]

Osborn acknowledges cases where it is necessary to translate an idiom or to insert background words (as when the KJV uses italics).[13] He also acknowledges that the term *dynamic equivalency* goes far beyond the cultural equivalents of Nida.[14] However, he thoroughly repudiates interpretation by translators. For example, he denounces the use of paraphrase to interpret and clarify the phrase "sin unto death." If God had made it clear, there would be no controversy over what He meant, and when a translator conveys what he thinks God meant, he has introduced his opinion into God's Word. Such addition dishonors God. Osborn likewise condemns the substitution of pigs for sheep since it affects the Old Testament picture of sacrificial animals and the Lamb of God himself.[15] Such a translation is unworthy of the word of God since it overlooks significant symbolism.

Carson points out the fallacy in the goal of dynamic equivalency. Trying to translate to obtain the same response on the part of the reader assumes that the modern translator knows the how the ancient recipients responded. Such information is rarely available and even when it is it may not be worth replicating. The Corinthians, he points out, did not always respond to Paul's letters in the Spirit.[16] Furthermore, he observes that paraphrasing the general idea can too easily cover the translator's failure in discerning "*all* the thoughts that are bound up in a text, reflected in *all* the words in this particular syntax, discourse, genre, and so on, and trying to render as many of them as possible in the receptor language in comparable space."[17]

Theological Bias

We have previously discussed some of the errors of the TEV. Its most serious flaw, however, is its theological bias. For example, *virgin* is mistranslated as "young woman" or *maiden* in order to deny the virgin birth—this is not a textual variant but a deliberate mistranslation. Such tampering is not surprising from those who hold so low a view of preservation that they, in addition to their paraphrasing and use of dynamic equivalency, indulge in radical eclecticism—including conjectural emendations in some two hundred passages in the Old Testament.[18]

Unfortunately, the TEV is not the only version that suffers from theological bias. Liberals frequently translate *blood* as *death* to escape the implications of the blood atonement in Scripture. The New Inclusive Translation (NIT) avoids all use of masculine pronouns for God to accommodate the feminist agenda.[19] Such tampering is done in spite of the fact that all Greek manuscripts use the word blood and all use the masculine pronoun for God. These are not issues of textual variants but translator's theological biases amounting to satanic attacks on the Word of God. The role of a translator is to communicate across languages what someone else said—not what the translator wanted him to say.[20]

Such versions are products of unregenerate hearts which see in the Scriptures a form of godliness, but deny the power thereof. No Bible-believing Christian can commend those who produce such versions any more than he would commend a liberal preacher, commentator, or theologian. Even though some passages may be translated well, God's people are correct to ignore and reject their efforts.[21]

Christians must be vigilant in doctrinal matters. We need to discern and reject translations of Scripture produced with intentional theological bias. Bias is evident if the translation adds, deletes, or colors words and phrases differently from the wording found in the manuscripts it purports to translate. In other words, all Christians can agree when someone has gone beyond the controversial issues of manuscripts and mishandled Scripture.

For instance, the *New World Translation* of the Jehovah's Witnesses used the name Jehovah 237 times in the New Testament, even though that Hebrew name never once occurs in any manuscripts of the Greek New Testament. Worse, all passages that refer to Christ as God are altered in slight ways so as to avoid this truth (which would contradict their doctrinal view).[22] Similarly, the name of the Holy Spirit is never capitalized because of their bias against his deity. Such bias is clear, and it would still be apparent regardless of which manuscripts it is judged against.

The *Jerusalem Bible* of the Catholics also contains bias. It not only contains the Apocryphal books, but it places them where they erroneously purport to go. Christians will be surprised to find 14 chapters in Daniel (the last two chapters being *Susanna* and *Bel and the Dragon*). The apocryphal additions to Esther are also spread throughout that book. The word *holocaust* for the burnt offering also reflects Catholic theology. While this translation is more restrained than older Catholic Bibles, these points show its theological bias.

Some Christians accuse all modern language Bibles of theological bias. This issue cannot be addressed in full, but the two most common arguments do not prove the case. One argument derives from the use of Greek manuscripts other than the Textus Receptus. We have already shown that no doctrinal variations arise regardless of which manuscripts are used. Thus, choice of manuscripts cannot result in a theological biased translation. Bias from Greek sources can only come from frequent use of conjectural emendation.

A second argument invokes differences of wording between the KJV and the version accused. Some such differences may seem to point to removing a doctrinal point. However, such lists of examples never include every reference to the doctrine. The NWT is doctrinally biased because *every* reference to the deity of Christ is circumvented. Though some verses in the NIV may seem to lessen Christ's deity, other verses still make it clear. Whatever its other faults, the NIV is not guilty of theological bias. There is a vast difference between the errors of the NWT and TEV that would be recognized by any Christian *regardless* of textual view and the alleged errors of the NIV which can be identified only from certain textual perspectives.

We have argued that theological bias does not depend either on selection of manuscripts or on translation of a few sample passages. The conservative modern versions (NASB, NIV, NKJV) do not display the kinds of deliberate theological bias found in the TEV and NWT. The theological bias of the NWT and TEV must be exposed and condemned, while the manuscript preferences of the conservative modern versions requires further evaluation and critique.

Conclusion

It seems the psalmist was most prophetic of our time in saying, "The Lord gave the word: great was the company of those that published it." (Ps. 68:11) The term "publish" as reflected in this psalm means simply to "proclaim" the Word rather than what the modern process of publishing involves using editors, printers and publishing companies. Still, publishing in the modern sense is one way of proclaiming the Word. And how "great" is the publishing of modern Bibles? Restricting ourselves solely to the 20th century, the number of different translations of the Bible (or portions of it) just in English exceeds 150.

Is this escalating number of English versions necessary? Is it wise? In no sense are 150 different modern translations either wise or necessary. Some are theologically biased or based on inadequate philosophies of translation. On the other hand, the more conservative modern translations cannot be dismissed so superficially and will be considered again in Chapter 12.

Endnotes

1. White, pp. 78-79.
2. Readers unfamiliar with Greek may wonder why there are more letters using English characters. This is because _ is usually rendered by *th*, _ by *ph*, and _ by *ch*. Also, the _ above first letters of words is transliterated by *h*.
3. D. A. Carson, *The Inclusive Language Debate: A Plea for Realism* (Grand Rapids: Baker, 1998), p. 68.
4. John Beekman and John Callow promote idiomatic translation as one which conveys the "meaning of the original by using the natural grammatical and lexical forms" of the receptor language. "His focus is on the meaning." See *Translating the Word of God* (Grand Rapids: Zondervan, 1974), p. 24.
5. Technically, a paraphrase restates an idea in the same language while translation converts meaning to another language. The term, however, has come to be used widely for versions that translate first and then paraphrase the translation. Beekman and Callow deny that such paraphrases are translations (though they acknowledge interlinears as translation!), see p. 21 footnote 4.
6. Carson points out the difficulty of translating Mark Twain with all the spellings that we interpret culturally as reflecting rural and colloquial pronunciations. Much explanation would be needed for a Chinese person to understand all the associations we have with such speech (*Inclusive Language Debate,* pp. 56-58). He also gives examples of verses in which translator has a choice of two alternatives each of which loses some aspect of the original (pp. 58-60).
7. Sakae Kubo and Walter F. Specht, *So Many Versions* (Grand Rapids: Zondervan, 1983), p. 178.
8. Eugene A. Nida, *Bible Translating* (London: United Bible Societies, 1947, 1961), p. 12.
9. Nida, pp. 130-45.
10. Nida, pp. 136-37. Nida repudiates the substitution of other animals for sheep even in the Marshal Islands which have no concept of them. He also

specifically states that when a cultural equivalent can be justified, it is "not dictated by a desire to make the Bible seem as though it were recording some events which took place just yesterday in the next town."

11. Carson, *Inclusive Language Debate*, p. 71, says that this term has been outdated since 1986, replaced by "functional equivalence." For purposes of general background and historic controversy, however, the term remains the most relevant.

12. Henry A. Osborn, Bernard Northrup, William Smallman, and Frederic A. Carlson, *Anchor Points for Scripture Translation Work* (Grand Rapids: Bibles International, 1988), p. 8.

13. Ibid., p. 11.

14. Ibid., p. 14.

15. Ibid., p. 12.

16. Carson, *Inclusive Language Debate*, p. 71.

17. Ibid., p. 70 [emphasis his].

18. Kubo and Specht, p. 184.

19. For example, in the Lord's prayer, "Father-Mother, hallowed be your name, May your dominion come" *The New Testament and Psalms: A New Inclusive Translation* (Oxford: Oxford University Press, 1995), Luke 11:2.

20. Beekman and Callow stress "Fidelity in Translation" as the primary responsibility of a translator, p. 33.

21. Sakae Kubo and Walter F. Specht list seven passages in which the *New English Bible* has an outstanding translation in spite of being translated by British liberals (pp. 205-206). Likewise, C. H. Spurgeon commended the *Revised Version* at several points in spite of its translators. In fact, Spurgeon in his Metropolitan Tabernacle Pulpit (1891, p. 90) quotes the RV at Isaiah 62:6 and comments "I quote the best translation" of that passage.

22. Kubo and Specht, pp. 98-116 for review of the NWT and pp. 99-101 cover the bias against the deity of Christ with sample passages in John 1:1, Titus 2:13, and Colossians 1:16-17.

Questions

1. In what four ways may translations differ?

2. Research the word *quick* and explain how its meaning has changed since 1611.

   In converting a text from one written language to another, how can you accomplish each purpose below?

3. convey the phonetic sounds

4. convey the vocabulary meanings

5. convey grammatical cues as well as vocabulary

6. convey syntax, grammatar, and vocabulary

7. Distinguish three types of translations.

8. Define dynamic equivalency.

9. What scholar first promoted dynamic equivalency?

10. Name two versions that show theological bias. Explain.

CHAPTER 12

SELECTING VERSIONS

Christians shopping for a Bible are confronted by literally dozens of Bibles from which to choose. It is no wonder that many Christians would like to know some of the differences so that they can make a wise choice.

In the last chapter we explained why translations based on extreme translation views such as dynamic equivalency (TEV) are unacceptable. We also warned Christians against translations that display theological bias (NWT, JB, NEB, NIT, etc.). This chapter will focus on other versions, those for which an analysis of the issues is more difficult.

Differences among Versions

Bibles differ in manuscript basis, translation issues, and publication purpose. All three should be considered by the purchaser. However, the purpose for publication is at least as important as the others and frequently overlooked.[1]

Publication purpose simply refers to the reason the publisher thinks you want a Bible. They consider their market, and want to publish a Bible you will want. If you do not consider why you want a Bible, you will likely not obtain the most useful one. Bibles differ in size from pocket Bibles to giant large-print Bibles. They also differ in marginal notes and helps in the back. Study Bibles have copious notes while pocket Bibles rarely have any. Some have pictures and helps for children, while others have key evangelism verses highlighted in red. Certainly consider the version, but also look beyond the version to what is included with the sacred text.

Bibles for Study

Publishers intend *study Bibles* for in-depth study. Study Bibles are available in most versions. Christians need to study God's Word, and the numerous helps in a study Bible facilitate this. Typical helps include: (1) introductory pages for each book of the Bible explaining the historical background, author, date, and theme, (2) margins with cross-references to other passges or explanations of difficult phrases, (3) appendices with maps, summary of Bible doctrine, concordance, time lines, harmonies, etc.

Each Christian will develop preferences for which helps are most useful. However, keep in mind that some such helps are more valuable to young Christians. Concordances in the back are rarely complete, and you will eventually want to own a complete concordance. Likewise, a Bible atlas will have many more maps and in more detail, while books on doctrine will surpass the summaries of Bible doctrine. Harmonies (chronologies that show where books overlap, such as the gospels or Kings-Chronicles) are also usually available separately, but since fewer people own a harmony, these may be the most useful. At any rate, you should consider which simplified resources you desire to have handy in the back of your Bible. Look through the helps before purchasing a study Bible.

Once you identify the helps you want, you will also need to select a version. In previous chapters we have showed that differences among manuscripts are few. Most differences among Bible versions in English are due to issues over how words should be translated rather than which manuscripts are the best. This means that a person buying a Bible need not get overly concerned about these issues. If the preceding chapters have helped you determine which manuscripts you would like to rely on, be sure to obtain a version based on them.

We have said that the key issue is not manuscript theory but translation philosophy. Literal translations stick as closely to the text as possible, while idiomatic translations and paraphrases interpret the meaning as well. Since the purpose of a study Bible is to promote your search of the Scriptures, it is self-defeating to use one that someone else has interpreted. Feeding your soul on God's Word and digesting properly requires that you search it and apply it for yourself. Eating predigested food may be appropriate for baby birds, but not for children of God.

The importance of this can be made clear by example. Suppose you wish to study *anointing* in the Bible. The TEV offers nothing to study because that cultural tradition has already been interpreted for you with the term *blessing* (see previous chapter). If you start looking up the word *blessing* to find the references to *anointing*, you will soon give up because *blessing* can translate many words and refer to many kinds of blessing other than anointings. Of course, the same could be said for paraphrases. Paraphrasing plays havoc with serious study of Scripture.

The advantage of a literal translation (KJV or NASB) over an idiomatic version (NIV) is that words are translated somewhat more consistently. The concordance study will uncover most every passage in which anointing is done just by looking up the two words anoint and oil separately. (You could speed this up with computer software that searches Greek words, using Strong's numbers, or even using a topical textbook.)

The literal translations have great advantages in word studies. For example, studying the names Jesus, Christ, Lord, and Savior would be much more difficult even in an idiomatic version. In a long confusing sentence with several pronouns, an idiomatic translation usually replaces some pronouns with the name of the person in view. This means that many references to Christ will not correspond to places where the word *Christ* occurred in the original. A serious study of the name *Christ* (anointed one) is greatly hindered by the translation principle of restatement. Similar when currency, weights, and measures are converted to dollars, pounds, and feet it becomes virtually impossible to study the various ancient units separately.

The King James Version is the version of choice by many Christians regardless of textual theory. It is traditional and time-tested and should be seriously considered. It is also a reliable literal translation. Further, since study includes memorizing and meditating on God's Word, many Christians regardless of textual views, find the King James Version the most beautiful prose and the easiest to memorize.

People who find the King James Version difficult to read or understand may want a more modern translation as a primary study Bible or as a secondary Bible to supplement their KJV. The most literal modern translation is the NASB, which stays as close to its Greek manuscript base as the KJV does. It therefore makes an important contribution for American Christians. Its main competitor, the New International Version, interprets frequently making it far inferior as a study Bible.

Those who desire a translation in modern English that is based on the same manuscript evidence as the KJV should obtain the New King James Version (NKJV). Both the NKJV and the NASB are conservative translations. If you purchase either as a primary study Bible, you should also obtain a concordance for it. This will be especially important as you begin to memorize from it.

Some people frown on owning multiple translations. These same people own commentaries, Bible atlases, Bible dictionaries, and Bible encyclopedias as tools to aid their study. If we can read a commentator's translation of a passage to help us understand it better, there is no reason why we should not read another translator's rendering of a passage to gain understanding. Since idiomatic and paraphrased Bibles must interpret to some extent, you can treat such versions as commentaries on the whole Bible. They provide a quick reference to the translator's interpretation. Versions translated by conservative scholars can be valuable secondary resources that supplement a literal study Bible.

Unfortunately, alternate translations are too often neglected as a tool for Bible study. Whatever you prefer as your main study Bible, consider owning a KJV, an NASB, and an NKJV as reference tools. In fact, owning a version that interprets such as the New International Version may also be a very useful reference tool. Consulting alternate versions can help you understand that confusing passage in your favorite study Bible.

Comparing several versions, however, can add a new type of confusion to your study. It can be disconcerting when one translation seems to say something quite different from another. However, this is also a useful tool if you choose to use it. Such translation discrepancies point you to issues worthy of further study. This is the best way for people who have not studied Greek to identify passages containing passages hard to translate well or alternate manuscript readings in the original languages. If you look up the verse in a commentary, you can often learn whether the difference is based on differing manuscripts or whether there has been disagreement over how a word should be translated. Sometimes you will learn that the differences are only apparent; perhaps the old English word in the King James means the same as the modern word in the NASB. Comparing versions can therefore help you study more deeply and to become aware of manuscript and translation issues.

Bibles for Children

We have already argued that God desires to communicate. He used common Greek rather than formal classical Greek for the New Testament. 1 Corinthians 14:9 and 19 show that the goal of any language (tongue) is to communicate and edify. Regardless of your ability to understand the King's English, you are foolish to ignore your audience. Two audiences are very important to God and should be to you.

While Bibles for children abound, many are simply picture books of favorite Bible stories. As children progress through elementary school, you will want them to graduate from pictures to a real Bible. However, few such children have the capacity to read old English with understanding. Of course, you can explain difficult passages to your child if you wish to use a King James Bible in family devotions. However, Christian parents will also want to encourage the child to read God's Word on his own.

How do you help a child read on his own? The child will not be "messed up" by a modern version or even a paraphrase. The child's study is not so deep that he will even notice whatever it is you do not like in a given version. However, if he reads a version without understanding, his interest will quickly flag. And why not? Who reads calculus texts or car repair manuals unless they understand such things? Reading without understanding is boring, and this is a frequent complaint of children forced to read a Bible version intended for an older audience. A Christian parent hearing this symptom should remedy the situation with a Bible aimed at his reading level.

A child needs to begin hearing God speak directly through His Word and not just through someone's explanation of God's Word. Consulting the age-level indicators on various Bibles and buying your child one at his level can greatly enrich his spiritual experience.

We have already indicated that the New International Version is a poor choice as a study Bible for an adult, however, its weaknesses are not significant for a child's level of understanding, and it can be used with benefit with children in junior high. The Living Bible, though poorer than the NIV, can also be used with young children. While we would never recommend this Bible as a Bible for casual reading for an adult (much less a study Bible), its intended purpose was for children and for that it is useful. All the modern versions have grade-level ratings lower than the beloved King James Version. Any Christian bookstore will gladly tell you reading levels for various Bibles and can guide you to those appropriate for your children.

Bibles for Evangelism

Several publishers make pocket New Testaments with commonly used evangelistic verses highlighted. Most of these are small and have no study helps, seeking to focus the listener's mind on the Scripture. These typically come in various versions, much as study Bibles do.

Two important considerations that apply to children also apply to non-Christians. First, God desires to communicate both His love and salvation in Christ to them, and second both groups have difficulty in understanding Scripture. The Bible is frequently incomprehensible to the unsaved, because unsaved people do not have the Holy Spirit to help them understand it. Thus, the Spirit's drawing to Himself is necessary regardless of version. The Christian only compounds the difficulty of understanding Scripture by relating God's Word in language that is antiquated. The use of such language encourages some people to pass the Bible off as antiquated and irrelevant for today's society. The version you read may be all some hearers will ever hear of God's Word, and it is that reading that they will associate with it. Consider using a modern language version for witnessing or for helping new converts.

The above remarks apply to people with no Bible in their household. If you visit a home to share the gospel, they may have a family Bible. Frequently, your witness will reach them more effectively if you can show them God's truths from their own Bible. Many families own a King James heirloom, but modern versions have also become very popular. Whichever version you prefer, get familiar enough with the other versions to guide a person to Christ from his own Bible. It is unnecessary to condone or critique their Bible at this time; that can come later once they get saved. If Paul, a Jew of God's chosen race, became as a Gentile to win the Gentiles, can we not become as an American (rather than an Elizabethan Englishman) and put version preferences aside for the sake of the gospel?

Finally, none of these remarks should be taken to an extreme. Of course, you cannot be familiar with every Bible on the market. Just because you may select some good passages for witnessing to Catholics from their Jerusalem Bible, does not mean that you need to consult it for Bible study. Likewise, witnessing in modern English does not require use of New York gutter slang (as explained in the previous chapter).

Worship Services

One of the concerns many pastors have with the proliferation of so many English versions, especially among their own church members, is the difficulty involved in congregational reading of Scripture as a part of the worship service. For this reason, many pastors have insisted on using only the KJV in their churches. Others, however, prefer to let church members choose their own versions and provide for congregational reading by displaying the passage to be read using an overhead projector.

Charity

Finally, there is the matter of exercising charity toward those holding other views of manuscripts, textual issues, and translation issues. As KJV advocate Philip Mauro has stated, the teachings of the New Testament are unaffected by any of the texts available to us. In light of this, we should temper our responses to those who differ over which of them to use. The apostle Paul insists that love (KJV—"charity")

> *suffereth long, and is kind; charity envieth not; charity vaunteth not itself, is not puffed up; Doth not behave itself unseemly, seeketh not her own, is not easily provoked, thinketh no evil (1 Cor. 13:4-5).*

This contrasts sharply with the many voices that condemn—not clear enemies of the cross, not the liberals who deny the gospel, or the Roman Catholics who adulterate the gospel, or the cults who preach another gospel, but—true believers, Christian brethren who simply disagree with their opinions about the transmission and translation of Scripture. The absense of love for anything but their own opinions is not a fruit of the Spirit.

Such love cuts both ways. KJV advocates must show love toward those using other versions, and those using modern versions must not scorn those using the KJV.[2] Criticism and condemnation of someone's treasured Bible creates a rift. Either their Bible is wrong or the critic is wrong. If the person decides the critic is wrong, the critic loses any opportunity to minister or share God's Word. If the person believes the critic instead, he begins to doubt his own Bible, from which he hears God speak. In neither case are the Bible and its Author honored.

It should be clear that pastors, especially, face difficult decisions. Decisions that affect our corporate worship and fellowship are close to the heart. Charity toward one another as brethren applies especially, then, to pastors who watch for our souls. Rather than criticism concerning such preferences, they need our prayers, prayers for the guidance of the Holy Spirit.

Remember them which have the rule over you, who have spoken unto you the Word of God: whose faith follow, considering the end of their conversation. (Hebrews 13:7)

Endnotes

1. Carson stresses the importance of evaluating versions based on their stated goals ("relevance theory") but not ignoring the responsibility of the translation to convey the inspired text to the readers (D. A. Carson, *Inclusive Language Debate*, p. 71).
2. James B. Williams stated six purposes for editing the book on the KJV issues (p. 8). These included exposing the extreme KJV Only advocates and the extreme KJV Discreditors but also preventing further division and healing wounds caused by this controversy.

Questions

1. Name three uses for Bibles.

2. Show from the Bible that God demands all three uses.

3. Considering only the modern versions, which is most literal and interprets least?

4. Fill in the table with conservative Bible translations. What do you notice?

	poetic Elizabethan English	modern English
eclectic manuscript base		
non-eclectic base		

5. Compare the King James Version with the New American Standard Bible on the following five passages. They mean exactly the same thing, if the words in the KJV are looked up in an old English dictionary rather than a modern one. Which is easier to understand for you? Which is easier to memorize?

   Matthew 28
   John 3:16-21
   1 Thess. 4:16-18
   1 Cor. 13
   James 1:1-18

6. Find the reading level for the King James Version, the New American Standard Bible, the New International Version, and the Living Bible by visiting or phoning a Christian bookstore.

7. Compare the King James Version, a modern version, and the Jerusalem Bible on your favorite evangelism passages. If you don't have favorites, look up John 3:16, the Romans road (Rom. 3:23, 5:8, 6:23, and 10:13), 1 John 5:12-13, and Revelation 20:15, 21:4, 8, and 22:17).

8. Which translation do you use for personal study? for teaching Vacation Bible School? for door to door evangelism? Why?

9. What version does your church use in the morning worship service. Why is this a good version to use?

10. What version do you bring to church and why?

CONCLUSION

We plead with the reader on this controversial topic to recall the first four chapters. Chapter 1 stressed that the Bible is the inspired and inerrant Word of God. Nothing else in this book is worth saying without that basis. The Bible is not only inspired but has been preserved to this day, and anyone who cares to look can see three amazing evidences of that fact. God has preserved his word since antiquity (see Chapter 2). The oldest manuscripts silence those Bible critics who think the books of the Bible were written long after the fact. He has also preserved His Word in great numbers (see Chapter 3). The agreement of the mass of manuscripts displays the miracle of preservation in comparison to any other ancient text. God has also preserved His Word throughout the ancient world (see Chapter 4). The distribution of quotations of the Fathers, ancient translations, and lectionaries for use in preaching show its progress across the known world and its constant use.

Having stressed that the Word of God is preserved, we have attempted to delineate the issues concerning exact wording of a small percentage of passages. None of these passages affect doctrine, and most do not even affect the meaning of the sentence. Nevertheless, these issues have become a source of bitter contention among some. Chapter 5 presented the two historic views that prompted some of this debate. Chapters 6-8 presented seven views currently held by those who have modified the historic views in various ways. We have tried to show that most of these views are within the bounds of the Christian faith and should not be tests of orthodoxy. The arguments concern tiny details in scattered passages, and no one is required to relinquish the facts of preservation outlined in the first four chapters.

The translators of the King James Version agreed and expressed their views in a preface to their 1611 translation of the Bible. See for yourself what they said about their version in Chapter 10. They claimed no divine insight or guidance beyond what any praying Christian may expect. Certainly none to match the direct revelation given to the prophets and apostles.

The translation controversies, then, derive from issues of translation. Of course, there are far more English translations than necessary, and many of them are poor—some even theologically biased. However, this cannot be said about all of them. Chapters 11 and 12 explained the various views of translation and the reasons why people select Bibles. If our desire is to know God, we each must desire to study a Bible that communicated God's Word as clearly as possible. While pastors, Bible dictionaries, commentaries, and other helps are important for communicating cultural background, we need not compound our difficulties with antiquated language. Translations, then, should be selected purposefully and with prayer from among the good conservative translations.

Neither the manuscript controversy nor the translation controversy need divide God's people. Of course, there are extremes in both issues that must be condemned. However, there is a wide variety of positions that do not contradict any commands or principles of Scripture. Is there not a place for charitability amongst Christians? Let us "love one another" and let us show that we are Christians by our love.

We submit this book with the hope that God will be glorified for inspiration, preservation, and providence, and that God's people will focus on obeying His Word instead of arguing over trivia. Such a book is worthwhile only if the exposure to the facts gives the people of God the background needed to be fair to their brothers in Christ. As it is written in Psalm 133, "Behold, how good and how pleasant it is for brethren to dwell together in unity!"

APPENDIX 1

SCHNAITER'S REPLY TO ACCUSATIONS

May 30, 1983

Dear Dr. Woodbridge:

I recently was given a letter that you wrote to Dr. Homer Massey, academic dean at Tabernacle Baptist Institute, Virginia Beach, Virginia, as an appendage to a letter by Roland Rasmussen dated April 7, 1983, to the same person. In your letter to Dr. Massey you name me as representing either Neo-Orthodoxy or, worse, rank heresy.

To say that I was surprised by what I read in your letter would be a severe understatement. I remember quite well a series of lectures that you delivered to the graduate class at Bob Jones University in 1967-68 when I was studying for my master's degree in Bible. At one point you quite excellently analyzed the Neo-Evangelical movement, detailing its progression through a series of "shifts." You outlined the progression as first a shift in mood that led to a shift of methods, which in turn led to a shift in message, and you predicted this would eventually culminate in a shift in morals. I have made use of your analysis to alert my students here at the University to the dangers of compromise evangelism and Neo-Evangelicalism many times since. I say this to indicate to you some of the profound respect that I have had for you as a man of character, conviction, and courage. You stood out, in my view, as one who carefully and sacrificially gave of himself to present strong warning against apostasy and modernism. Perhaps you can have some idea, then, of the effect that your letter to Dr. Massey had upon me.

As one who was snatched by the grace of God from the brink of Roman Catholocism and brought to the knowledge of salvation through the atoning death of our resurrected Lord, and as one who has since that time desired only to serve that Savior and Lord, I can only implore you to allow me to clarify what may have been not well stated in my Biblical Viewpoint article to which you made reference. You quote from my article:

> However, the presence of manuscript variations leads us to analyze more carefully the considerations of preservation into two categories: (1) THE PRESERVATION OF THE AUTHORITATIVE MESSAGE OF GOD, and (2) THE PRESERVATION OF THE PRECISE WORDING OF THAT MESSAGE . . . . However, such PROMISES OF PRESERVATION in view of the wording variations CAN ONLY APPLY TO THE MESSAGE OF GOD'S WORD, NOT TO ITS PRECISE WORDING. It is therefore reasonable to assume that God's providence is at work to preserve His revelation in spite of the minor variations in its wording. To realize this should encourage fundamentalists to relax their concern over minor variations that do not affect the teachings of God's Word . . . . [emphasis yours]

You then suggest that I am on "dangerous theological ground," that I make a "perilous disjunction between the Scriptural text and the Scriptural message," and that "EVERY TRAINED CHRISTIAN THEOLOGIAN OF [your] ACQUAINTANCE, who really believes the Bible, WOULD LOOK UPON THIS DISJUNCTION, TO SAY THE LEAST, AS 'NEO-

ORTHODOXY' and, TO SAY THE MOST, AS 'RANK HERESY.'" [emphasis yours]

Please let me make clear at the outset that I had no intention of intimating that I do not believe in the preservation of the precise wording of the text. I do, in fact, wholeheartedly believe that God has preserved not only the message of His Word, but even the precise wording of that message as it appeared in the original autographs. However, I did intend to make a distinction in my discussion, but one that I believe is validly indicated by the Scriptural data and the manuscript phenomenon. Let me explain.

I believe that the presence of copyists' errors or translator's errors or publishers' errors in EVERY copy of the New Testament (even though most of these are so minute in significance as to give no pause for reflection, let alone cause for alarm) justifies the conclusion that God has not preserved the precise wording of the text which would thus include the above-mentioned errors) in any PARTICULAR manuscript or copy or translation, but that He HAS indeed preserved BOTH wording and sense. The sense is preserved in EVERY copy since each is generally unaffected by the wording variations; the precise wording of the text of the New Testament autographs is preserved in the plethora of copies that we have. I maintain that only in the original autographs themselves can we find error-free precise wording of the text of the New Testament. Thus my distinction is between the autographic text and what some have called "The Bible as it is today." This distinction, I believe, is not any different from such distinction made by the Westminster Assembly as reflected in the Confession of Faith (i.8) which distinguishes between the original text of Scripture, the transmission of that text, and the translations of that text. It boils down, as one sage put it, to precisely this question: "But what is it that distinguishes 'The Bible as it is' from the original autographs? Just scribes' corruptions and printers' errors; nothing else." That statement came from the pen of Benjamin B. Warfield, and it accurately reflects what the manuscripts and copies show us. Now I am well aware that there are many men on the horizon today who are crying out with alarm about making such a distinction because of the supposed ramifications of such a distinction upon the Bible as we have it today. But again, I do not agree to their alarms. The famous statement of Richard Bentley still holds:

> The real text of sacred writers is competently exact; . . . nor is one article of faith or moral precept either perverted or lost . . . choose as awkwardly as you will, choose the worst by design, out of the whole lump of readings.

As staunch a defender of verbal-plenary inspiration as B. B. Warfield ratified that statement (cf. *An Introduction to the Textual Criticism of the New Testament.* London: Hodder and Stoughton, 1889, p. 14.) and I do also. Incidentally, the truth of it should, I would think, make rather moot the contentiousness concerning Westcott and Hort's theological aberrations, since they would have had no opportunity to perpetrate any of them (real or imaginary) through textual criticism. They were confined to work with manuscript readings of previous ages in the edition of their text. And although the readings they chose may or may not be the readings of the autographs (no one can prove one way or another at this point), nevertheless, they were readings used by Christians of a previous age and ratified by such use in the early chruch as far as we can tell. My point is, therefore, that God's providential care of the New Testament is undisturbed by the manuscript variants.

My dispute, Dr. Woodbridge, is not with anyone who maintains the plenary-verbal inspiration of the Scripture in its original, autographic text. My dispute is with those who would argue for the plenary-verbal inspiration of a particular version and would thus include all the copyists' variants and publishing errors as well as translators' variants of that version as part of divine authorship. More particularly, my dispute is with those who maintain that there is one line of textual transmission that alone providentially was kept from errors of scribes and copyists, translators and publishers, and that any manuscript that varies in wording from such a text-line is to be *ipso facto* adjudged as corrupt, when in fact there is strong textual evidence to the contrary. Finally, my dispute is with those who insist that, as a corollary to their theories about a single, pure text-line there is only one version of the Scripture that is the authoritative Word of God and that can qualify to be called the "Bible." My position is that, insofar that it agrees with the autographs, any version of Scripture is the Word of God. In this way I do not ascribe to God the printers' and publishers' errors of the King James Version, nor in fact of any other version. I recognize the King James Version to be the Word of God, therefore because its agreement with the manuscripts is exceedingly close. The variances of it from the autographs are so minute and insignificant that they are unworthy of serious discussion for the most part. But this is also true of other versions, not only in English but in other languages as well. Those versions of which this is not true (and admittedly there are some) stand out well as reflecting some sort of cultic bias (as the Jehovah's Witnesses' New World Translation, the "Cotton-patch" Version, etc.).

As Fundamentalists, we have an obligation to avoid these, I believe. But, in my view, the obligation is based upon the fact that unbelievers and cultic infidels have tampered with the translation, not the text. Considerably more harm can be done in tampering with Scripture by mistranslation or by distorted translation than by manipulating the ancient manuscripts, in my opinion. The TEV (Today's English Version) by Robert Bratcher is a good example. Bratcher has tried to impose his unbelieving opinions upon Scripture by, among other things, mistranslating the words *parthenos* (virgin) and *haima* (blood). He could not under any circumstances do this by manipulating the manuscripts in order to say what he wants. But he can and has by translating *virgin* as "young woman of marriageable age" and *blood* as "death." I am in agreement also that we do not need the overwhelming number of "modern" versions that we have seen proliferate since the 1950s. But is there harm in reading as a study guide the New American Standard Bible or the Amplified Bible? Evidently the King James Version translators would not have thought so. They stated in their Translators' Preface:

> . . . We affirm and avow, that the very meanest translation of the Bible in English set forth by men of our profession . . . containeth the Word of God, nay, is the Word of God: As the King's speech which he uttereth in Parliament, being translated into French, Dutch, Italian, and Latin, is still the King's speech, though it be not interpreted by every translator with like grace, nor peradventure so fitly for phrase, nor so expressly for sense, everywhere . . . . No cause therefore why the Word translated should be denied to be the Word or forbidden to be current, notwithstanding that some imperfections and blemishes may be noted in the setting forth of it . . . variety of translations is profitable for the finding out of the sense of the Scriptures; . . . they that are wise had rather have their judgments at liberty in differences of readings than to be captivated to one, when it may be the other . . . . It is better to make doubt of those things that are secret, than to strive about those things that are uncertain.

I trust, Dr. Woodbridge, that I have herein clarified my position sufficiently to demonstrate that I am neither Neo-Orthodox nor rank heretic in my views. As nearly as I can tell, I am following the "faith of my fathers" in terms of what some of the greatest defenders of the faith (Luther, Calvin, Knox, Tregelles, and Warfield) held in this area. Am I wrong in this position? I sincerely invite you to demonstrate to me if I am. Thank you for your kind attention to what is necessarily a protracted letter. I eagerly solicit the counsel and wisdom of Godly men who have preceded me in the faith. I await your response.

Sincerely yours,
Sam Schnaiter

APPENDIX 2

QUOTATIONS

We have argued that there is no perfect translated version and that this does not reflect on the inspiration of the Bible. The translators of the King James Version made similar statements in their day (see chapter 10). The following is a collection of quotations from Christians on such issues.

John Quincy Adams

Lecture 8: The Establishment of the Correct Principle of Biblical Translation.

In presenting this theme, let me inquire, I. What is the Correct Principle on which Translations of the Holy Scriptures should be made? To this I reply, that they should be conformed, as nearly as possible, to the inspired originals. Let it be remembered, that the Bible which we possess is a translation. The words of our English version are invested with Divine authority, only so far as they express just what the original expresses. I present this thought because there is, in the minds of many, a superstitious reverence for the words and phrases of our English version. This being a translation, partakes more or less of the imperfections of the translators; and, in every instance where the original is not clearly and fully translated, it is the word of man, and not the Word of God. The

Old Testament was originally written in Hebrew, and the New Testament in Greek. In translating, therefore, into English, or Burmese, or French, or German, or Bengali, or any other language, it is evident to any one, that the Hebrew and the Greek should be the standard to which these translations should be conformed.[1]

E.M. Bounds, on Prayer

God's method is men. God has chosen to use men, godly men, scholarly men, to carefully and prayerfully study and compare all of the Greek texts of the New Testament, and in this way to arrive at the correct Greek text on which the translation of His Word into all other languages (including English) is based.[2]

Adam Clarke, D.D.

Though I believe our translation to be by far the best in any language, ancient or modern; yet I am satisfied it stands much in need of revision.[3]

Donald K. Drake, president
Piedmont Bible College

Those who earnestly contend for an inspired King James Version are missing the really critical issue of the day . . . Christians are missing the issue entirely because they have been lured into a battle that is neither proper nor productive.[4]

Erasmus

You must distinguish between Scripture, the translation of Scripture, and the transmission of both." "the only way to determine the true text is to examine the early codices."[5]

Fundamental Baptist Fellowship

The FBF recognizes that discussion and debate concerning the biblical manuscripts continues to attract national attention. The FBF affirms belief in the Bible, both the Old and New Testaments (66 canonical books), as the inspired, inerrant, and infallible Word of God as originally written. We believe in the verbal inspiration of the Scriptures. We believe that any version must reveal faithfulness in translating the best manuscripts. We reject as fallacious any theory of double inspiration. We reject the concept that a translation can be used to correct the autographs, or that the Holy Spirit so superintended a particular translation as to make it infallible. We recognize that any issue involving the Word of God is, of necessity, important and should be dealt with carefully, intelligently, and prayerfully. We resolve that this Fellowship take note of the large number of men who love the Lord and are faithful to the Scriptures on both sides of the debate and that we encourage these men and schools in further scholarly discussion and publication in a spirit of courtesy and consideration for the godly, fundamental men with whom they disagree.[6]

Louis Gaussen

It is said: of what consequence is it to me that the third operation is effected by the Spirit of God, if the last be accomplished only by the spirit of man? In other words, what avails it to me that the primitive language be inspired, if the translated version be not so? But people forget, in speaking thus, that we are infinitely more assured of the exactness of the translators, than we could be of that of the orignal text, in the case of all the expressions not being given by God.[7]

Now although all the libraries in which ancient copies of the sacred books may be found, have been called upon to give their testimony; although the elucidations given by the fathers of all ages have been studied; although the Arabic, Syriac, Latin, Armenian, and Ethiopian versions have been collated; although all the manuscripts of all countries and ages, from the third to the sixteenth century, have been collected and examined a thousand times over, by countless critics, who have eagerly sought out some new text, as the recompense and the glory of their wearisome watchings; although learned men, not content with the libraries of the West, have visited those of Russia, and carried their researches into the monasteries of Mount Athos, Turkish Asia, and Egypt, there to look for new instruments of the sacred text;— 'Nothing has been discovered,' says a learned person, already quoted, 'not even a single reading, that could throw doubt on any one of the passages before considered as certain. All the *variantes,* almost without exception, leave untouched the essential ideas of each phrase, and bear only on points of secondary importance;' such as the insertion or the omission of an article or a conjunction, the position of an adjective before or after its substantive, the greater or less exactness of a grammatical construction.[8]

We know the perplexities of the excellent Bengel on this question; and we know that these led, first, to his laborious researches on the sacred text, and, next, to his pious wonder and gratitude at the preservation of that text.[9]

Hence we will venture to say, that were some able and ill-meaning person (such as we may supposed the wretched Voltaire or the too celebrated Anthony Collins to have been in the last century) to study to select at will, out of all the manuscripts of the East and the West, when placed before him, the worst readings and the variations most remote from our received text, with the perfidious intention of composing at pleasure the most faulty text— such a man, we say (even were he to adopt such various readings as should have in their favour no more than one sole manuscript out of the four or five hundred of our libraries), could not, in spite of all his mischievous inclination, produce a Testament, as the result of his labours, that would be less close to that of our Churches than Martin is to Osterwald.[10]

Nevertheless, we must once more conclude, that not only was the Scripture inspired on the day when God caused it to be written, but that we possess this word inspired eighteen hundred years ago; and that we may still, while holding our sacred text in one hand, and in the other all the readings collected by the learned in seven hundred manuscripts, exclaim with thankfulness, I hold in my hands my Father's testament, the etenal word of my God![11]

J. R. Graves

There may be errors in the transcription of the ancient manuscripts; there may be errors in translation, and errors many in interpretation, but that the original Scriptures are the Words of the living God, He most explicitly declares them to be.[12]

Dr. James M. Gray, late Dean of Moody Bible Institute

Let it be stated that the record for whose inspiration we contend is the original record—the autographs or parchments of Moses, David, Daniel, Matthew, Paul, or Peter as the case may be, and not any particular translation or translations of them whatever.[13]

Matthew Henry

But then we must see to it very carefully that it be really the Christian faith that we believe, profess, propagate, and contend for: not the discriminating badges of this or the other party, not any thing of later date than the inspired writings of the holy evangelists and apostles.[14]

Bob Jones, Sr.

But now what do we mean by "inspiration of Scripture"? Well, here's what we mean. We mean that in the original language, the

Holy Spirit directed in the words that the men used, and the very words themselves were chosen by the Holy Spirit. Now notice—this doesn't mean that the Holy Spirit took Paul's vocabulary and turned over to Peter. It doesn't mean that Peter's vocabulary was turned over to Paul; it doesn't mean that. It doesn't mean that the Holy Spirit merely dictated like you dictate to a secretary; it doesn't mean that. It does mean that Paul retained his style, Peter his style, and all the other writers retained their style. But out of Paul's vocabulary and out of Peter's vocabulary, and all the other people that wrote the Bible, the Holy Spirit chose the words that men used out of that vocabulary, at least directed them in the words. Do you know that if he didn't, you'd have confusion confounded? Now that's what orthodox Christians have always believed, and that's what the Bible says. The Bible says that "it came to us not in the words which human wisdom teaches, but in the words which the Holy Spirit teaches." Now get that clear.

Now the Bible is a God-breathed book; now that's in the original language. It doesn't mean that in the translations that the translators were not inspired. I think God directed the folks that translated the King James; I think it's the best translation we've ever had. But it doesn't mean that they were inspired men, and it doesn't mean that in translating one language to another that somebody may not have made a mistake, but we still have the original language. We still have the Greek and the Hebrew. God preserved those languages; we have 'em still. And here's the Greek and here's the Hebrew; and there are still scholars, great orthodox Bible scholars, and they are not denying what the original Greek said or what the original Hebrew said and meant. They don't deny that.

These modernists come along and just simply say, "Well, they were mistaken; 't isn't that way. They thought so, but they were misguided men." Now you see what's happening? Well now that means you have no longer an authoritative Bible if you go along.[15]

Adoniram Judson

The Bible, in the original tongues, comprises all the revelation now extant which God has given to this world.[16]

Homer Kent, president of Grace Theological Seminary

In summation, the King James Version is a fine and readable version. It is 'inspired,' however, only to the extent that it conveys the meaning of the autographs, just as any other translation. In general it does this very well But it is not perfect. Two problems must be noted. (1) There are some poor or erroneous translations. Word usage has changed since 1611. Furthermore, there are some translations which rest on exceedingly poor manuscript authority. One example is 1 John 5:7-8, for which there is no Greek manuscript evidence at all earlier than the fifteenth century. (2) The King James Version is becoming less and less intelligible to young Americans (whether we like it or not), and if its archaic expression do not speak meaningfully to them, to that extent it is failing to communicate God's inspired revelation.[17]

Robert Lowth, D.D.

As to style and language, it [KJV] admits but of little improvement; but in respect of the sense and the accuracy of interpretation (translation), the improvements of which it is capable are great and numberless.[18]

J. Gresham Machen, Professor at Princeton University.

In the first place, then let it be said that we believers in the plenary inspiration of the Bible do not hold that the Authorized Version or any other form of the English Bible is inspired. I beg your pardon for saying anything so obvious as that, but, do you know, my friends, it is necessary to say it. There are scarcely any limits to the ignorance which is attributed to us today by people who have never given themselves the trouble to discover what our view really is. Let it be said then very plainly that we do not hold that the Authorized Version or any other form of the English Bible is inspired. We are really quite well aware of the fact that the Bible was written in Hebrew and in Greek. The Authorized Version is a translation from the Hebrew and the Greek. It is a marvelously good translation, but it is not a perfect translation. There are errors in it. The translators were not supernaturally preserved from making mistakes. It is not inspired.

In the second place, we do not hold that any one of the hundreds, even thousands, of the Greek and the Hebrew manuscripts of the Bible is free from error. Before the invention of printing the Bible was handed down from generation to generation by means of copies made by hand. Those copies were written out laboriously by scribes. Before one copy was worn out or lost another copy would be made to take its place, and so the Bible was handed down. Hundreds of thousands, perhaps—no one knows how many—of such copies or "manuscripts" were made. Several thousand of them, some of these containing of course only parts of the Bible or only parts of either Testament, are now in existence. These are just remnants from among the vast number that are lost. Now we believers in the inspiration of the Bible do not believe that the scribe who made any one of these manuscripts that we have was inspire. Every one of the manuscripts contains errors; no one of them is perfect. What we do believe is that the writers of the Biblical books, as distinguished from scribes who later copied the books, were inspired. Only the autographs of the Biblical books, in other words—the books as they came from the pen of the sacred writers, and not any one of the copies of those autographs which we now possess—were produced with that supernatural impulsion and guidance of the Holy Spirit which we call inspiration.[19]

Alfred Martin, a Textus Receptus advocate

One cannot say that the Textus Receptus, for example, is verbally inspired. It contains many plain and clear errors as all schools of textual critics agree.[20]

Philip Mauro, KJV only advocate

But no two of these thousands of manuscripts are exactly alike; and every discrepancy raises a distinct question requiring separate investigation and separate decision. While, however, the precise reading of thousands of passages is affected by these differences, it must not be supposed that there is any uncertainty whatever as to the teaching and testimony of the New Testament in its entirety.

The consoling facts in that regard are: (1) that the vast majority of the variant readings are so slight (a mere question of a single letter, or an accent, or a prefix, or a case ending) as not to raise any question at all concerning the true sense of the passage; and (2) that the sum of all the variant readings taken together does not give ground for the slightest doubt as to any of the fundamental points of faith and doctrine. In other words, the very worst Text that could be constructed from the abundant materials available would not disturb any of the great truths of the Christian faith.[21]

Doug McLachlan, president of Central Baptist Seminary

It has always been Central's position that this is an issue over which good fundamental men and ministries can differ without dividing. This was as true under Dr. Richard V. Clearwaters' ministry—our founder and first president—as it is today. Those who have chosen to transmute perfectly legitimate preferences into inflexible absolutes and elevate them to the core beliefs of fundamentalism have, in our opinion, caused a terrible and unnecessary division within our ranks.[22]

L. W. Munhall

Many of these gentlemen [Higher Critics] are dishonest because, *First,* they know that most of these apparent errors and contradictions were long ago satisfactorily answered, even to the silencing of the infidel scoffers; and, *Second,* they know that no one believes that the transcribers, translators, and revisers were inspired. The doctrine of verbal inspiration is simply this: The original writings, *ipsissima verba,* came through the penmen direct from God; and these gentlemen are only throwing dust into the air when they rail against verbal inspiration and attempt to disprove it by pointing out the apparent errors of the authorized and revised texts.

But some may say, "Since we do not have the original writings, what is the use of insisting upon the doctrine of verbal inspiration" I answer, there are two sufficient reasons: *First.* If the original writings were not inspired of God verbally, then we have no Word of God. *Second.* Is there no difference between an inexact copy of an inerrable record and a faulty copy of an uncertain record? I think there is.[23]

John R. Rice, evangelist and editor of "Sword of the Lord"

Where in the Bible does God guarantee that any translator of the Bible, will be infallibly correct? There is no such Scripture. The doctrine of infallibility of the translation in the King James is not a Bible Doctrine; it is a manmade scheme by some partly ignorant and some partly influenced by bad motives.[24]

C. I. Scofield

The discovery of the Sinaitic manuscript and the labours in the field of textual criticism of such scholars as Griesbach, Lachmann, Tischendorf, Tregelles, Winer, Alford, and Westcott and Hort, have cleared the Greek Textus Receptus of minor inaccuracies while confirming to a remarkable degree the general accuracy of the Authorized Version of that text. Such emendations of the text as scholarship demands have been placed in the margins of this edition; which therefore combines the dignity, the high religious value, the tender associations of the past, the literary beauty and remarkable general accuracy of the Authorized Version, with the results of the best textual scholarship.[25]

Dr. Miles Smith, key translator of A.V. 1611

We affirm and avow, that the very meanest translation of the Bible in English set forth by men of our profession . . . is the Word of God: as the King's speech which he uttered in Parliament, being translated into French, Dutch, Italian, and Latin, is still the King's speech, though it be not interpreted by every translator with the like grace, nor peradventure so fitly for phrase, nor so expressly for sense, everywhere.[26]
Variety of translations is profitable for the finding out of the sense of the Scriptures.[27]

John Smyth, d. 1612

The holy Scriptures viz. the Originalls Hebrew & Greek are given by Divine Inspiration & in their first donation were without error most perfect and therefore Canonical . . . no translation can possibly express all the matter of the holy originalls, nor a thousand things in the Grammar, Rhetoric, & character of the tongue.[28]

Charles Haddon Spurgeon

I do not hesitate to say that I believe that there is no mistake whatever in the original Holy Scriptures from beginning to end. There may be, and there are, mistakes of translation; for translations are not inspired; but even the historical facts are correct . . . there is not an error in the whole compass of them. These words come from him who can make no mistake, and who can have no wish to deceive his creatures.[29]

Do not needlessly amend our authorized version. It is faulty in many places, but still it is a grand work taking it for all in all, and it is unwise to be making every old lady distrust the only Bible she can get at, or what is more likely, mistrust you for falling out with her cherished treasure. Correct where correction must be for truth's sake, but never for the vainglorious display of your critical ability.[30]

There is one fact which the most illiterate Christian can understand. Do not our pulpits perpetually resound with the words, "in the original it is so and so"? Do we not almost every Sabbath hear our ministers amend and correct the translation? Why is this? Why not make the translation true to the original? Why leave it to every pretender to a little Greek and Hebrew for ever to contradict the Bible of the English people? Surely it is not to be the special prerogative of the clergy to read God's Word in its purity, and for ever to condemn the unlearned to draw their spiritual nourishment from a book in which God's Word is marred by man's ignorance, sectarianism, and kingcraft. If God's Word is worthy of all reverence, it is a crime of the highest magnitude to dilute it with error; and the sin is grievously increased, when the error is so apparent that the wayfaring man is aware of it. The cant and fudge which cries out against the least alteration of the old version of our forefathers, as if it were positive profanity, are nothing to me. I love god's Word better than I love King James' pendantic [sic] wisdom and foolish kingcraft. We want God's own Book pure and unaltered. It is our firm belief that the present version is so good, that it will abundantly repay for revision. If it were utterly base, we would cry "Away with it;" but because it is to a great degree faithful, and never contrary to sound doctrine, we desire to see it yet further purified till it shall be as near perfection as a human translation of the Divine Book can possibly be brought. Do I love my friend any the less because I desire to brush away the dust which has accumulated upon his time-honoured portrait? No; it is because I love him, that I desire a correct likeness of him; and it is because I think that likeness a good one, that I desire to have every spot removed from it. And it is because I love the most Holy Word of God that I plead for a faithful translation; and from my very love to the English version, because in the main it is so, I desire for it that its blemishes should be removed, and it faults corrected. It is of course an arduous labour to persuade men of this, although in the light of common sense the matter is plain enough. But there is a kind of Popery in our midst which makes us cling fast to our errors, and hinders the growth of thorough reformation: otherwise the Church would just ask the question, 'Is this King James' Bible the nearest approach to the original?' The answer would be, 'No; it is exceedingly good, but it has many glaring faults.' And the command would at once go forth,—'Then ye that have learning amend these errors; for, at any cost, the Church must have the pure Word of God.

As for the present version, I think it a kind of treason to speak of rejecting it for another. It is almost miraculously good. Its noble Saxon, its forcible idioms, its sweet simplicity, its homely sentences, all commend it to the Englishman as a treasure to be preserved with scrupulous care. I ask, from very love of this best of translations, that its obsolete words, its manifest mistranslations and glaring indecencies, should be removed. In God's own word there are no vulgarities; why should they be retained in the Englishman's Bible? Why must we use expressions which are as foreign to our present language as the untranslated Hebrew? These are matters of revision upon which we should all be agreed; at least let these be done.[31]

Cornelius R. Stam, missionary to China

Even as I spoke, in 1984, a secret movement was already afoot to promote a KJV ONLY theory, an extreme philosophy concerning our beloved King James Version that does not have one scintilla of Scriptural support. This theory, so far from being edifying to the saints, resulted in heated debates, prolonged arguments, widespread division and deep bitterness, with the breaking up of churches, families and close friends.[32]

W. H. Griffith Thomas

Bible of Today = Bible of 16th Cent. = mss of 4th cent. (‫א‬, A, B) = 2nd cent. versions; There is no reasonable doubt that we possess today what has always been regarded as the Scriptures of the Christian Church.[33]

R. A. Torrey

No one, as far as I know, holds that the Authorized Version, or any English translation of the Bible is absolutely infallible and inerrant. The doctrine held by me and by many others who have given years to careful and thorough study of the Bible is, that the Scriptures as originally given were absolutely infallible and inerrant and that our English translation is a substantially accurate rendering of the Scriptures as originally given. We do not possess the original manuscripts of the Bible. These original manuscripts were copied, many, many times with great care and exactness, but, naturally some errors crept into the copies that were made. We now possess so many good copies that by comparing one with another, we can tell with great precision just what the original text was. Indeed, for all practical purposes the original text is now settled. There is not one important doctrine that hangs upon any doubtful or uncertain reading of the text.[34]

B. B. Warfield, professor at Princeton Seminary

The [Westminster] Confession affirms the providential preservation of the inspired Scriptures in purity in the originals, and the adequate purity of the Word of God in translations.

The necessity of looking upon the original Scriptures only as "authentical," that is, authoritative in the highest sense, and appealing to them alone as final authorities "in all controversies of religion," is based by the Confession on the fact that these original Scriptures, and they alone, are the inspired Bible. The Confession uses the strongest phrase of technical theological terminology to express their divine origin: "Being immediately inspired by God." It thereby points to the originals as the very Word of God, authoritative, as such, in every one of their deliverances of whatever kind. The possibility of appealing to the original Scriptures, as we now have them, as the Word of God, is based on the further fact that they have been, "by God's singular care and providence kept pure in all ages." The Confession thus distinguishes between the autographic text of sacred Scripture, which it affirms was "immediately inspired by God," and its subsequent transmission in copies, over the course of which it affirms, not that an inspiring activity of God, but that a providential care of God has presided, with the effect that they have been kept pure and retain full authority in religious controversy. This distinction cannot be overlooked or explained away; it was intentional, as is proved by the controversies of the day in which the framers of the Confession were actively engaged.

When it is affirmed that the transmission has been "kept pure," there is, of course, no intention to assert that no errors have crept into the original text during its transmission through so many ages by hand-copying and the printing press; nor is there any intention to assert that the precise text "immediately inspired by God," lies complete and entire, without the slightest corruption, on the pages of any one extant copy. The difference between the infallibility or errorlessness of immediate inspiration and the fallibility or liability to error of men operating under God's providential care alone, is intended to be taken at its full value. But it is intended to assert most strongly, first, that the autographs of Scripture, as immediately inspired, were in the highest sense the very Word of God and trustworthy in every detail; and, next, that God's singular providential care has preserved to the Church, through every vicissitude, these inspired and infallible Scriptures, diffused, indeed, in the multitude of copies, but safe and accessible. "What mistake is in one copy is corrected in another," was the proverbial philosophy of the time in this matter; and the assertion that the inspired text has "by God's singular care and providence been kept pure in all ages," is to be understood not as if it affirmed that every copy has been kept pure from all error, but that the genuine text has been kept safe in the multitude of copies, so as never to be out of the reach of the Church of God, in the use of the ordinary means. In the sense of the Westminster Confession, therefore, the multiplication of copies of the Scriptures, the several early efforts towards the revision of the text, the raising up of scholars in our own day to collect and collate MSS., and to reform the text on scientific principles—of our Tischendorfs and Tregelleses, and Westcotts and Horts—are all parts of God's singular care and providence in preserving His inspired Word pure.

No doubt the authors of the Confession were far from being critics of the nineteenth century: they did not foresee the course of criticism nor anticipate the amount of labor which would be required for the reconstruction of the text of, say, the New Testament. Men like Lightfoot are found defending the readings of the common text against men like Beza; as there were some of them, like Lightfoot, who were engaged in the most advanced work which up to that time had been done on the Biblical text, Walton's "Polyglot," so others of them may have stood with John Owen, a few years later, in his strictures on that great work; and had their lot been cast in our day it is possible that many of them might have been of the school of Scrivener and Burgon, rather than of that of Westcott and Hort. But whether they were good critics or bad is not the point. It admits of no denial that they explicitly recognized the fact that the text of the Scriptures had suffered corruption in process of transmission, and affirmed that the "pure" text lie therefore not in one copy, but in all, and is to be attained not by simply reading the text in whatever copy may chance to fall into our hands, but by a process of comparison, i.e. by criticism. The affirmation of the Confession includes the two facts, therefore, first that the Scriptures in the originals were immediately inspired by God' and secondly that this inspired text has not been lost to the Church, but through God's good providence has been kept pure, amidst all the the crowding errors of scribes and printers, and that therefore the Chruch still has the inspired Word of God in the originals, and is to appeal it, and to it alone, as the final authority in all controversies of religion.

The defense of the right of the people to translations of Scripture in their mother tongue, is based by the Confession on the universality of the Gospel and the inability of the people at large to read and search the Scriptures in the original tongues. In making good this right, the competence of translations to convey the Word of God to the mind and heart is vigorously asserted, as well as the duty of man to make diligent use of translated Scripture, to the nourishing of the Christian life and hope. The sharp distinction that is drawn between the inspired originals and the uninspired translations is therefore, not permitted to blind men to the possibility and reality of the conveyance in translations adequately for all the ordinary purposes of the Christian life and hope, of that Word of God which lies in the sense of Scripture, and not in the letter save as in a vessel for its safe conduct. When exactness and precision are needed, as in religious controversies, then the inspired originals only can properly be appealed to. But just because of the doctrine of the perspicuity of Scripture, as set forth in section 7, and that of its perfection, as set forth section 6, translations suffice for all ordinary purposes, and enable those who truly seek for it to obtain a thorough knowledge of what is "necessary to be known, believed, and observed for salvation." The use of translations is thus vindicated by the Confessional doctrine of the properties of Scripture.

But something more than the right of translations is here vindicated. The duty of making translations "into the vulgar language of every nation" under heaven, is laid upon the consciences of the people of God.[35]

Daniel Waterland, D.D., 19th century minister and scholar

Our last English translation, though a very good one, and upon the whole scarce inferior to any, yet is undoubtedly capable of very great improvements.[36]

Noah Webster

Whenever words are understood in a sense different from that which they had when introduced, and different from that of the original languages, they do not present to the reader the Word of God.[37]

John Wesley

I really believe our English translation with all its faults, is the best translation of the Bible now in the world.[38]

Robert Dick Wilson

If, however, the original document cannot be produced, certified copies of the original, or copies approximating as nearly as possible to the original, may be introduced as evidence, and will have value for all parties to a controversy in proportion as they are recognized as genuine copies of the original. It is this fact that makes the question of the transmission of the text of the Old Testament fundamental to all discussions based upon the evidence of that text. Only insofar as we can establish a true copy of the original text shall we have before us reliable evidence for our inspection and interpretation. In regard to the Old Testament therefore, the first question to determine is whether we have a reliable copy of the original text. It is my purpose to convince my readers that the answer of experts to this question must be an unhesitating admission that in the text of our common Hebrew Bibles, corrected here and there, especially by the evidence of the ancient versions and through the evidence of paleography, we have presumptively the original text. That is, we have it with sufficient accuracy to be reliable as evidence on all great questions of doctrine, law and history.[39]

Endnotes

1. John Quincy Adams, *Baptists: The Only Thorough Religious Reformers* (Rochester, NY: Backus Book Pub., 1982 reprint), pp. 128-129 {ed. Doug Kutilek cites this as a textbook used at Spurgeon's college}.

2. Quoted by Homer Duncan in "What a Shame!" in the Nov. 1, 1988 issue of *The Biblical Evangelist*, Ingleside, Texas.

3. *Adam Clarke's Commentary* (London: T. Mason and G. Lane, 1840), vol. 2, p. 341 on 2 Samuel 12:31.

4. *Daybreak*, Nov./Dec., 1981 (Piedmont Bible College publication).

5. Roland Bainton, *Erasmus of Christendom* (New York: Charles Scribner's Sons, 1969), p. 135.

6. "Regarding the Biblical Manuscripts Controversy." *Fundamental Baptist Fellowship Resolutions* (Tempe, Ariz.: Tri-City Baptist Church, June 14-16, 1994), p. 2.

7. Gaussen, *The Divine Inspiration of the Bible* (Chicago: Moody Press, 1949 reprint of 1841 work entitled *Theopneustia: The Plenary Inspiration of the Holy Scripture*), p. 155.

8. Ibid., pp. 170-71.

9. Ibid., 167.

10. Ibid., pp. 175-76.

11. Ibid., p. 197.

12. Seven Dispensations, p. 24.

13. R. A. Torrey, A. C. Dixon, and others, eds. *The Fundamentals: A Testimony to the Truth* (Grand Rapids: Baker, 1910, reprinted in 1972 in four volumes), vol. 2, pp. 13-14.

14. Matthew Henry, *Commentary*, vol. 6, p. 1109.

15. Jones, Bob Sr., Tape of radio message in the series Dr. Bob Jones says" entitled "The Inspiration of the Bible," January 21, 1958.

16. Francis Wayland, *A Memoir of the Life and Labours of the Rev. Adoniram Judson D.D.*, 2 vols. (London: James Nisbet, 1853), vol. 2, p. 236.

17. "The King James Only?" *Brethren Missionary Herald*, Nov. 1979, p. 35.

18. Former Professor of Hebrew at the University of Oxford, where he lectured on the Sacred Poetry of the Hebrew, later Bishop of London. The quote is from the Preliminary Dissertation, p. 72.

19. J. Gresham Machen, *The Christian Faith in the Modern World* (Grand Rapids: William B. Eerdmans, 1936), pp. 38-39.

20. Alfred Martin, "A Critical Examination of the Westcott-Hort Textual Theory", in *Which Bible?* (pp. 253-82) ed. by David Otis Fuller, p. 258. Although Martin criticizes the TR, his article favors the traditional text but recognizes that Erasmus' edition was a good but not perfect edition of it. "But it [the TR] embodies substantially the text which even Westcott and Hort admit was dominant in the church from the middle of the fourth century on. The text used by the Church Fathers from Chrysostom's time on was not materially different from the text of Erasmus and Stepahanus. This is not a conclusive proof of the superiority of the text—far from it, but, taken in connection with other factors discussed in this dissertation, does it not present a strong presumption in favor of the reliability of this text? namely the Textus Receptus."

21. Philip Mauro, "Which Version?" in *True or False?* ed. David O. Fuller, p. 62.

22. Doug McLachlan, *Central Testimony*, 1998. p. 5. Response to the PCC Video *The Leavening of Fundamentalism.* Another excellent reply in the same issue (by Kevin Bauder, pages 4-5) summarizes a video response by Central Baptist Theological Seminary.

23. L. W. Munhall, *The Highest Critics vs. the Higher Critics* (Philadelphia: E. & R. Munhall, 1896), pp. 20-21.

24. J. R. Rice, ed., *Sword of the Lord,* March 30, 1979.

25. C. I. Scofield, *Scofield Reference Bible* (New York: Oxford Univ. Press, 1909), see introduction, p. iv.

26. Translator' Preface, King James Version, 1611. The entire preface is printed in Chapter 10. To see the quote in context, see the subheading "Objections of Roman Catholics Answered."

27. Translator' Preface, King James Version, 1611. See Chapter 10 for the quote in context (toward the end of the subheading "Marginal Notes on Alternate Readings"). See also the subheading "Scripture's Power Conveyed through Translations" for further relevant comments.

28. W. T. Whitley, ed. *The Works of John Smyth, fellow of Christ's College* (Cambridge: University Press, 1915), vol. 1, pp. 279-80.

29. C. H. Spurgeon, *Metropolitan Tabernacle Pulpit,* 1889, p. 257.

30. C. H. Spurgeon, *Commenting and Commentaries*, pp. 24-25.
31. C. H. Spurgeon, preface to *The English Bible* by Mrs. H. C. Conant (London: n.p., 1859), pp. vii-xii.
32. C. R. Stam, "A Plea for Renewal: To Close the Chapter on the KJV Only Controversy," *Berean Searchlight*, Sept. 1988, p. 172.
33. W. H. Griffith Thomas, *How We Got our Bible* (Chicago: Moody Press, 1926), pp. 15-16.
34. Reuben Archer Torrey, *Is the Bible the Inerrant Word of God?* (New York: George H. Doran Co., 1922), p. 76.
35. B. B. Warfield, pp. 11, 13. Warfield was Professor of Didactic and Polemic Theology at Princeton, 1887-1921.
36. Daniel Waterland, "Scripture Vindicated," part 3, p. 64 in *The Works of Rev. Daniel Waterland, D.D.*, 6 vols. (Oxford: Oxford University Press, 1856), vol. 4, p. 341.
37. *The Holy Bible in the Common Version with Amendments of the Language*, 1833, see preface.
38. John Telford, ed., *The Letters of John Wesley*, 8 vols., (London: Epworth Press, 1931), vol. v, p. 37.
39. Robert Dick Wilson, *A Scientific Investigation of the Old Testament* (Philadelphia: Sunday School Times Co., 1926), pp. 68-69.

ANSWERS TO QUESTIONS

Chapter 1

1. 2 Timothy 3:16 describes all Scripture as *inspired*, meaning God-breathed. This clearly refers to the Scripture (product) rather than the human writers (means) since people are not God-breathed. However, this is not to deny that God used human writers: 2 Peter 1:21 reminds us that holy men of God spake as the Spirit moved them.

2. The term *inerrant* emphasizes that the Bible is without error; whereas *infallible* means that it teaches no falsehood. *Authoritative* means that man is responsible to obey what God commands in the Bible and to submit to God's Word.

3. *Verbal* inspiration describes that every word and letter of the Bible is inspired, while *plenary* (full) inspiration describes the Bible as complete, lacking nothing that God would have us know.

4. No councils decided on the canon of Scripture. The canon consists of the books God inspired (His act, not the church's). The two councils at Hippo and one at Carthage correctly identified the inspired books but the books had been previously recognized by the recipients and by some Christians in each intervening period (2 Pet. 3:15-16).

5. The Spirit's illumination, apostolic authority, spiritual content, accurate fulfillment, universal reception.

6. The Word of God is eternal (will stand forever) and is settled in heaven. The Bible does not restrict this to any given manuscript or version.

7. The theory of inspired copyists is appealing in terms of seeing the same authority in a translation as the original autographs. The disadvantages are that variations in translations may conflict with one another; that a separate miracle would be required for each translation project; that this additional hypothesis cannot be proved from Scripture; and that this still would not protect a translation from printing errors.

8. Higher Criticism judges the content of Scripture (against evidence from science, history, archaeology, etc.) while Lower Criticism, or textual criticism is the study toward identifying the original wording of Scripture in the original languages.

9. B.B. Warfield

10. The variations among the manuscripts tempt some to doubt the preservation of Scripture, while others react in the other extreme clinging to a view of preservation that admits no human error at all.

Chapter 2

1. Greek, Hebrew, and Aramaic

2. Homer wrote in classical Greek, whereas the New Testament is in Koine Greek, the common Greek spoken and written on a daily basis in the first century.

3. The Rylands Papyrus is the oldest known manuscript and is significant because it proves that the gospel of John is as old as it claims to be. Vaticanus and Sinaiticus are the most complete of the oldest manuscripts and are significant for that fact.

4. Parchments are leather writing surfaces. A palimpsest is an erased parchment with another text copied on it. Vellum is the finest quality parchment.

5. A scroll is a long strip of pages pasted together and rolled

from side to side in order to be read; a codex is in the form of a modern book with pages that can be turned.

6. C
7. A
8. D
9. E
10. B

Chapter 3

1. Bengel
2. codex Sinaiticus, codex Vaticanus, the Textus Receptus
3. Syrian conflations, lack of Syrian readings in the early church fathers, and internal evidence (of scribal tendencies for mistakes)
4. Burgon
5. Westcott and Hort
6. B
7. D
8. A
9. E
10. C

Chapter 4

1. A patristic quotation is a Bible quotation by one of the church fathers.
2. Any five: Athanasius, Augustine, Origen, Irenaeus, Polycarp, Theodore of Mopsuestia. The first three should be among the five listed since they are bold terms.
3. A lectionary consists of Bible portions arranged as readings for services according to the church calendar.
4. A manuscript is a copy of a text in the same language, while a version is a translation of the text into a different language.
5. Old Latin 6. Latin Vulgate

7. Jerome 8. targums
9. 1) the translation of Scripture into Aramaic (Neh. 8:8) for the people, 2) the inspiration of the New Testament in Koine (common) Greek rather than classical Greek or Hebrew, 3) I Cor. 14:19 stresses that Paul would rather speak five words with understanding to teach others than five thousand that fail to be understood. His desired to communicate God's truth.
10. When the New Testament quotes the Old Testament, it may follow the Hebrew wording, the Septuagint version, or Paul's own translation occasionally. These facts prove that Jesus and the apostles used translations that differed at points.

Chapter 5

1. J. A. Bengel
2. Sinaiticus for Tischendorf, Vaticanus for Westcott and Hort, the Traditional (Textus Receptus) for Burgon.
3. First, the conflation of the Syrian readings (which combine Western and Alexandrian readings and must therefore be later). Second, Syrian readings are never quoted by church fathers until after A.D. 350. Third, the "full" and "smooth" readings of the Syrian text were deemed late according to their canons of scribal tendency (prefer shorter and harder readings).
4. Burgon 5. Westcott and Hort
6. B
7. D
8. A.
9. E.
10. C.

Chapter 6

1. The lack of neutrality in the term Neutral text type.

2. Westcott and Hort spoke of the Neutral, Alexandrian, Western, and Syrian text types. Today, we refer to the Alexandrian, Western, Byzantine, and Caesarean types. Today's Byzantine type renames the former Syrian type. Also, today's Alexandrian combines both the Neutral and Alexandrian types of Westcott and Hort; and the new fourth type is the Caesarean (identified by Streeter). Metzger and Aland helped standardize the new terms.

3. Metzger and Aland

4. Failure to explain and emphasize inspiration and preservation as the context for their theories.

5. The switch to an eclectic text rather than promotion of a single text or text type.

6. External evidence concerns things about the manuscripts (such as date of copying), while internal evidence concerns content and is divided into intrinsic probability (evidence from such things as style) and transcriptional probability (evidence from scribal habits). External evidence is the least subjective. Within internal evidence, transcriptional probability is less subjective than intrinsic probability.

7. The oldest manuscript is not universally followed because scholars have recognized that no single manuscript is completely free of all copying errors.

8. Contributions of Hills include his clarifying his position (TR) from similar ones and his willingness to concede and retract an argument recognized as weak based on current research (early date of Peshitta). His greatest contribution, though was his emphasis on inspiration and preservation including his rejection of conjectural emendation.

9. His acceptance of the logic of faith to argue that only spiritual Christians recognize the preservation of Scripture in the Textus Receptus condemns other views as satanic. This cannot be proved from Scripture and is uncharitable toward Christians holding any other view.

10. Answers will vary. If you check closely you will probably not find a flawless copy (although in the case of a single short book, it is not impossible). Students will not be intentionally changing text since they are trying to make the most accurate copy possible, however, point out which of their errors are classified as intentional (especially harmonizing to a parallel passage). This might be more obvious if you have them copy a passage from Luke (birth of Christ, Lord's prayer).

Chapter 7

1. The reading most likely to be correct at any given variant is the one found in the majority of manuscripts at that passage. This is not always the same as the text of Erasmus, called the Received Text.

2. Unlike some other eclectic scholars, conservative eclectic stress the inspiration of Scripture and reject all use of conjectural emendation in the New Testament.

3. The distinctions are important because each side tends to erect straw arguments against other positions that may be relevant to one but not both of the confused positions. This happens often when one of the two is easier to refute, but the carries no weight against the other. It is essential that eclectic scholars direct arguments to the TR or Majority Text views that are relevant to the view in question. Likewise, non-eclectic scholars tend to lump the various eclectic positions and fail to recognize that the argument applies only to critical eclecticism but not conservative eclecticism.

4. The reading most likely to be correct is the one found in a majority of text types.

5. The Majority Text summarized the remaining weaknesses of eclecticism and presented an alternative, thus forcing a healthy reevaluation of views of textual scholars and greater caution in generalities. Its focus on the Greek text rather than relying on traditional texts such as the Comma Johanneum gave it an

advantage over the TR view. Conservative Eclecticism retains the contributions of eclectic scholars (such as willingness to consider certain Byzantine readings) without resort to conjectural emendation. The main contribution of the Independent Text Type view is to focus attention on the potential value of Byzantine readings and to merge strengths of various views.

6. The main weakness of the Majority Text view is the lack of manuscripts reflecting the Majority text that are as old as Vaticanus. The main weakness of Conservative Eclecticism is the difficulty in explaining the agreement among the mass of later manuscripts. The main problem of the Independent Text Type view involves explaining how to select the correct reading when no two of the three main text types agree.

7. Majority Text: a, d, e; Conservative Eclecticism: b, c; Independent Text Types: f.

8. a. Majority text (and TR) b. Conservative (and critical) eclecticism

9. The oldest New Testament manuscripts comprise a small group of manuscripts that disagree with one another frequently, displaying evidence of being copied poorly (or at best copied well from a poor copy). Their survival in the dry climate is possible evidence that owners set them aside, recognizing that they were poor copies.

10. The vast majority of New Testament manuscripts were copied in the monasteries and churches of the Byzantine empire because it alone remained untouched by the dominance of Latin in the West after A.D. 350. The liturgy, the lectionaries, and the preaching of Chrysostom and others tended to stabilize the Byzantine text. The same tendency to resist change from a traditional text is visible today in English.

Chapter 8

1. G.D. Kilpatrick and J.K. Elliott

2. The four distinctives of Radical Eclecticism are that it 1) rejects text types, 2) abandons use of external evidence, 3) adopts readings from any source (even versions, fathers, etc.), 4) indulges in or conjectural emendations as often as desired.

3. Only the final point since it flatly denies preservation and makes the inspiration of Scripture subjectively dependent on human whims.

4. Radical Eclectic scholars have contributed detailed studies of the styles of the human authors of Scripture, which are valuable as background studies and for interpretation issues.

5. Philip Mauro (most balanced), and any two of the following: D. A. Waite, Benjamin Wilkinson (first), David Otis Fuller, J. J. Ray, Gail Riplinger, Peter Ruckman

6. The main contribution of the KJV Only position is its attempt to stress the inspiration of Scripture in a simple manner understandable by any layman.

7. Weaknesses include misrepresentation of eclecticism, promotion of the logic of faith to attack all other positions, ignores historical facts (blessing on the Vulgate, existence of copyist errors and translation errors in all versions).

8. Ruckmanism is the extreme branch that is heretical, in the sense of engendering strife, divisiveness, and factionalism.

9. Since a distinctive of radical eclecticism is heretical, it is unfair to characterize other eclectic scholars this way and then condemn them for beliefs they do not hold.

10. Eclectic scholars recognize the value of the Greek manuscripts and have little time for KJV Only positions concerning tradition or the logic of faith. It is unfair of them to treat Majority or Textus Receptus postions as though the same were true of them.

Chapter 9

1. Match Kilpatrick and Elliott to Radical Eclecticism; Aland and Metzger to Critical Eclecticism; Carson and Custer to Conservative Eclecticism; Sturz to Independent Text Types;

Pickering and Hodges to the Majority Text; Hills to the Textus Receptus; and Mauro and Ruckman to the KJV Only.

2. Biblical, coherent, and adequate
3. The Western text type consists of only as many manuscripts as the Alexandrian type, but they are not as old. This leaves little to commend them as primary and explanations to explain both the lack of oldest manuscripts and conflicts with the mass of manuscripts would fail the criterion of simplicity (if not also accuracy).
4. Radical Eclecticism, consistency, external evidence
5. KJV Only, copyist's errors
6-8. Answers will vary.
9. Best manuscripts
10. Textus Receptus, KJV Only

Chapter 10

1. Scripture is perfect, but it is sealed until it is understood
2. Greek (Septuagint) and Latin (Vulgate) because these were lingua franca (languages of trade known across the ancient world) that brought the Scriptures to many peoples. Apostolic use of the Septuagint shows that God intends translations to be made to spread His Word afar. He did not intend the Old Testament to be limited to those who spoke Hebrew. Also, both the Septuagint and Vulgate were often revised in the hopes of making them more consistent with the Hebrew original.
3. a. John, Bishop of Sevil b. Jerome c. John Trevisa d. Efnard (and later Peter Waldo) e. Ulfilas f. Bede (and later King Alfred) g. Methodius
4. Roman Catholic Church
5. a. All translations (even poor ones) are the Word of God and deserve respect; b. Good translations have been made by heretics, so translations should not be evaluated by the habits, views, or orthodoxy of the translators; c. As in any endeavor,

truth is paramount and corrections should be made not resisted.

6. Hebrew Old Testament and Greek New Testament
7. The translation team a. spent some three years or more ("over twice 7 times 72") preparing their translation in contrast to the rushed job of 72 days of the Septuagint translators; b. improved their work through revisions unlike Jerome whose pages were published as he completed them; c. consulted many other translations recognizing that theirs was not the first labor of this kind (unlike Origen who made the first ever commentary and could not consult others)
8. It would not engender doubts because the alternatives do not affect the doctrine of salvation (doubt of such clear truths would be unbelief), but it would also leave unclear the things God left unclear (acting certain where God left questions is presumption).
9. words that occur only once in Scripture (such as certain plants) can be very difficult to determine precise meanings.
10. They hoped to achieve an honest and understandable translation. The Catholics used unnecessarily difficult words in their translations to conceal meaning from the laity; while the Puritans made the meaning clearer by selecting words that tended to support their own views.

Chapter 11

1. manuscript basis, language development, translation mehtods, theological bias
2. The word *quick* initially meant "living" (the first three meanings given in the Oxford English Dictionary relate to this and are documented from the 800s well into the 1800s). This explains its usage in 9 of its 10 occurences in the KJV (including "the quick and the dead" in Acts 10:42, 2 Tim. 4:1, 1 Pet. 4:5; the tenth, Isa. 11:3 refers to a quick mind). Modern dictionaries label the above meaning as archaic and

define the word in terms of speed or swiftness, meanings known in 1600 (see OED meanings 23 and 24) but not as common as later. (Cf. quicken, quickened, quickening).

3. transliteration
4. glosses
5. interlinear
6. translation
7. Translations may be literal, idiomatic, or paraphrased.
8. Dynamic equivalency involves conveying cultural information in order to give the reader the same reaction that the original recipients had.
9. Eugene Nida
10. Any two of the four. TEV, which translates virgin as young women to avoid the virgin birth; the Inclusive Version, which avoids masculine pronouns for God to make Scripture consistent with the feminist agenda; NWT, because it inserts Jehovah 237 times in the New Testament or because it doctors passages on the deity of Christ; JB, which includes the apocryphal books or because it uses the term holocaust for burnt offerings.

Chapter 12

1. study, children, evangelism
2. study: 2 Tim. 2:15 children: Prov. 22:6 evangelism: Acts 8:30-35, Acts 17:2
3. NAS
4. —NAS, NIV KJV NKJV
   No translations are available that use Elizabethan English but follow eclectic manuscripts.
5. Answers will vary.
6. Grade 12 for KJV, 11 for NASB, 8 for LB, 7 for NIV
7-10. Answers will vary.

GLOSSARY

Alexandrian: a text type based on Greek manuscripts from Egypt, especially Vaticanus and Sinaiticus.

Alexandrinus: the name of an early uncial manuscript, codex A.

apocrypha: 14 intertestamental books not given by inspiration of God and therefore never accepted as canonical by God's people.

apologists: defenders of the faith against doctrinal error and philosophical attacks.

Aramaic: the language of Aram (western Syria) and of several small portions of the Old Testament as well as the native language of Jesus and the disciples.

authoritative: the quality of Scripture that makes it the sole guide to truth, faith, and living.

autographs: the original documents of the books of the Bible.

Byzantine: a text type based on Greek manuscripts from Asia minor.

Caesarean: a text type identified only in the gospels and based on manuscripts associated with Palestine.

canon: a standard or rule. Applies to the books of the Bible as the rule for which books are to be recognized as inspired, consequently the 66 books themselves. Applies to textual criticism to describe rules of scribal tendencies.

codex: an ancient book with pages written on both sides and turned as our modern books (compare to *scroll*).

collation: systematic comparison of a given manuscript with others to identify and organize its variant readings.

Comma Johanneum: the name given to the text of 1 John 5:7-8 in view of its textual history.

conflation: the combining of two distinct readings from different manuscripts by a scribe into the new copy.

conjectural emendation: the adoption of a reading with no manuscript support based on speculation.

Conservative Eclecticism: see Eclecticism.

Coptic: describing the Copts, especially the church, language, and writing of pre-Islamic Egypt. The Coptic version of the Bible is dated from the third century.

corrupt: containing an error. In textual criticism, corrupt readings involve copyist errors. In theology, corrupt doctrine involves false teaching.

Critical Eclecticism: see Eclecticism.

criticism: the analysis, interpretation, and evaluation of literary works. With regard to Scripture, the field is divided into higher criticism and lower criticism.

criticism, higher: also called historical and literary criticism; evaluates the dates, sources, genre, authorship, and unity of Scripture portions (often without regard for the claims of Scripture on these matters as typified by the German rationalistic higher critics).

criticism, lower: also called textual criticism; compares known manuscripts to catalog their variations from one another for the purpose of identifying the autographic text.

cursive: minuscule script with letters joined together in a flowing style; may describe such a manuscript as well (not just its script).

Dead Sea Scrolls: writings from the Qumran community near the Dead Sea including the oldest known manuscripts of the Old Testament.

discourse: aspects of a written work concerned with paragraphs or larger units; examples include genre and theme.

dynamic equivalency: the theory of translation that seeks to convert the message so that people in the modern culture respond to the text in the manner of the ancient readers.

eclecticism: the practice of selection from among options. In textual criticism, the scholar selects readings from various manuscripts. Eclectic theories are distinguished by their use of conjectural emendation. It is never applied in conservative eclecticism, rarely in critical eclecticism, and as often as desired in radical eclecticism.

extant: a manuscript that is still available

external evidence: evidence from the manuscripts other than the words, including the number of manuscripts that support a reading, the age of those manuscripts, and the locations where they were produced.

family: a group of manuscripts with readings that distinguish it from other such groups within a text type.

genre: a written document classified by its form or purpose, such as poem, letter, recipe, play, narrative, fiction, etc.

gloss: a brief translation; often describing the selection of a word as an approximate equivalent of a word in another language.

grammar: the way parts of speech are expressed in a language

Greek: the language of Greece and of the New Testament.

Hebrew: the primary language of Israel and of the Old Testament.

higher criticism: see criticism, higher.

idiomatic translation: translations that focus on converting meaning into natural English rather than literally.

Independent Text Types: a theory of textual criticism that adopts the reading of the most text types (not the most manuscripts).

inerrancy: without error, applied to Scripture.

inspiration: God-breathed, applied to Scripture as containing exactly what God intended to communicate.

interlinear: a text with glosses between the lines; such glosses take into account grammar but will not have the correct word order for meaningful reading.

internal evidence: evidence for one variant as opposed to another based on the words of a text as judged by intrinsic probability and transcriptional probability.

intrinsic probability: consideration of author's style, vocabulary, background, and culture, to determine which variant the author would most likely have written.

inversion: as applied to textual matters, a conflation of text types with either the Western or the Byzantine text as a source rather than recipient.

KJV Only: the view that the King James Version of the Bible in English is as inspired and authoritative as the Greek originals.

Koine: the Greek word for *common,* used to designate the dialect of Greek used by the common man in Bible times.

Latin Vulgate, the translation of the Bible into the common form of Latin of the late fourth century.

lectionary: Bible passages organized for reading in services according to the church calendar.

literal translation: a translation that attempts to preserve word choice and word order as much as possible within the parameters of meaningful translation.

logic of faith: descriptive of spiritual truth as distinct from human reasoning; often applied to suggest that spiritual people recognize the traditional text of Scripture as best preserved.

Majority Text: a text produced from a theory of textual criticism that adopts the reading with the most manuscript support.

Masoretic Text: the standard text of the Old Testament in Hebrew as preserved through the group of scribes called Masoretes.

manuscript: a hand-written copy of the Bible or a portion of it as opposed to copies duplicated through use of printing press.

minuscules: manuscripts written in the lower-case Greek letters (see also cursive).

Neutral (text type): the text type identified and considered by Westcott and Hort as closest to the autographs; it has since been reclassified as part of the Alexandrian type.

Old Slavonic: the ancient language of the Slavs, especially the ninth century version of the Bible using the Cyrillic alphabet.

ostraca: broken pottery shards with writing on them.

palimpsest: a manuscript, usually parchment, upon which a text has been copied over a previous text that has been erased.

papyrus: a writing surface made from overlapping strips of the papyrus reed.

paraphrase: a translation that seeks to communicate paragraph-by-paragraph the same impressions as those communicated by the originals.

parchment: a leather writing surface made from young sheep, goats, cattle, or antelope skins.

patristic: of or concerning the church fathers, usually referring to their writings.

phonetic: representing the sounds of a language

plenary: full; refers to the divine revelation as complete and as inspired fully.

Radical Eclecticism: see Eclecticism.

reading: see variant reading.

Received Text: the text produced by Erasmus as later designated by the Elzevir brothers. Also called Textus Receptus.

recension: an official edition of the Bible that becomes the most popular or traditional edition in a region.

Ruckmanism: the term popularly given to the view of Peter Ruckman, the most extreme of the various KJV Only positions.

Rylands Papyrus (P52): oldest New Testament manuscript known (early second century), contains only five verses from John 18.

scroll: writing surfaces joined end to end and rolled up in contrast to a codex (see codex).

Septuagint, the translation of the Hebrew Old Testament into Greek; name comes from the seventy translators.

Sinaiticus: famous Greek manuscript found at Mt. Sinai and dated to the fourth century.

stele: upright metal or stone slab engraved with royal conquests or other commemoration.

style: the way an author writes including word choice, distinctive phrases, complexity of sentence structure, etc.

syntax: word order in a language.

Syriac Peshitta: the common version of the Bible in the language of the Syrians and dated from about the fifth century.

tablet: writing surface made from clay

targum: commentary on the Old Testament in Aramaic

text: the words of a written passage or work.

text type: one of four groups of manuscripts sharing similarities at specified test passages.

textual criticism: see criticism, lower.

Textus Receptus: Latin for Received Text.

transcriptional probability: study of scribal habits to identify typical mistakes made in copying (transcription).

translation: converting a communication from one language into another with attention to vocabulary, grammar, and syntax of both languages (contrast to transliteration, gloss, interlinear)

transliteration: the substitution of equivalent letters of one language for those of another to express the sound (rather than the meaning) of a foreign word.

uncial: an upper case Greek letter or a manuscript written in a script consisting entirely of such letters.

variant reading (or variant): the wording of one manuscript in a passage where it differs from at least one other manuscript.

Vaticanus (B): famous Greek manuscript in the Vatican library dated to the fourth century.

vellum: the finest parchment often written with gold or silver ink.

verbal: of words; used of the inspiration of Scripture to indicate that it extends to every word.

version: a translation of the Bible into a language different from the original Greek, Hebrew, or Aramaic.

vocabulary: the words of a language.

Western: a text type based on key Greek manuscripts found in Italy from which the Old Latin version was translated.

BIBLIOGRAPHY

Aland, Kurt and Barbara. *The Text of the New Testament.* Leiden: E. J. Brill, 1987.

Archer, Gleason L. *Encyclopedia of Bible Difficulties.* Grand Rapids: Zondervan, 1982.

Bainton, Roland H. *Erasmus Of Christendom.* New York: Charles Scribner's Sons, 1969.

Baxter, John, Peter Clarkson, Elizabeth Cruwys, and Beau Riffenburg. *Wonders of the World.* Stamford, CT: Longmeadow Press, 1995.

Beale, David O. *A Pictorial History of our English Bible.* Greenville: Bob Jones Univ. Press, 1982.

Beekman, John, and John Callow. *Translating the Word of God.* Grand Rapids: Zondervan, 1974.

Bengel, John Albert. *Gnomon of the New Testament.* Vol. 1. Edinburgh: T. and T. Clark, 1877.

Black, David Alan. *New Testament Textual Criticism: A Concise Guide.* Grand Rapids: Baker Book House, 1994.

Boyer, Carl B. *A History of Mathematics.* Princeton: Princeton Univ. Press, 1985. See pages 111, 131.

Breese, Dave. *Seven Men Who Rule the World from the Grave.* Chicago: Moody Press, 1990.

Brotzman, Ellis R. *Old Testament Textual Criticism,* Grand Rapids: Baker, 1994.

Bruce, F. F. *The Books and the Parchments.* Old Tappan, NJ: Fleming H. Revell, 1950 (reprint 1984).

———. *History of the Bible in English.* New York: Oxford University Press, 1978.

———. *The New Testament Documents: Are They Reliable?* Downers Grove, IL: Inter Varsity Press, 1943, 1978 reprint.

Burgon, John William. *The Causes of the Corruption of the Traditional Text of the Holy Gospels.* Posthumously completed and edited by Edward Miller. London: George Bell & Sons, 1896.

———. *The Last Twelve Verses of the Gospel According to Mark.* Ann Arbor: Sovereign Grace Book Club, 1959.

———. *The Revision Revised.* Paradise, PA: Conservative Classics, 1883; reprint 1977.

Burgon, John William. *The Traditional Text of the Holy Gospels Vindicated and Established.* Posthumously completed and edited by Edward Miller. London: George Bell & Sons, 1896.

Cairns, Alan. *Dictionary of Theological Terms.* Belfast: Ambassador-Emerald, International, 1998. See especially "Dead Sea Scrolls"

(p. 113), "JEDP Theory" (p. 199), "Textual Critic" (pp. 370-1), and "Textual Criticism" (pp. 371-402).

Carson, D. A. *The Inclusive Language Debate: A Plea for Realism.* Grand Rapids: Baker, 1998.

———. *The King James Version Debate.* Grand Rapids: Baker Book House, 1979.

Carson, D. A., ed. *Biblical Interpretation and the Church.* See author's preface. Exeter: Paternoster Press, 1984.

Carson, D. A. and John D. Woodbridge, eds. *Hermeneutics, Authority, and Canon.* Grand Rapids: Academie Books, 1986.

Cloud, David W. *New Age Bible Versions: A Critique.* Oak Harbor, WA: Way of Life Literature, 1994, 1998.

———. "Is the KJV Advanced Revelation?" *O Timothy,* vol. 12, May, 1995 (pp. 1-5).

Custer, Stewart. *The Truth about the King James Version.* Greenville, Bob Jones University Press, 1981.

Davis, John J. *Biblical Numerology.* Grand Rapids: Baker Books, 1968.

Delitzsch, F. *Psalms.* Trans. by Francis Bolton. In *Commentary on the Old Testament* by C. F. Keil and F. Delitzsch. Vol. 5. Grand Rapids: Eerdmans, 1990.

Dorey, T. A. *Ersamus.* Albuquerque: University of New Mexico Press, 1970. See pages 81-113 for "Erasmus: Biblical Scholar and Reformer" by B. Hall.

Eldon J. Epp, "The Twentieth Century Interlude in New Testament Textual Criticism," *Journal of Biblical Literature,* XCIII (1974), 389 f.

Faulkner, John Alfred. *Erasmus the Scholar.* Cincinnati: Jennings and Graham, 1907.

Fee, Gordon D. "The Textual Criticism of the New Testament" in the ten-volume *Expositors Bible Commentary,* vol. 1, pp. 417-433. Grand Rapids: Zondervan, 1979.

_____. "Book review of *The Byzantine Text-Type and New Testament Textual Criticism.*" *Journal of the Evangelical Theological Society,* June, 1985 (Vol. 28, no. 2), pp. 239-242.

Finegan, Jack. *Encountering New Testament Manuscripts: A Working Introduction to Textual Criticism.* Grand Rapids: Eerdmans, 1974.

Froude, J. A. *Life and Letters of Erasmus.* New York: Charles Scribner's Sons, 1894, 1912.

Fuller, David Otis. *Counterfeit or Genuine? Mark 16? John 8?* Grand Rapids: Grand Rapids International Publications, 1975.

Fuller, David Otis, ed. *True or False?* Grand Rapids: Grand Rapids International Publications, 1973, 1978. Pages 56-122 contain Mauro's article "Which Version?"; pages 123-215 condense Burgon's *Revision Revised,* while pages 216-295 contain Pickering's thesis on "The Contribution of John William Burgon to New Testament Textual Criticism."

_____. *Which Bible?* second ed. Grand Rapids: Grand Rapids International Publications, 1970. Reproduces Zane Hodges' article for Bibliotheca Sacra (pp. 25-38), and articles by Edward

Hills (on Burgon, pp. 49-68), Benjamin Wilkinson (pp. 93-235), and Alfred Martin (pp. 253-282).

Geisler, Norman L. and William E. Nix. *A General Introduction to the Bible.* Chicago: Moody Press, 1968.

Goulburn, E. M. *Life of Dean Burgon,* 2 Vols.; London: John Murray, 1892, I, vii.

Greenlee, J. Harold. *Introduction to New Testament Textual Criticism.* Grand Rapids: William B. Eerdmans Pub. Co., 1964.

Hills, Edward F. *Believing Bible Study.* Second Ed. Des Moines, IA: Christian Research Press, 1967, 1977.

——. *The King James Version Defended.* Des Moines, IA: Christian Research Press, 1956, 1973.

Hodges, Zane C. "Rationalism and Contemporary New Testament Textual Criticism," *Bibliotheca Sacra* CXXVIII (January-March, 1 71), 27.

Hodges, Zane C. and Arthur L. Farstad. *The Greek New Testament According to the Majority Text.* Nashville: Thomas Nelson, 1982.

Hodges, Zane C. and David M. Hodges. "The Implications of Statistical Probability for the History of the Text" in *Identity of the New Testament Text,* Appendix C, pp. 159-169 by W. N. Pickering.

Hort, Arthur F. *Life and Letters of Fenton John Anthony Hort,* London: Macmillan, 1896.

Kaiser, Walter C., Jr. *Toward Redicovering the Old Testament.* Grand Rapids: Zondervan, 1987.

Kenyon, Frederick. *Handbook to the Textual Criticism of the New Testament.* Oxford: Clarendon Press, 1977.

Kubo, Sakae and Walter F. Specht. *So Many Versions.* Revised and Enlarged Ed. Grand Rapids: Zondervan, 1983.

Letis, Theodore P. "B. B. Warfield, Common Sense Philosophy and Biblical Criticism." *American Presbyterians,* Fall 1991.

Mazar, Amihai. *Archaeology of the Land of the Bible 10,000—586 B.C.E.* New York: Doubleday, 1992.

McDowell, Josh. *Evidence that Demands a Verdict.* Revised ed. San Bernadino, CA: Campus Crusade for Christ, 1979.

Metzger, Bruce Manning. "Explicit References in the Works of Origen to Variant Readings in the NT MSS."

____. *The Text of the New Testament.* New York: Oxford University Press, 1968.

Miller, Edward. *A Guide to the Textual Criticism of the New Testament.* 1886. Reprint Collingswood, N.J.: Dean Burgon Society, 1986.

New Testament and Psalms: A New Inclusive Translation. Oxford: Oxford University Press, 1995.

Nida, Eugene A. *Bible Translating.* London: United Bible Societies, 1947, 1961.

Osborn, Henry A. and Bernard Northrup, William Smallman, and Frederic A. Carlson. *Anchor Points for Scripture Translation Work.* Grand Rapids: Bibles International, 1988.

Pickering, Wilbur Norman. *The Identity of the New Testament Text.* Revised Ed. Nashville: Thomas Nelson Publishers, 1980.

Ray, Jasper James. *God Wrote Only One Bible.* Junction City, OR: Eye Opener Publishers, 1955, 1976.

Riplinger, G.A. *New Age Bible Versions.* Munroe Falls, OH: AV Publications, 1993.

Robertson, A.T. *Introduction to the Textual Criticism of the New Testament.* Nashville, TN: Boardman Press, 1925.

Ruckman, Peter S. *The Christian's Handbook of Manuscript Evidence.* Pensacola, FL: Pensacola Bible Press, 1970.

———. *Custer's Last Stand.* Pensacola, FL: Bible Baptist Bookstore, 1981.

Schultz, A. C. "Exile," *Zondervan Pictorial Bible Encyclopedia,* Vol. 2 (pp. 423-28). Edited by Merrill C. Tenney. Grand Rapids: Zondervan, 1976.

Seebohm, Frederick. *The Oxford Reformers.* New York: AMS Press, 1867, 1913.

Sightler, James H. *A Testimony Founded For Ever.* Greenville: Sightler Pubs., 1999.

Sturz, Harry A. *The Byzantine Text-Type and New Testament Textual Criticism.* Nashville: Thomas Nelson, 1984.

Tagliapietra, Ron. *Better Thinking and Reasoning.* Greenville: Bob Jones University Press, 1995.

Thiessen, Henry Clarence. *Introduction to the New Testament.* Grand Rapids: William B. Eerdmans, 1943.

Tischendorf, Constantin von. *Codex Sinaiticus.* London: Lutterworth Press, 1934 reprint.

Tregelles, Samuel P. *An Account of the Printed Text of the Greek New Testament: With Remarks on Its Revision Upon Critical Principles.* London: Samuel Bagster and Sons, 1854.

van der Waerden, B. L. "Euclid" in *Encyclopaedia Britannica.* Chicago: Helen Hemingway Benton, 1983. Vol. 6., pp. 1019-21.

Waite, D. A. *Dean John Burgon's Prerequisites for Major Revision of the New Testament Greek Textus Receptus and the English King James Version New Testament.* Collingswood, NJ: The Bible for Today, 1980.

_____. *Defending the King James Bible.* Collingswood, NJ: The Bible for Today, 1992.

_____. *The New Testament Majority Greek Text Defended.* Collingswood, NJ: The Bible for Today, 1976.

_____. *The Theological Heresies of Westcott and Hort.* Collingswood, NJ: The Bible for Today, 1978.

Warfield, B. B. *An Introduction to the Textual Criticism of the New Testament.* London: Hodder and Stoughton, 1896.

Westcott, B. F. and F. J. A. Hort. *Introduction to the New Testament in the Original Greek.* 1882. Reprinted. Peabody, MA: Hendrickson Publishers, 1988.

———, eds. *The New Testament in the Original Greek*, 2 vols. New York: Harper, 1882.

White, James R. *The King James Only Controversy.* Minneapolis: Bethany House, 1995.

Williams, James B. *From the Mind of God to the Mind of Man.* Greenville: Ambassador-Emerald, International, 1999.

INDEX

(Endnotes, questions, and helps after page 310

are not indexed)

Aland, Kurt 48, 104 5, 110-14, 129, 136-37, 139-40, 143, 151, 154, 174, 182
Alexandrian (text type) 87, 91, 112 15, 118-19, 133-34, 137, 139 42, 162, 172, 179
Apocrypha(l) 22, 85, 93, 263
Apologist(s) 56-57
Aramaic 35-36, 63-65, 240, 251
Arian,—ism,—s 57, 78
Armenian (version) 60, 149, 292
Athanasius 57
Augustine 57, 192-93, 197, 202, 205-6, 210-12, 215

Bengel, J. A. 81-84, 86-88, 91, 96-97, 110, 112-13, 292
Bodmer Papyri 39
Burgon, John W. 79, 90-96, 98, 103-4, 110, 113, 115-16, 122, 130-32, 140, 143, 147, 156-57, 304
Byzantine (text type) 113-16, 120-22, 128, 131-33, 136-37, 139-42, 172, 176, 179-80

Caesarean (text type) 103, 113-14, 129, 172

Cairns, Alan 130-131, 177
Canon,—ical,—icity (of Scripture) 20-23, 33, 40, 56, 58, 93, 112, 291, 299
Canon(s) (of scribal errors) 82-83, 86, 88, 91, 107, 110, 128-29, 135, 138
Carson, D.A. 136-37, 143, 175, 255, 258, 261
Chester Beatty Papyri 39, 41
Codex 38-42, 46, 49, 77, 79, 83, 85
Collation(s) 80-81, 83, 86, 88, 141
Colwell, E. C. 131-32
Comma Johanneum 77-80, 84, 96, 115-16, 130, 177-79
Complutensian Polyglot 74-76
Conflation(s) 88, 91, 128, 131-33, 139
Conjectural Emendation 111, 122, 137, 141, 151, 153-54, 162, 173-75, 179-81, 262-63
Conservative Eclecticism 135-39, 143, 148, 154, 162, 175, 179-180
Coptic (version) 24, 59, 86, 151
Critical Eclecticism 103-4, 110, 122, 135-37, 143, 148, 154, 162-63, 174, 179-81
Custer, Stewart 136-37, 143, 175

Damasus 61
Dead Sea Scrolls 46-47
Dorpius 78
Dynamic Equivalence,—cy 260-262, 268

Eclectic(ism) 104, 106, see conservative, critical, radical
Elliott, J. K. 147-49, 153, 173
Erasmus 9, 49, 73-82, 89, 96-97, 104, 115-17, 130, 134, 159, 177, 180-81, 198, 207, 226, 236, 247, 290
Ethiopic (version) 60, 149
Euclid 51-52
External Evidence 105, 109, 147-48, 152-54, 173-75

Family 13 50
Froben, Johann 74
Fuller, David O. 31-32, 155, 178

Genre 256, 261
Gloss,—es,—ing 252-54, 256
Gothic (version) 60, 232
Grammar 94, 106, 108, 182, 252-53, 255, 257, 299
Greek 9-10, 13-14, 16, 18-19, 24, 36-37, 41, 43, 47, 49, 52,
    55-56, 58-59, 61-66, 73-87, 89, 92, 95-96, 104, 107-8,
    110, 112, 115-16, 119-20, 127, 129-30, 149, 151, 156-
    62, 174, 176-78, 180-82, 185, 194-98, 205, 210-11,
    213-14, 222-27, 233-34, 237-40, 242-43, 247, 250-51,
    253-54, 256, 260, 262 63, 270-73, 290, 294-96, 298-
    300
Griesbach, Johann Jakob 86-88, 109-10, 113, 298

Hebrew 21, 24, 35-36, 62-67, 107, 119-20, 159, 161, 179,
    181, 194-95, 197-99, 206, 210-11, 213-14, 222-23, 225-
    27, 233-34, 238-40, 242-43, 256, 258, 263, 289-90, 294,
    296, 299-301, 306
Higher Criticism 29-30, 46-47, 50, 298
Hills, Edward F. 27-28, 116-21, 130-32, 140, 143, 156-57, 177,
    182
Hodges, Zane 50, 129, 132, 143, 162, 177
Homer 36-37, 51-52
Hort, F.J.A. 9, 79, 86-92, 94-97, 103-4, 107, 110-14, 117, 122,
    128, 131-35, 138, 140, 147, 153, 155-56, 160, 164, 176,
    182, 247, 286, 298, 304

Idiomatic Translation 256-57, 259, 270-72
Independent Text Types 139, 141, 143, 173, 175, 179-80
Inerrancy 16-17, 22, 30, 33, 94, 117, 136, 279, 291, 302

Inspiration 15-23, 26-30, 32-33, 51, 63-67, 77, 81, 111-12, 117, 127, 131, 136-37, 152, 155-56, 161, 163, 170-71, 178, 180, 192, 279, 281, 286, 289-91, 293-99, 302-5
Interlinear 253-54
Internal Evidence 87, 94, 105-6, 109-10, 147-49, 151, 153, 173-74
Intrinsic Probability 106, 109, 111
Inversion(s) 133-34, 139

Jerome 55, 57, 59, 61-62, 80, 88, 91, 96, 161, 220-22, 225-27, 230-31, 234-35, 238-39, 241
Jesus 16-19, 23-25, 36, 42, 62, 65-67, 92, 107-8, 118, 159, 191, 209, 215, 219, 237, 245, 271

Kilpatrick, G. D. 140, 147-48, 153, 165, 173, 182
King James Only, KJV Only 121, 154-61, 163-65, 173, 178-79, 181, 297, 301
King James Version, KJV, Authorized Version, A.V. 7, 49, 92, 115-17, 120, 130, 154-65, 175, 177-79, 185-86, 200, 209, 214, 229, 247-50, 254, 256, 259, 261, 263, 270-72, 276, 280, 290, 295-96, 299-302
Koine Greek 37, 43, 63

Lectionary 57-58, 67, 279
Lee, Edward 78
Literal Translation 256, 260, 270-71
Lower Criticism 79
Lucian(ic) 88, 110, 128, 198, 226

Majority Text 93, 115, 121, 127-33, 135, 137, 139, 141, 143, 149-50, 152-53, 157-58, 162, 165, 173, 176-77, 179-80
Marcion 22, 56, 93, 119
Masoretes 27, 130

Masoretic Text 46, 119, 161
Mauro, Philip 156, 160, 162, 178, 297
Metzger, Bruce M. 51, 104-5, 110, 112-14, 129, 136-37, 140, 143, 147, 151, 154, 174
Miller, Edward 90-91
Mills, John 81
Minuscules 18, 45, 48-49, 50, 53

Neutral 87-88, 103, 112-14, 133, 172
Nida, Eugene 259-61

Old Latin (version) 59, 61-62, 87, 117, 151
Old Slavonic (version) 61
Old Syriac (version) 60, 149
Origen 56-57, 103, 110, 196, 206, 211, 225, 239
Osborn, Henry A. 260-61
Ostraca 38

Palimpsest 41
Papyri,—rus 37-41, 48, 56, 113, 128, 132 140
Paraphrase 67, 84, 256-57, 259-62, 270, 272-73
Parchment(s) 40-42, 48-49, 85, 293
Patristic 55-57, 59, 67, 85, 95, 98, 110, 116
Phonetic 251
Pickering, Wilbur N. 127-35, 137-39, 143, 153-54, 157, 165, 177, 182
Plenary 16-17, 33, 81, 286, 295
Polycarp 56-57
Preservation,—ve,—ved,—ves,—ving 11, 13-15, 20, 23-29, 31, 33, 35-36, 40, 43, 45-46, 48-53, 55, 58, 66-67, 71, 81, 83-84, 92, 94, 96-98, 111, 113, 116-22, 127-28, 131, 136-37, 148-56, 160-61, 163-64, 170-71, 174-81, 185, 232, 251, 257, 262, 279-81, 284-85, 292, 294, 296, 301-4

Radical Eclectic,—ism 135, 137, 147-54, 162, 173, 179-80, 262
Ray, J. J. 155-57, 160-61, 178
Recension 88, 91, 96, 110, 122, 128-29, 137, 140
Riplinger, Gail 162
Ruckman, Peter S. 158, 162, 164, 178
Rylands Papyrus 39-40, 48

Scroll 38, 46
Septuagint 62, 64-67, 85, 119-20, 161, 179, 181, 210, 212,
    224-26, 233-34, 239, 241
Sinaiticus 41, 85-87, 90, 93, 96, 113, 154
Smith, Miles 7, 299
Stele 38
Streeter, B. H. 103, 113
Sturz, Harry A. 139-43, 176, 179
Style 11, 18, 37, 40, 105-6, 109, 111, 148-49, 173-74, 185,
    243, 255, 257-58, 294-95
Syntax 254-57, 261
Syriac 60, 86, 91, 121, 149, 151, 227-28, 240, 291
Syriac Peshitta (version) 60, 91, 121-22

Tablet 38
Tacitus 50, 52
Targum 63
Text Type 13, 81-84, 87-88, 90-91, 103-4, 110, 112-16, 118-
    20, 122, 127-29, 131-34, 139-43, 148-50, 158, 164, 172-
    73, 175-76, 179-80
Textual Criticism 29-30, 56-57, 73, 83, 86, 95-96, 98, 104-5,
    113, 115, 118, 138-39, 147-48, 151, 153-54, 156, 163,
    170-72, 174, 176, 185, 286, 298
Textus Receptus, TR 28, 80, 87, 89, 92, 95, 103, 114-18, 121,
    130-31, 134, 137, 143, 155-58, 160-61, 164-65, 173, 177,
    179-81, 247, 263, 297-98
Tischendorf, Constantin von 41, 85-86, 88, 96-97, 113, 298, 304